PENGUIN BOOKS

THE GATEWAY TO FRANCE

James Bentley is an experienced travel writer whose books include *The Loire*, *Life and Food in the Dordogne*, *Secrets of Mount Sinai*, *Oberammergau and the Passion Play*, *West Germany and Berlin*, *The Languedoc*, which won the first Thomas Cook award for an illustrated travel book, *A Guide to Tuscany* (Penguin 1988) and *Alsace* (Penguin 1989). His *A Guide to the Dordogne* (Penguin 1986) led the *Evening Standard* to write: 'France with a Bentley – it's the only way to travel.' His other travel books include *Normandy*, *Umbria*, *Rome* and *Castile*.

JAMES BENTLEY

THE GATEWAY TO FRANCE

FLANDERS, ARTOIS AND PICARDY

PENGUIN BOOKS

PENGUIN BOOKS

Published by the Penguin Group
Penguin Books Ltd, 27 Wrights Lane, London W8 5TZ, England
Penguin Books USA Inc., 375 Hudson Street, New York, New York 10014, USA
Penguin Books Australia Ltd, Ringwood, Victoria, Australia
Penguin Books Canada Ltd, 10 Alcorn Avenue, Toronto, Ontario, Canada M4V 3B2
Penguin Books (NZ) Ltd, 182–190 Wairau Road, Auckland 10, New Zealand

Penguin Books Ltd, Registered Offices: Harmondsworth, Middlesex, England

First published by Viking 1991
Published in Penguin Books 1992
1 3 5 7 9 10 8 6 4 2

The author and publishers are grateful to Faber & Faber Ltd for permission to quote
from two poems by Siegfried Sassoon: 'The General' and 'The Blighters', which appear on
pages 52 and 59. Copyright 1918 by E. P. Dutton, renewed 1946 by Siegfried Sassoon.
Reprinted by permission of Viking Penguin, a division of Penguin Books USA Inc.

Printed in England by Clays Ltd, St Ives plc

To Emma-Louise Davson

CONTENTS

LIST OF ILLUSTRATIONS

Illustration Acknowledgements

The author and the publishers are grateful to the following for permission to reproduce photographs: French Government Tourist Office, London: 1, 2, 3, 4, 5, 6, 7, 8, 9, 10, 11, 12, 13, 14, 15, 16, 17, 18, 19, 22, 23, 28, 29, 30, 31, 32, 33, 34, 35, 36; C.R.T./Nord-Pas de Calais/P. Mercier: 20; C.R.T./Nord-Pas de Calais/ P. Morès: 21, 27; Office du Tourisme, Laon: 24, 25, 26.

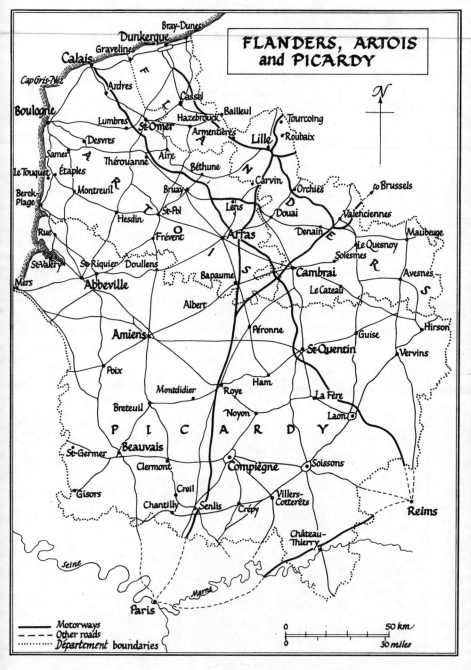

FLANDERS, ARTOIS and PICARDY

N

Bray-Dunes
Dunkerque
Gravelines
Calais
Cap Gris-Nez
Ardres
Cassel
Boulogne
Bailleul
Hazebrouck
Tourcoing
Lumbres
St Omer
Armentières
Lille
Roubaix
Desvres
Aire
Samer
Thérouanne
Béthune
Le Touquet
Étaples
Carvin
Orchies
Montreuil
Bruay
Berck-
Plage
St-Pol
Lens
Douai
Valenciennes
Rue
Hesdin
Denain
Maubeuge
Frévent
Arras
Le Quesnoy
St Valéry
St Riquier
Doullens
Solesmes
Avesnes
Mers
Bapaume
Cambrai
Abbeville
Le Cateau
Albert
Hirson
Amiens
Péronne
Guise
St-Quentin
Vervins
Poix
Ham
Montdidier
Roye
Breteuil
Noyon
La Fère
Laon
P I C A R D Y
St-Germer
Beauvais
Clermont
Compiègne
Soissons
Gisors
Creil
Chantilly
Senlis
Crépy
Villers-
Cotterêts
Reims
Château-
Thierry
Seine
Marne
Paris

to Brussels

F L A N D E R S
A R T O I S

Motorways
Other roads
Département boundaries

0   50 km
0   30 miles

xi

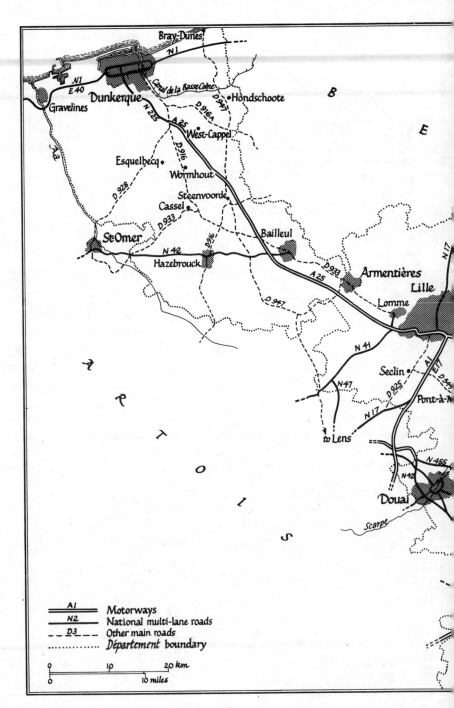

Bray-Dunes

N1

Canal de la Basse Colne

N1
E40
Gravelines
Dunkerque
N 225
A25
West-Cappel
D 916A
D 947
Hondschoote

B

E

Esquelbecq
D 916
Wormhout
D 928
Steenvoorde
Cassel
D 933
Bailleul
St Omer
D 916
N 42
Hazebrouck
A 25
D 933
Armentières
Lille
D 947
Lomme

Aa

A
R
T
O
I
S

N 41
Seclin
A1
E17
D 549
D 925
Pont-à-N
N 47
N 17
to Lens

N 455
N 42
Douai
Scarpe

N 17

A1	Motorways
N2	National multi-lane roads
D3	Other main roads
....	*Département* boundary

0   10   20 km
0   10 miles

xii

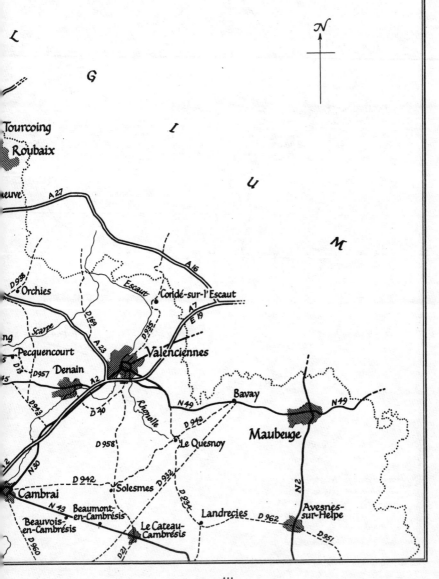

FLANDERS

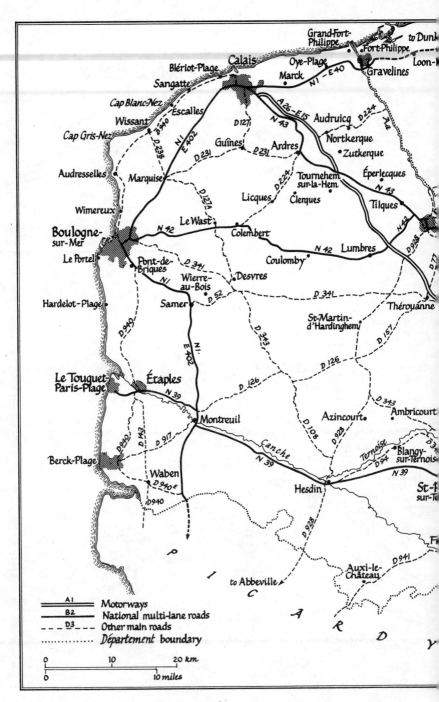

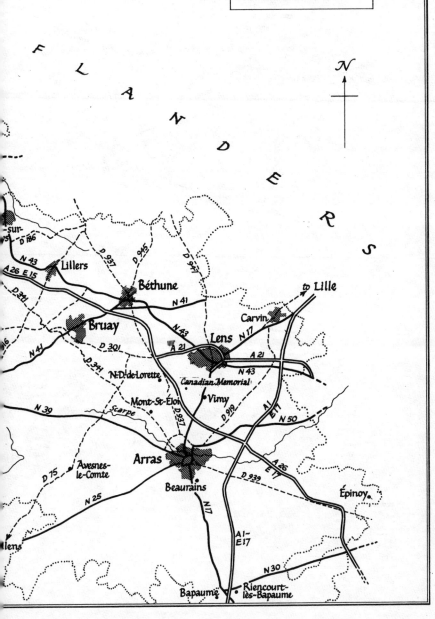

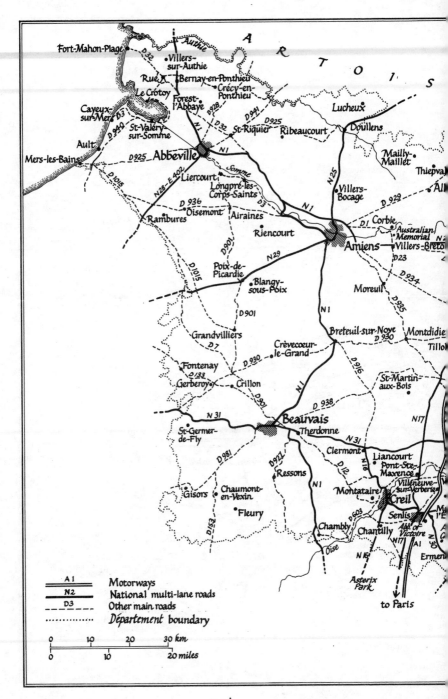

ARTOIS

Fort-Mahon-Plage
D 32
Villers-sur-Authie
Rue
Bernay-en-Ponthieu
Le Crotoy
Crécy-en-Ponthieu
Forest-l'Abbaye
D 928
D 941
Lucheux
Cayeux-sur-Mer D3
D 32
St-Riquier
D 925
Ribeaucourt
Doullens
St-Valéry-sur-Somme
Ault
D 940
N 1
Mailly-Maillet
Mers-les-Bains
D 925
Abbeville
N 1
Thiepva
Liercourt
Somme
N 25
Villers-Bocage
Al
N 28 – E 402
Longpré-les-Corps-Saints
D 929
Corbie
D 1015
D 936
D 3
Oisemont
Airaines
N 1
D 1
Australian
Memorial
N 2
Rambures
Riencourt
Amiens
Villers-Breto
D 901
Poix-de-Picardie
N 29
D 23
D 934
Moreuil
D 1015
Blangy-sous-Poix
D 935
N 1
D 901
Breteuil-sur-Noye
Montdidie
Grandvilliers
Crèvecoeur-le-Grand
D 930
Tillol
D 7
D 916
Fontenay
D 133
D 930
St-Martin-aux-Bois
Gerberoy
Crillon
N 1
D 938
N 31
Beauvais
N 17
St-Germer-de-Fly
Therdonne
N 31
D 901
Clermont
Liancourt
D 981
D 921
D 12
N 16
Pont-Ste-Maxence
Ressons
Villeneuve-sur-Verberie
Gisors
Chaumont-en-Vexin
Montataire
Creil
M
l'E
D 603
Fleury
N 1
Senlis
A
Chambly
Chantilly
Mus. of
Victoire
N 17
A 1
A
D 153
Oise
N 16
Ermen
Asterix
Park
to Paris

A 1 ————— Motorways
N 2 ————— National multi-lane roads
D 3 ------- Other main roads
.... *Département* boundary

0   10   20   30 km
0   10   20 miles

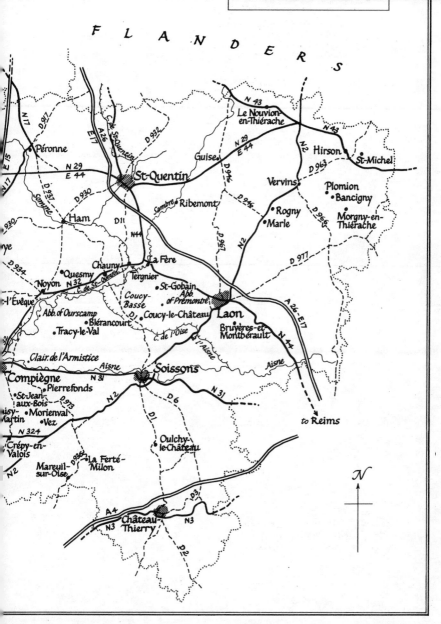

PICARDY

FLANDERS

N 43

Péronne

N 17

A 26

E 17

D 917

D 932

N 29
E 44

E 15

N 17

Le Nouvion-
en-Thiérache

N 43

N 29
E 44

Guise

N 2

Hirson

St-Michel

St-Quentin

D 946

Vervins

Plomion
Bancigny

D 963

D 930

D 937

Somme

Sambre

Ribemont

Rogny
Marle

D 946

Morgny-en-
Thiérache

D 965

D 977

Ham

D II

N 44

D 930

D 934

D 951

N 2

rye

Chauny

La Fère

Quesmy

Noyon

N 32

C. de St-Quentin

Tergnier

St-Gobain
Abb.
of Prémontré

A 26-E 17

l'Évêque

Coucy-
Basse

Coucy-le-Château

Laon

Abb. of Ourscamp

Blérancourt

D I

C. de l'Oise

Bruyères-et-
Montbérault

Tracy-le-Val

l'Aisne

N 44

Clair. de l'Armistice

Aisne

Aisne

Compiègne

Pierrefonds

N 31

Soissons

St-Jean-
aux-Bois

D 973

N 2

D 6

N 31

to Reims

Morienval
Vez

D I

Martin

N 324

Crépy-en-
Valois

Oulchy-
le-Château

N 2

Mareuil-
sur-Oise

D 936

La Ferté-
Milon

D I

A 4

D 2

Château-
Thierry

N 3

N 3

D 2

N

PREFACE

Travelling through northern France in the late eighteenth century Arthur Young commented that there was nothing to see. This normally astute observer must have missed the remarkable, sheer cliffs at Mers-les-Bains. He must also have been blind to the great collegiate church of Saint-Vulfram at Abbeville, not to mention Amiens cathedral. Evidently he failed to relish the half-timbered houses of the *département* of the Aisne and the intimate cobbled streets which wind up into Senlis. He had perhaps little time for the forests and lush pastures of this region, cut through as they are by noble rivers, one of which (the Thérain) was dubbed by the poet Anna de Noailles 'a blonde Loire'.

I shared Arthur Young's prejudices. Having bought a house in south-west France I would drive heedlessly through Flanders, through Artois, through Picardy, anxious only to reach home. Then, fearful of driving so relentlessly that I might demolish not only a wall but myself as well, I began to stay overnight, and then longer, exploring the gateway to France. This was a much overdue conversion, if only because in its tragic and glorious history this region has for centuries been connected with Britain. Julius Caesar chose the Somme estuary from which to launch his assault on our country. When the Spanish Armada threatened the realm of Elizabeth I, its base was not Spain but Flanders. Four centuries later British and Commonwealth blood was shed on the killing fields of northern France.

Today I can say with Paul Claudel, who was born in this part of France, that I retain the most delightful memories of a humane corner of the world. In this book I have set out to describe its history, its gastronomy, its art, its merriment, its great and humble monuments and something of the temper of its people. I have done so by means of suggested tours which take in not only every great town and city in the whole region but also humbler, enchanting spots, pointing out where a reader might follow his or her own particular inclinations on the way. No such guide can claim to have covered every possible monument. (After all, the two most recent authoritative guides to French châteaux list 226 in the *département* of the Pas-de-Calais alone, and another 160 in the neighbouring *département* of the Nord.) I have selected as best I know how.

Many people have helped me in writing this book, including those who were simply willing to talk to me on my way. Here I would like especially to express my thanks to Mme Pascale Delgrange, Chef de Projet Tourisme at the Chambre de Commerce et d'Industrie, Arras; to Mme Chantal Duraffourd, who so generously showed me around the abbey of Saint-Jean-des-Vignes well outside normal opening hours; to Mme Théodoulitsa Kouloumbri, Directrice of the Office du Tourisme at Laon; to Mme Anne-Marie Goales, Directrice of the Comité Départemental du Tourisme de la Somme; to M. Jean-Marie Lasblais of the Comité du Tourisme de la Somme, Amiens, who devoted to me an enormous amount of his time and enthusiasm; to M. Jean-Michel Lefebvre of the Comité Régional du Tourisme de Picardie, not just for much practical help but also for inspiration; and finally for the abundant kindness shown to me, as always, by Mrs Pauline Hallam, Public Relations Director of the French Government Tourist Board in London.

THE OPAL COAST

Running from Belgium to Normandy, the Opal Coast, so-called because of the milky-white seas which wash it, is craggy with estuaries sheltering fishing villages and ports. We owe the name to a long-forgotten painter, who dubbed these creeks and beaches the Opal Coast in 1911. In truth I find them opalescent, the waters sometimes golden, sometimes blue. Its northernmost point of entry, sheltered by the Flanders hills and set where the River Colne flows into the Channel, is the port of Dunkerque (or as the British prefer to spell it, Dunkirk).

The fourth most important fishing and commercial port in France, flourishing on chemical plants and oil refineries, Dunkerque derives from a tiny Merovingian hamlet named Saint-Gilles. Only in the ninth century did it adopt its present Flemish name, '*Dune-Kerke*', which means 'church of the dunes'. Besieged and sacked no fewer than six times during the Middle Ages, the town was given no respite during the sixteenth and seventeenth centuries, when the Spanish, the British, the Dutch and the French repeatedly fought over it. Turenne took twenty-eight days to wear down the citizens' resistance after the Battle of the Dunes in 1658. Oliver Cromwell had committed 8,000 Ironsides to the side of Turenne and took Dunkerque as his reward, but in 1662 the English monarch Charles II sold the town back to Louis XIV for 5,000,000 *livres*. Louis now commanded the brilliant military engineer Sébastien Le Prestre de Vauban to build its fortifications, among the first of the many major works he undertook for the French monarchy. Vauban lived long enough to build another entrenched camp at Dunkerque in 1703.

So much of Dunkerque was destroyed during the Second World

War that the town was almost completely rebuilt. Fortunately a few of its most characteristic monuments were saved. One was the statue of Jean Bart, France's most celebrated corsair. Sculpted by David d'Angers, he stands in Place Jean-Bart, pistol in hand and brandishing his sword, as well as bestriding an enemy cannon. Bart was born at Dunkerque into a fisherman's family in 1650. His first job was as a sailor in the Dutch navy, but he soon came over to the French side. In the 1690s the British bombarded Dunkerque no fewer than four times. Their misfortune was that Bart was commanding a squadron of ships in the North Sea which sank a good number of British ships and even made a daring landing near Newcastle. In 1694 he also took on the Dutch fleet, capturing a number of corn-ships and bringing them and their cargo back to Dunkerque. When the British captured Bart and imprisoned him in Plymouth, he escaped in a fishing smack back to his native land. Small wonder that when Louis XIV honoured him, Jean Bart responded with the words, 'Well done, sir.' The courtiers laughed until the sovereign rebuked them with the remark, 'His answer reveals a man who knows his own worth.'

Just around the corner in Rue de Président-Poincaré you find a *crémerie* which with its *brie de Meaux* and Dutch cheeses reminds us how close we are to the Low Countries. And to the north of Place Jean-Bart rises another monument saved from destruction in the Second World War, Dunkerque's 59 m high belfry. A belfry in Flanders still denotes immense civic pride – it was a symbol in the Middle Ages of urban freedoms. This fat square tower, built in brick and growing more graceful as its rises for six storeys, was erected in 1440 as the belfry of the church of Saint-Éloi. Today it serves both as a war memorial and the Dunkerque tourist office. Although the belfry itself withstood the bombardments of 1940, its clock-tower and carillon of forty-eight bells alas perished. Happily, the carillon has been restored. On the quarter-hour its forty-eight bells ring the traditional chime *talire, taloure*. At the half-hour the chime is the so-called *carillon de Dunkerque*. At a quarter before the hour the bells ring out a tune celebrating the Viking Reuze, who ravaged these shores until he became a Christian. The citizens took him in when he lay wounded, after which he became their protector rather than their persecutor. Inevitably, on the hour every bell sings the *cantate à Jean Bart*.

Reuze is also commemorated by one of the four giant puppets of Dunkerque. The others represent his wife Gentille and their two children. All four emerge for the carnival which takes place around Shrove Tuesday, paraded through the town by fishermen and their families to the sound of fifes and drums. The citizens, bizarrely dressed and made up as clowns (with some women dressed as men and some men as women), sing the *cantate à Jean Bart* as well as such quaint dialect ditties as '*Donne un zo à mon oncle Cô qui revient d'Islande*' (Give a kiss to my uncle Cô who has just returned from Iceland). Anyone who responds and kisses ugly uncle Cô with his long nose and black wizard's hat is rewarded with a piece of *wamme*, or smoked herring. Fishing is the theme of this whole carnival, for its origins lie in a feast to inaugurate the sallying forth of Dunkerque's fishermen to Iceland. '*Des kippers, des kippers,*' the crowd outside the Town Hall cries, and the mayor of Dunkerque and his councillors throw kippers into the crowd from the balcony.

Surrounded by a few pretty brick houses is the church of Saint-Éloi, which stands on the opposite side of the road from the belfry. Though severely damaged, it too survived the Second World War. Its own tribulations date from earlier epochs. St Éloi was a bishop of Noyon whose first church, built on this spot, gave the city the name 'church of the dunes'. Built as a last gasp of the Gothic in 1570, the present Saint-Éloi was severely damaged by a fire of 1667, after which it was restored in its original style. Next, part of its nave was demolished to make way for a new road, and from 1784 to 1889 Saint-Éloi presented a classical façade to the world. In the latter years, however, the French Gothicists saw fit to rebuild the façade in the flamboyant style that it retains to this day. The ravages of the First World War were made good in the 1920s. In consequence Saint-Éloi boasts a stone façade, while the rest of the church is built in pale yellow brick. The rose window at the west end is both huge and graceful. Walk around the outside of the church to relish the chapels radiating from the choir. Saint-Éloi has no transepts but consists of a nave and four aisles. Inside, look for the tombs of both Jean Bart, who died on 27 April 1702, and his wife Marie-Jacqueline Tugghe.

A little more than 100 m west of the belfry church of Saint-Éloi, near the Bassin du Commerce, rises the building the people of Dunkerque call their 'little church', the eighteenth-century

Saint-Jean-Baptiste. It once served as the chapel of the order of Franciscan monks known as the Recollects, set up in France in the sixteenth century to revive what they took to be the true spirit of St Francis of Assisi. To the north of Saint-Éloi, along Rue Clémenceau and already visible from the church, rises Dunkerque's nineteenth-century glory, the rich, almost raucous Hôtel de Ville which Louis-Marie Cordonnier built in the Flemish Renaissance style between 1896 and 1901. Its belfry, from which you have a splendid view of the surrounding countryside and seascape, rises for 75 m. The equestrian statue over its main doorway represents, inevitably, Jean Bart, with a pigeon or two usually perched on him and his nag.

That we are in Flanders is indicated by the menus offered by the local restaurants (such as the *auberge* in the town hall square). Seafood makes its welcome appearance (mussels, *gratinée Mer du Nord*) as well as less appetizing pizzas. Rue Jean-Jaurès takes us from here to the waterside itself. Cranes rise over the docks. In the holiday season you can take a cruise from here through the busy commercial port of Dunkerque. On the quayside stands an octagonal tower, known as the Tour de Leughenaer, which is all that survives of Dunkerque's fourteenth-century defences. In Flemish *'leughenauer'* means 'liar', but no one has yet satisfactorily explained why this tower should bear such an appellation, save for the legend that someone once gave a false alarm from its summit. The Tour de Leughenaer was once accompanied by twenty-seven others rising from Dunkerque's ramparts.

Beside it is a fish market known as the Mynck, whose open-air stalls give off a tangy scent. Stroll further east to reach another seafarer's resource, the chapel of Notre-Dame-des-Dunes (known in Dunkerque as the *'petite chapelle'*, as distinct from the *'petite église'* of Saint-Jean-Baptiste). It houses a statue of the Blessed Virgin which is said to have been washed ashore here in 1403. Where it landed, a fountain jetted forth. Soon mariners came to regard this miraculous Virgin as their special protector. The chapel was transformed into an arsenal at the time of the Revolution. Unfortunately the arsenal exploded. Rebuilt in 1816, Notre-Dame-des-Dunes once again houses the statue of the Virgin. She is a tiny little thing, but hundreds of ex-voto plaques inside the chapel testify to her efficacy in protecting mariners. Model sailing ships hang from the ceiling, which is spotted with stars in homage to Our Lady, Star of the Sea.

Twentieth-century Dunkerque has exerted herself for tourists by founding a casino, which offers English and American roulette as well as a piano bar. The city also boasts a tourist train, a sort of pseudo-puffing billy which in summer will take you as far as the British war memorial as well as along the beach. Throughout the year you can visit the exhibition of 110 model ships in the Musée des Beaux-Arts, an exhibition which in my view is far more fascinating than the minor baroque and rococo Flemish works in the same gallery. A slightly bizarre treat is to visit the modernistic Musée de l'Art Contemporain, set in a park filled with contemporary sculptures.

Just beyond the chapel of Notre-Dame-des-Dunes is a column set up in 1793 by the Convention to record its gratitude for the faithful Revolutionaries of Dunkerque. Drive left here and follow the signs for the Casino and the Kursaal (the Congress Hall) to reach Dunkerque's splendid beach. Along the seafront itself the wide Promenade with its shops and restaurants runs north-eastwards along 4 km of lovely sand to reach Malo-les-Bains, which, though contiguous with Dunkerque, flourishes not as a commercial port but as a seaside resort. Its restaurants, like those of Dunkerque, boast of their beer soup, their scallop shell-fish dishes garnished with cream of endives, and their *potje vleesch* (a cold terrine of veal, pork, chicken and rabbit in jelly). Blessed with a casino, mini-golf courses, rows of caravans and fine sandy beaches along which career wind-surfers, Malo-les-Bains is over a thousand years younger than Dunkerque, for it was founded by an enterprising shipping magnate named Gaspard Malo only in 1865. However, the *Fort des Dunes* brings a trifle more history into its modern face, for here in 1658 Turenne fought his successful Battle of the Dunes. From this beach too some 325,000 British and 40,000 French soldiers, retreating under the murderous fire of the advancing Germans, embarked in 1940 for England. (They are commemorated by a stele which rises on the seafront.) As for the beautiful beaches of Bray-Dunes on the border with Belgium and reached by the D60 which runs alongside the dunes, their seaside resort is even younger than Malo-les-Bains, founded as a bathing spot by another shipping magnate, Charles-Alphonse Bray in 1883. A long row of bathing huts lines its spotless beach. From here an attractive route back to Dunkerque is along the N1, which runs beside the still busy Canal de Furnes.

The N1 continues from Dunkerque to Calais, the ferry-terminals well signposted, as are the villages, industrial towns and beaches along the way. The first of these is Fort-Mardyck, which Louis XIV set up as a commune of citizens devoted to his rule because he decreed that each newly born child was to be given twenty acres of land. Louis XIV also transformed the little village of Mardyck into an alternative port to Dunkerque, when he lost the latter as a result of the Treaty of Utrecht. Mardyck still retains an ancient church, last rebuilt in the late sixteenth century, and enclosing a chapel dedicated to St Anne which houses a couple of sixteenth-century statues. One, not surprisingly, represents an admiral. Next comes the sparklingly clean beach of Loon-Plage (which the locals pronounce as Lone-Plage).

From here you drive 3½ km west through the hamlet of Huttes to reach Gravelines, outside which in 1588 the English fleet routed the Spanish Armada. Today yachts shelter in little bays, while larger vessels ply out at sea. The town lies on the right bank of the River Aa, still surrounded by its ramparts and its glacis, a sloping bank down which attackers could be subject to a murderous fire. The glacis, created in 1160, is today shaded with trees and additionally protected by a double moat. Long ago, in the twelfth century, Philippe d'Alsace, Count of Flanders, deflected the course of the Aa through the town. Then Gravelines came into the possession of the dukes of Burgundy, and Emperor Charles V fortified the town in 1528. Its strife-torn history did not end then. The emperor's fortifications were not strong enough to withstand the attack of the troops of Gaston d'Orléans, who took Gravelines in 1644 and demolished them, an action which made it easier for Archduke Leopold to take it back eight years later. Finally Turenne recaptured Gravelines for the French monarchy, whose rights were confirmed by the Treaty of the Pyrenees in 1659. Louis XIV judiciously set Vauban to building new fortifications, those which today are surrounded by peaceful grassy banks. Its citadel, known as the arsenal, remains equally intact, and its belfry dominates the red-roofed houses of a charming and irregular square.

Before being beset by dynastic struggles Gravelines was a small village surrounding a church founded in the early eighth century by the Northumbrian missionary St Willibrord, 'an outstanding priest of radiant virtue', as the Venerable Bede testified. Its major parish church is still dedicated to him, spelt in the French fashion as Willibrod. Saint-Willibrod in its present form is a very late flamboyant Gothic church with a Renaissance doorway carved in 1598. The hanging bosses of the choir are matched in excellence by the superb seventeenth-century woodwork inside the church, along with some splendid tombs (notably that sculpted by Girardon for the governor of Gravelines, Claude Bertier de Metz, who was killed at the siege of Saint-Venant in 1657, and the tomb of Jean and Louis du Hamel, who died in 1642). Beside the church is a quaint cistern, built in 1729 to supply the town with water during any lengthy siege.

Gravelines has its own beach, 2 km north-west at the fishing village of Petit-Fort-Philippe, whose name recalls the history of the town, for it derives from King Philippe II of Spain. In 1557 his army had beaten the French troops at Saint-Quentin. They performed the same feat at Gravelines a year later, and Henri II was forced to sue for peace. Philippe constructed here a superb lock, and Petit-Fort-Philippe took his name. The pretty village, with its low Flemish houses, lies like Gravelines on the right bank of the River Aa. Grand-Fort-Philippe stands on the other bank of the river, its dunes and beach seemingly unending, its lighthouse visible for miles around. Naturally enough, the restaurants here offer you eels, mussels, oysters, *coquilles* and above all herrings. They dub a fish soup *la waterzoï*. I can think of few more satisfying dishes than the eels of the Opal Coast done with leeks, or the herrings of the region served along with potatoes laced with vinai-grette.

Drive west now along the dunes to the beach of Oye-Plage (which is known as Les Huttes d'Oye) and then continue south to Oye-Plage itself. Although the parish church was rebuilt in 1865 it preserves its lovely fifteenth-century belfry with a strangely un-embellished octagonal stone *flèche*. Near by are the remains of the Château d'Anseria, and 7 km south-west along the N1 you reach Marck, today a suburb of Calais but once a Roman camp named Marci, manned in the fourth and fifth centuries by a legion of Dalmatian cavalry. Flanked for the most part by rows of low white houses, Marck is an exceedingly long town and in my experience seems even longer if you are in a hurry to reach a ferry at Calais.

Calais itself is a double-city, the northern part (the *vieille ville*) devoted to seafaring, swimming and bathing and much damaged during the Second World War, the southern section an industrial town of curiously regular streets. The sufferings of the Second World War are movingly evoked in the town's Musée de la Guerre. Calais, which enters written history only in the early twelfth century, prospered not only from fishing and sea-commerce but also from the manufacture of fine silk net (this nowadays beautifully displayed in the city museum). The town even imported lace-makers from Nottingham in 1817 to create its lace industry, and Boulevard Jacquard (today a fashionable shopping street) is named after the looms they used, they in turn named after the Frenchman who invented them.

In 1347 the English, flushed with victory after the Battle of Crécy, laid siege to the town. Calais capitulated. Six leading citizens, the burghers of Calais, named Eustache de Saint-Pierre, Jacques and Pierre Wissant, Jean d'Aire, Andrieus d'Andres and Jean de Fiennes, presented themselves to King Edward III, offering their own lives if he would spare the rest of the citizens. Bare-headed and dressed in their shirts, ropes around their necks, they carried, history relates, the keys of the castle and the city in their hands. Only the intervention of Edward's queen, Philippa of Hainaut, saved their lives.

The English held on to Calais until 1558, when an eight-day siege by François de Guise took it from them. In November of the same year the English Queen, Mary Tudor, died. According to the chronicler Holinshed she remarked, 'When I am dead and opened, you shall find "Calais" lying in my heart.' The English never took the town again, though in 1596 it fell to the Spaniards, who held on to it for no more than a couple of years. As we have come to expect, Vauban fortified the town, and you can still see the remains of his massive Fort Risban.

The way in from Mardyck crosses the Canal de Saint-Omer and becomes the Boulevard Lafayette, passing on the left a square housing a delicious curiosity, the church of Saint-Pierre, seemingly built in the thirteenth century but really the work of Jacques-Émile Boeswillwald who, in the 1890s, some thirty years later, was to finish the reconstruction of the remarkable cathedral of Périgueux. The boulevard reaches a square in which stands the opulent baroque theatre of Calais. In front of it is a statue of Joseph-Marie Jacquard himself. A silk-weaver from Lyon, he lived

from 1752 to 1834, and in the first decade of the nineteenth
century created the loom which was to enable a humble working
man or woman to match the patterns which previously only the
most skilled weavers had been able to accomplish. Luddites inevitably hated his invention, but Napoleon Bonaparte honoured the
inventor and his pioneering work eventually triumphed. He
stands here delicately resting a hand on his contraption, admiring
women and children at his feet.

Turn right down Boulevard Jacquard to make your way to
what is visually undoubtedly the most impressive monument in
Calais, its Town Hall, built in the style of the Flemish Renaissance
between 1910 and 1922 to plans of an architect named De-
brouwer. Chimneys and dormer windows, balustrades and a long
balcony add glamour to the building. Its belfry, with a majestic
carillon, rises to 75 m. In spite of the grandeur of this building,
the celebrated bronze statue of the Burghers of Calais, created by
Rodin in 1895 and today standing in front of the Town Hall,
exudes yet more glamour as well as pathos. A former German
bunker opposite suitably forms the basis of Calais' war museum.

Drive north from the Hôtel de Ville along another excellent
shopping street, Rue Royale. Rue Richelieu leads off to your
right to the Musée de la Dentelle. The next street off to the right
from Rue Royale, Rue du Duc-de-Guise, takes you to the sumptuous church of Notre-Dame, which is surrounded by the most
utilitarian houses imaginable. Though it dates back to the twelfth
century, this today is a Gothic church built in the English rather
than the French style and left in ruins after the last World War.
(It was in a bad enough state even before: John Ruskin paradoxically adored 'the large neglect, the noble unsightliness of it', and
its resemblance to some old fisherman, beaten grey by storm.) We
would call its style perpendicular, and there is not another such in
France. The beautiful pinkish yellow brick tower is in truth
scarcely English perpendicular in style, but the windows decidedly
are. Walk through the little arch to the left of the west façade to
admire the fortified south aisle with its wide and high elegant
window. A plaque on the south wall tells you that Captain
Charles de Gaulle and Mlle Yvonne Vendroux were married in
this church on 7 April 1921.

Massive pillars, alternately cylindrical and octagonal and
sculpted at the top, support the five aisles of the nave. The round

columns of the nave bear still finer leafy decorations. Its massive high altar is a curiosity. A Genoese ship sank in the Channel as it was carrying to the Low Countries this Italian marble treasure, sculpted by Adam Lottmann in the 1620s. The painting of the Assumption of the Blessed Virgin which it enshrines was done by the Antwerp master Gérard Seghers in 1628. The sculptures on either side of the high altar are by Gaspard Marsy.

From the church you can see the lighthouse of Calais, its octagonal tower rising 58 m above sea-level. Make your way along the first street to the north side of the church and then along Rue de la Paix to find the forlorn-looking Tour du Guet which Philippe de Boulogne built in 1224. It dominates the south-west side of huge Place d'Armes in the *vieille ville*. The tower partly fell down during an earthquake of 1580 and was not repaired until 1806. Place d'Armes offers two other engaging treats: the Fraismarché supermarket and an excellent cheese emporium. The Wednesday market spreads itself into this square, while the Thursday and Saturday markets at Calais occupy Place Crèvecœur. (Mention should also be made here of the massive supermarket Le Continent, if only because it attracts some 50,000 British day-trippers a year.) Cross Place d'Armes and we are back in Rue Royale. Then turn right across the western basin. On our right over the so-called Bassin du Paradis you can see old fishermen's houses, restored after the Second World War, and the moored ferry boats (whose predecessors began crossing the Channel in 1821, a cautious development in the wake of Louis XVIII's accession to the French throne). Ahead are the ruins of Vauban's Fort Risban, along with the Tour du Guet all that remains of the once powerful defences of Calais.

Before leaving we should not forget that Calais is a city of parks and, away from the immediate vicinity of the port and the supermarkets, intimate restaurants, where the noisier day-trippers are replaced by airily garrulous French. Another fine monument worth seeking out in the town is the Palais de Justice which dates from the mid-nineteenth century. Our way out of the town begins just beyond Fort Risban at a roundabout centring on a bronze monument which resembles a dolphin but on closer inspection turns out to be an angel hovering over a half-submerged submarine, the *Pluviose*, which sank in Calais harbour in 1910. Turn left here to follow the route 'Boulogne par la Corniche'.

As you drive south-west along this coastal road you pass
Blériot-Plage, with its pillboxes and comical holiday homes. The
village derives its name from Louis Blériot's successful attempt to
fly the Channel in 1909. He accomplished this feat in a 24-horse-
power monoplane, and his courage is commemorated in an insignificant monument on the right, on which is engraved his
ramshackle vehicle. New forms of travel are continually devised,
and the next village, Sangatte, was chosen as the mouth of the
exceedingly expensive Channel Tunnel. Sangatte still preserves
both its old-fashioned bathing huts and some Second World War
pillboxes. You reach it by driving alongside the dunes, beach huts
and more holiday homes. The first Channel Tunnel was suggested
to Napoleon Bonaparte by an engineer named Mathieu nearly
two centuries ago. Another attempt at digging a tunnel was
abandoned in the 1870s. The 1986 decision to try again advertises
itself by means of an 'international' Musée du Tunnel sous la
Manche and the company decided to provide a look-out ramp
over the tunnel building-site – not surprisingly, for the project is
breathtaking – and by 1990 tunnelling was costing the Anglo-
French consortium a staggering two million pounds a day.

Here we begin to climb to Cap Blanc-Nez, whose magnificent
views are matched by its beach, passing on the right another
monument to an aviator. This one was set up for H. Latham in
1922. He stands gallantly here, his cap sheltering his head from
the winds, his scarf tossed nonchalantly around his neck. If you
wind up the path to the 133 m high summit of Cap Blanc-Nez,
where the cliffs of chalk and clay drop steeply into the sea, you
can on a clear day see across to England. Here an obelisk commemorates the famous Dover Patrol which kept German U-boats
and ships out of the Channel from 1914 to 1918. With every
kilometre the route is growing more delightful, as we pass through
the hamlet of Escalles and then Wissant with its graciously curving
beach. The canny French have recently dubbed this part of the
Opal Coast the stairway to the sky (or *Côte d'Escalles*). From
Wissant Julius Caesar set sail in 55 BC to conquer Britain. On this
spot once lived a holy virgin named Wilgeforte, whose father
insisted she should marry. The saint prayed to be rendered
horrible in the eyes of her suitors, at which God decreed that she
should grow a long beard. The suitors retired, horrified, and
Wilgeforte's father crucified her.

Dunes and sand run from here as far as Cap Gris-Nez, whose lighthouse rises some 80 m above sea-level. Cap Gris-Nez is a mere 28 km from the English coast, and from its cliffs you can see the Dover coast as well as over to Boulogne and back to Cap Blanc-Nez. Blanc-Nez and Gris-Nez are both corruptions of English words, that is 'Black Ness' and 'Craig Ness'. From the eminence of Cap Gris-Nez you can also see the craggy Jurassic rocks plunging down to the sea (which the locals call the *épaulards*, or killer whales), the lighthouse and also the column set up where Napoleon Bonaparte's Grande Armée planned to set out to conquer the British. In its solitary copse this column pokes its finger into the sky, the statue of Napoleon on top like an elongated false fingernail.

Drive from here by way of the hamlet of Framzelle back to the D940 and then south-west to the fishing village of Audresselles. Fishermen and holidaymakers bustle in and out of the port, the former selling seafood from their own cottages. Audresselles boasts another fine beach and a church with a twelfth-century tower. It houses a celebrated statue of the Virgin Mary known as Notre Dame du Cran-aux-Oeufs, since in the Middle Ages she was discovered at that spot 4 km to the north. The little town is also celebrated for lobsters so succulent that, suitably washed down one's throat, they remind one of a remark by a friend of James Boswell, the actor Richard Cumberland, who observed that he loved the great biographer above all 'when his vivacity and his heart were exhilarated by the circulation of the glass and the grateful odour of a well-broiled lobster'.

Fleeing Britain in 1689, King James II landed at the pebble-beach of Ambleteuse, 2 km south of Audresselles. Ambleteuse is guarded by the crumbling Fort-Vauban, one of seven Vauban built along the Opal Coast in 1680. Most mild days the rocks are crowded with visitors catching lobsters and crabs. Blessed by a spring, near the church of Saint-Pierre, which is said to have gushed out when the corpse of a drowned abbot of Canterbury named Peter was washed up here, the village lies due north of the pretty seaside town of Wimereux. On the way there you pass by Pointe-aux-Oises (Pointe-à-Zoie), where in 1840 Louis-Napoleon, who had sought exile in England, foolishly decided to land in order to rule France. Instead he was ignominiously captured and sentenced to perpetual imprisonment – later to escape and return to become first president of France and then Emperor Napoleon III. As for Wimereux, which boasts a windy nineteen-hole golf links, bathers here rest beside an eighteenth-century tower called the Tour Napoléon, though it has nothing to do either with Napoleon Bonaparte or Napoleon III. On Tuesday mornings a busy market sets itself up by the River Wimereux. Wimereux can boast another cross-Channel 'first', for in 1899 Guglielmo Marconi was here, sending the first ever wireless telegraph signals from France to Britain, and he is commemorated with a suitable memorial on Avenue de la Mer.

As you drive on to Boulogne the views out to sea are magnificent. You pass through Terlincthun where in 1544 Henry VIII set up his headquarters during the siege of Boulogne, and by the marble column of the Grande Armée which we spotted from as far away as Cap Gris-Nez. Napoleon assembled 132,000 soldiers and 2,000 ships here, before calling off his attack on Britain. Thus thwarted, he never finished building the column. In 1821 Louis XVIII thought that to complete the work would fittingly celebrate the restoration of the Bourbon monarchy. The 54 m high Doric column was finished, however, only in 1841. Napoleon Bonaparte's statue on top looks not towards Britain which helped to defeat him but towards Austerlitz, where, on 2 December 1805, he had taken on and beaten the combined forces of Russia and Austria.

Almost instantly we arrive at Boulogne-sur-Mer, which stands on a couple of steep hills where the River Liane flows into the sea. The road from Terlincthun enters Boulogne through the Porte de Calais, once known as the Porte Flamenque, whose towers were built in 1632. A statue of the Virgin Mary in its niche on the wall between the towers is accompanied with her motto: *Urbis et orbis domina* (Ruler of the city and the universe).

The Porte de Calais is but one gateway of four set in the impressive thirteenth-century walls, a rectangle 400 m or so by 325 m, built by Count Philippe Hurepel in 1231. Walk a few paces south from the Porte de Calais and continue along Boulevard Eurvin which flanks the walls. The boulevard was named after a mayor named Antoine Eurvin who refused to capitulate to Henry VIII and was betrayed by a craven fellow-citizen. The boulevard sports nine outdoor tennis courts and leads to the château of Boulogne, built at the same time as the walls, a massive irregular octagon, protected with ditches and round towers.

Porte de Calais leads into Rue de Lille, on the north side of which rises the basilica of Notre-Dame-de-Boulogne. I cannot say that I like it. Built between 1827 and 1866 this basilica replaced the twelfth- and thirteenth-century cathedral, which was destroyed at the time of the French Revolution. In 1308 Isabella of France had married Edward II of England in the former cathedral (going on to murder him nineteen years later). Vast and cold, its dome supporting a huge statue of Our Lady, today's basilica stands over the Romanesque crypt built to shelter a statue of the Madonna which, legend relates, was washed ashore in an unmanned boat in the year 633. In consequence, Boulogne became a famed centre of pilgrimage. As Geoffrey Chaucer wrote of one of his pilgrims:

> And she had been three times to Jerusalem,
> She had crossed many a foreign river,
> She had been to Rome and to Boulogne,
> To St James in Gallicia and to Cologne.

In spite of the wealth these pilgrims brought to the city, in 1567 the Huguenots first buried the Madonna of Boulogne in a dung-heap and then threw her down a well. Rescued, she was replaced in the cathedral in 1607, only to be burnt to cinders by the Revolutionaries on 18 December 1793. Scholars, musing over her representation on coins and medallions, presume that the statue was really carved not in the seventh but in the twelfth century. The present statue of Notre-Dame-de-Boulogne in the apse was carved out of oak by Louis Duthoit only in 1885.

Another Madonna and Child in this cathedral, the 'Vierge du Grand Retour', then became almost as renowned as the original Madonna and was taken on a tour of France in 1938 which lasted for ten years. As for the present high altar, it was made in Rome by Vatican workmen and incorporates 147 different sorts of marble. Weighing 16 tonnes, it was hauled here in 1866 in nine pieces pulled by relays of thirty horses. North of the basilica is the elegant eighteenth-century bishop's palace, while to the south, in Rue du Château is a house where in his eightieth year Alain René Lesage, author of the novel Gil Blas, died in 1747.

If you turn right along Rue Saint-Martin at the end of Rue du Château, you will find another of the four gateways of Boulogne, the Porte du Gayole, whose name is close enough to the English word 'gaol' to indicate that its squat towers once served as the town's prison. Outside this gate at the south-west corner of the city walls is a statue of the English physician Edward Jenner by Eugène Paul, set up here in 1865, thirty-two years after Jenner's death, because Boulogne was the first city to try out his vaccine.

Walk north along Boulevard du Prince-Albert as far as the third gateway piercing the fortifications of Boulogne, the Porte des Degrés, which was rebuilt in the 1530s. As you stroll through to the centre of the upper city from here, you pass on the left the eighteenth-century Hôtel des Androuins, which is now called the Imperial Palace because Napoleon Bonaparte used to stay here. The façade of this eighteenth-century *hôtel* is impressive but also, I find, bleak, in spite of its pilasters and powerful pediment, with no artifice adorning the windows. Beyond it is the Place Godefroy-de-Bouillon. Godefroy de Bouillon was probably born here – though some say in Brabant. Certainly he was the son of a count of Boulogne and, as leader of the first crusade, captured Jerusalem. Though proclaimed its king, his piety would not allow him to claim the title of his Saviour, and Godefroy remained content to be called Defender of the Holy Sepulchre. In the square named after him rises the Town Hall of Boulogne, built in 1734 and restored in the mid-nineteenth century. It replaces a palace where, the citizens say (wrongly, I fear), Godefroy was born. Behind it rises the splendid belfry, once the keep of the palace. The powerful square lower storey dates from the thirteenth century, the octagonal tower which it carries added in the seventeenth and bearing a bell weighing over 4,000 kg and named '*Estourmie*'.

To the north you reach the city's classical Palais de Justice, built in 1852. Beyond it is the fourth of the gates of Boulogne. The Porte des Dunes was restored in the mid-nineteenth century and leads into a little park in which stands a statue of King Henri II by David d'Angers. It was set up to commemorate the return of Boulogne from England to the French in 1550 when Henri II was on the French throne. To the left rises Boulogne's subprefecture, which was begun in 1776 and finished eighty years later, and to the right is the shady Esplanade Auguste-Mariette, where I have often slept for half an hour after eating well in this city. The monument to Auguste Mariette in this esplanade fittingly mimics an Egyptian pyramid, for Auguste Édouard Mariette (better known as Mariette Pasha), who was born at Boulogne in 1821, reached Egypt in 1850 where his researches culminated in excavating the Sphinx.

Make your way past the park with David d'Angers's statue of Henri II and along the Grand'Rue to find at no. 105 the house in which the Argentinian patriot and liberator of both Peru and Chile, General José de San Martín, died in 1850. He had been made president of Peru in 1821, but retired to Boulogne the following year. Beyond the Casa San Martín is Boulogne's municipal museum, whose collection reminds us that we are strolling through a city founded by the Gauls. Place Dalton takes us as far as the church of Saint-Nicolas, which should by no means be neglected. Its nave dates only from the eighteenth century, but the vaulting of the transept is a hundred years older. The Flemish influence in this whole region of France is evidenced by a Deposition housed in the church which was painted by Jacob Jordaens in 1675. This Antwerp master had become a Calvinist two decades earlier, but he still continued to earn a profitable living painting for Catholic churches such as Saint-Nicolas.

Every Wednesday and Saturday morning the hubbub of a food and flower market fills the Place Dalton, the Place Saint-Nicolas and the surrounding streets, while a clothes market sets itself up on the same days in Boulevard Clocheville. Finally, walk by way of Rue Thiers and Rue Victor-Hugo to find at no. 16, in the busy shopping street of Rue Faidherbe, the house where in 1804 was born the brilliant literary critic Charles-Augustin Sainte-Beuve.

For years a celebrated cheese merchant named Philippe Olivier who plies his trade on Rue Thiers has been attracting customers to the city. To eat in the pedestrianized upper town further up from here is an invariable treat, especially if you try a traditional fish dish *à la chaudière*, where, along with a handful of crabs claws and *langoustines*, at least four varieties of fish (selected from monkfish, plaice, cod, mullet, bream, mackerel, conger) will be served steaming hot in a broth of garlic, parsley and vegetables. The name *chaudière* derives from the old-fashioned matelots' pot in which their catch would be cooked in sea-water. Eating not long ago in our favourite Boulogne restaurant, my wife and I were asked by the proprietor's wife who were the English party occupying a couple of her tables, all of them wearing name badges. We inquired, and learnt that one of the companies digging the Chan-

nel Tunnel had brought them all across to get to know each other
better. 'We haven't ever met each other, and our wives have
never met,' one of them observed. 'So,' said the twinkling hostess,
'they are here to begin enjoying each other's wives.' Thus en-
tertained and sated, carrying their cheese and wine (mostly
bought at a gigantic warehouse of a supermarket), thousands of
British visitors rejoin their Channel-crossing ferries, scarcely noticing as they make their way down to Pont Marguet a bronze
statue of the nautical engineer Frédéric Sauvage, who created the
modern screw propeller in 1832.

To the south of Boulogne the nearest beach is at Le Portel.
Though technically 4 km away from Boulogne by way of the
D119, Le Portel is in fact contiguous with the city. As you cross
the estuary and climb, the cathedral of Boulogne seems surprisingly impressive as it towers above the city. Surrounded with
cliffs, Le Portel is blessed with mild-mannered rocks, where the
natives clamber to find mussels and run out to the remains of a
fort built by Napoleon. If you do not want to search for mussels
yourself, buy them on the markets, which take place at Le Portel
on Tuesdays and Fridays.

For a time the cliffs further south become more dangerous,
where the 51 m high Cap d'Alprech with its quaint lighthouse
approached by a spiral staircase juts out into the sea. The dunes
stretch as far as the pretty beach of Equihen-Plage. Here the road
turns inland to Saint-Étienne-au-Mont, where it veers right and
plunges into the Écault forest, which is rich in rare wild plants and
flowers, to reach the hamlet of Condette. Keep a look out as you
reach the village for the sign pointing towards the lake and the half-
ruined, wildly picturesque Château d'Hardelot. Today canoeists
and fishermen exploit the two lakes which once filled its moat.
Philippe Hurepel, Count of Boulogne, built the first château here
probably around 1230 or a trifle earlier, and over the centuries it
became a favourite hunting lodge of his successors. This was where
the ambassadors of Henry VIII and Françoise I met in 1544 to
draw up plans for a peace treaty between England and France.
Polygonal walls and seven circular or semi-circular towers retain
the feudal aspect of this château, though part of its supposedly
medieval self was built by the Englishman Sir John Hare between
1846 and 1864. Condette has created a leisure centre for youngsters,
and a sail on its placid 'lake of mirrors' is entrancing.

Charles Dickens loved to stay here with the actress Ellen Ternan, and at Condette he was inspired to write both *Bleak House* and *Hard Times*. From Condette the D113E runs south-west to Hardelot-Plage, whose admirable, long beach is dotted with plane trees. The development of this beach into today's resort was the inspiration of another Englishman, Sir John Robinson Whitley, in 1906. He would surely not have approved of the monstrous buildings that today line part of its magnificent beach. That apart, the beach, the Olympic riding school and the wooded hinterland conspire to make this resort a haven for sunbathers, riders and hikers alike. Golf courses too are respecters of the countryside, and Hardelot, blessed with a fine links, runs annual golfing competitions.

This country evidently much inspired nineteenth-century literary geniuses, for some 15 km inland from Condette lies Samer, the haunt of Sainte-Beuve. The remarkable church here consists in truth of a couple of Gothic sanctuaries which were once quite separate, joined together only in the nineteenth century. It stands in a triangular cobbled square made up of eighteenth-century houses. The young Sainte-Beuve spent holidays staying with his cousin in the château at Wierre-au-Bois north-west of Samer, and here he fell in love for the first time. The château is still in private hands, and you can scarcely see its dour fifteenth-century tower from the D215 north-west of the village. Happily Sainte-Beuve himself evoked it for us in his '*Volupté*' (under the name 'Château de Couaën'). His statue stands in the main square at Wierre-au-Bois, whose church boasts a twelfth-century font and sixteenth-century statues. Since we have made this detour it is worthwhile driving a little further inland to Desvres, which the Romans called Divernia. It lies on a tributary of the River Lierne at the foot of two of the tallest hills in the region. Its nineteenth-century church has a choir of 1604 and stands on an eleventh-century crypt. Before driving back to Condette, spare time at Desvres for a visit to the ceramic factories or the ceramic museum in the Town Hall. Delicate blue and white, or glittering with chinoiserie, the china made at the little town has been famed since the seventeenth century.

Without visiting Hardelot-Plage you can drive directly south from Condette through the Hardelot forest. The curious hill that rises 152 m above sea-level is known as Mont Saint-Frieux, after the saint who was martyred on its summit in the fifth century. You pass by Dannes whose sixteenth-century Gothic church possesses a Romanesque font, eighteenth-century furnishings and a very stern, square tower. The next little town, Camiers, with its campsites, sandy woods and rush-lined, limpid lake is a turning-off point for a couple more excellent beaches (Plage Sainte-Cécile and Plage Saint-Gabriel), while the main road continues southwards to the shipbuilding port of Étaples, birthplace of yet another literary genius, the humanist Lefèvre d'Étaples, who translated the Bible into French in 1530.

The approach to Étaples passes by the huts of shipbuilders and ship's chandlers, with some rusty old vessels occupying the quayside. On the left you reach a little maritime museum on the river front. Its model ships, ancient fishing tackle and traditional mariners' costumes constitute a fitting shrine to a port whose strategic position, where the widening River Canche flows into the sea, made Étaples important both for the Gauls and the Romans. Opposite is an open fishmarket selling kippers, sprats, mussels, whelks, long juicy cod and conger eels waiting to be sliced, herring fillets, burbot (*lotte*), white marlin (*merlin*), brill (*barbue*), turbot, clams, Norway lobster (*langoustines*) – in short a fish-lover's paradise. The shop also sells white wine to accompany its catches, and is topped by a fish restaurant. Naturally enough the people of this region have developed succulent fish dishes which also incorporate the typical vegetables of the Pas-de-Calais. For me a cassoulet of mussels and leeks (*cassoulet de moules aux blancs de poireaux*) is an unmissable treat here.

Étaples was important enough to have been destroyed by the Normans in the ninth century and by the English in 1346. Henry VII and Charles VIII of France signed a peace treaty here in 1492. The fishermen's quarter of the town is extremely attractive, low houses with gables lining its twisting little streets. At the Tuesday and Friday markets the mariners sell their catch, setting up their stalls in the triangular Town Hall square, whose classical brick-and-stone Town Hall was built in 1889. Outside market days you can park here and enjoy a Flemish beer as you lean against the polished wooden bar of the *Palais de la Bière*. An eighteenth-century house in the same Place du Général-de-Gaulle has been known as the Maison Napoléon ever since Bonaparte and Marshal Ney paid it a visit when they were encamped at Boulogne.

More luxurious and infinitely younger is Le Touquet-Paris-Plage. In 1876 the spot was still a mere hamlet, surrounded by a forest and marked by a lighthouse, when a M. Villemessant conceived the idea of transforming it into a fashionable bathing station, with sumptuous villas and a casino adding to the attraction of its white sand. Today Le Touquet boasts two casinos (the Casino de la Forêt and the Casino des Quatre Saisons), golf and tennis courts, a pony club and a polo club, yachting and a race track. A promenade laid out with flowers runs alongside its long sandy beach. A welcome hint of its less sophisticated past is provided by its morning markets on Mondays, Thursdays and Saturdays. The arcades of the market square are quiet and homely. The Hôtel de Ville was built in 1931 in an 'Anglo-Norman' style (albeit with a belfry and a carillon), whereas the church of Sainte-Jeanne-d'Arc just to the north dates from 1911 and mimics the Romanesque. Concerts take place in the shade of the pine woods, which offer cool walks. The indoor swimming pool (which is slightly pompously promoted as the 'aquatic leisure park') naturally includes a solarium and a sauna. If you like seawater, there is an open-air swimming pool filled with it. Le Touquet today has exploited the iodine and mineral salts of its waters to develop itself as a health resort whose establishments claim to alleviate asthma, arthritis and, simply, general listlessness.

So the seaside resorts continue southwards: Stella-Plage, Merlimont-Plage and above all Berck-Plage, whose waters are said to cure arthritis. Stella-Plage is the most recent of the seaside resorts of the Opal Coast, and its lawns and pine trees offer a peaceful breathing-space from its often crowded beach. In the huge and crudely enjoyable zoo and pleasure park of Bagatelle, Merlimont offers an extra treat to the usual golf links, campsites, pony clubs and tennis courts. From the end of March to the beginning of October you can thunder down the so-called River Splatch to end up wet to the skin, ride on a donkey or the narrow-gauge railway, row on the lake or scare yourself in the ghost-train. Following the normal custom of French pleasure parks, once you have paid to get in most of the amusements are free.

As for modern Berck-Plage, like Le Touquet this is a creation of the nineteenth century, though its repute arose not through the exertions of a canny entrepreneur but through the fame of a

humble woman named Marianne Brillard. The widow of a fisherman, Marianne Toute Seule, as she came to be known, began to
look after sick children sent to her by a doctor from Montreuil-
sur-Mer. Disporting themselves on the beach, the crippled infants
made remarkable recoveries. Berck-Ville began to grow around a
little hospital which the doctor and charitable Parisians built for
Marianne Toute Seule in 1861. Alongside the huge maritime
hospital which is the successor to Marianne's, Berck-Ville houses
numerous hospices for those who come to seek a cure here for
various respiratory and orthopaedic ailments. The resort today
also boasts its casino, a wide esplanade stretching for nearly
600 m and a beach whose sand is as fine as that at Le Touquet-
Paris-Plage. The locals periodically entertain their visitors by
parading with gigantic statues of fisherfolk. Visitors entertain
themselves by careering along the beach, windsurfing.

Fort-Mahon-Plage, a seaside resort since 1778, lies further south
across the bay of the River Authie and is altogether more homely. I
wish I could warm to its modern church of the Assumption, but I
cannot. The town still offers visitors the chance of fishing or
shooting game birds, as does its neighbour, Quend-Plage-Les-Pins.
Both offer well-kept campsites and weekly markets, that at Fort-
Mahon-Plage a sizeable affair on Tuesdays and Fridays during the
summer months, that at Quend on Mondays and Thursdays. The
village of Quend itself lies further inland from its beach, reached
from Fort-Mahon-Plage by the D940, and boasts a couple of
châteaux and a seventeenth-century church dedicated to St Vaast.

The road takes you south-west on to the capital of the Marquenterre region, the exquisite town of Rue. Rue, which once stood
by the sea before the sands encroached, developed in the Middle
Ages as a stronghold of the counts of Ponthieu, though its fame
began earlier for a pilgrimage centred on the tomb of St Vulphy,
who was born and died here in the seventh century. Pilgrimages
picked up after 1101, when an unmanned boat landed on the
nearby coast carrying a crucifix, one of three said to have been
discovered under the supposed house of Nicodemus near Golgotha
in Jerusalem. (The other two, similarly transported, landed respectively near Lucca in Italy and at Dives-sur-Mer on the
Normandy coast.) When the people of Abbeville tried to take
possession of the miraculous crucifix, the horses conveying it from
its rightful home refused to move.

Rue in consequence prospered, and the church of Saint-Vulphy in particular was lavishly endowed. Although most of it was rebuilt in 1826 (though the church retained its fine fifteenth-century stalls), the chapel of the Saint-Esprit on its north side remains a magnificent flamboyant Gothic gem. Begun in the fifteenth century and finished in the next, it carries a wealth of statuary, including sculptures of the four evangelists and the early church fathers, as well as Charlemagne, St Louis and Charles VIII. Its double porch, whose doors were carved in the fifteenth century, is sculpted with scenes from the Passion of Jesus and the Seven Sorrows of Mary. The cloister is similarly rich, with statues among others of Louis XI and Isabeau of Portugal, and more carvings elaborating the story of the miraculous crucifix. The interior with its hanging bosses is exquisite. Four nails are housed here, all that remain of the Jerusalem crucifix. As for the treasury, that too is beautifully sculpted, with scenes from the infancy of Jesus.

To cope with the pilgrims, the citizens built a hospice, which still stands in the Grand'Rue, its chapel dating from the sixteenth century, the brick-and-stone quarters from 1780. The Gothic Town Hall, with its Flemish belfry whose corners are guarded with four round towers wearing pointed hats, dates from the fifteenth century, though the upper section was added only in 1860. The buildings which flank it have ogival decoration over their windows and delightful spiky dormers. Inside you can visit a museum devoted to the brothers Caudron, an intrepid couple of early aviators. Rue also sports the brick-and-stone Château du Boroutel, built in the eighteenth century out of material from its demolished citadel. At any time between April Fool's Day and All Saints' Day Rue is an excellent base from which to take your binoculars and explore the beautifully laid out 2,300 hectares bird sanctuary of Le Marquenterre to the west, a stretch of land which was rescued from the sea. You can visit the sanctuary daily from April to November, yellow signposts guiding you past birds who stare back as curiously as you stare at them. More determined ornithologists hide themselves in little huts to observe some 300 species of rare birds.

Market day at Rue is Saturday, and on Whit Monday the town is enlivened by a pilgrimage to the chapel of the Saint-Esprit. Le Crotoy, 6 km south-west, stands on a little promontory jutting out into the bay of the Somme. Villas, chalets and the remains of the château overlook the superb bay and its fine beach. Fishing smacks mingle with the yachts of holidaymakers. Le Crotoy has the requisite casino. But all this belies its past, for until 1674 when the town was almost entirely demolished what overlooked the bay was a fortress. Here Joan of Arc was imprisoned in 1430 before being taken for her trial and death at Rouen. Parts of the fortifications remain, as well as two powerful towers.

Joan of Arc's statue was erected in Place Jeanne-d'Arc in 1880. From this square runs Rue Jules-Verne, in which the novelist lived between 1865 and 1870, writing here parts of his *Vingt mille lieues sous les mers*. Colette too frequented this spot, as did Toulouse-Lautrec. Though the medieval church of Le Crotoy was rebuilt in 1865, it retains its fifteenth-century oaken reredos. And a chapel of Saint-Pierre houses fascinating models of sailing ships. As for markets, that at Le Crotoy flourishes on Fridays. On its patronal festival (the first Sunday in July) the parish priests bless the sea. On Sunday mornings the local fishermen will sell you and the natives of Le Crotoy their *crevettes* (shrimps), cockles, mussels and turbot. And during the summer season Le Crotoy also enjoys the blessings of the little tourist train of the Somme bay, which steams along a single track from here by way of Noyelles-sur-Mer and Saint-Valéry-sur-Somme to Cayeux-sur-Mer.

Noyelles-sur-Mer lies 7 km south-east, boasting from antiquity a Roman villa, as well as two medieval châteaux, a sixteenth-century church dedicated to the Assumption of the Blessed Virgin Mary and a First World War cemetery with the graves of Chinese soldiers who fought alongside the British and French. They came from Indo-China and died not from bullets but from Spanish flu. You turn west here, driving through a countryside supporting beetroot, cereals and fat cattle. Crossing the Canal maritime de la Somme which here runs straight as an arrow for 13 km, to turn into Saint-Valéry-sur-Somme, across the estuary from Le Crotoy. Staying here in 1837, Victor Hugo wrote his exceedingly gloomy 'Oceano nox':

> *Oh! Combien de marins, combien de capitaines*
> *Qui sont partis joyeux pour des courses lointaines,*
> *Dans ce morne horizon se sont évanouis!*

Combien ont disparu, dure et triste fortune!
Dans un mer sans fond, par une nuit sans lune,
Sous l'aveugle océan à jamais enfouis!

[Oh! How many sailors, how many captains
Who set off merrily on long voyages,
Have disappeared over that doleful horizon!
How many, hard and sad fate, are dead!
In a fathomless sea, on a moonless night,
For ever buried beneath the blind ocean!]

While the modern quarter (or Ville-Basse) of Saint-Valéry-sur-Somme stretches rather dully along the waterside (for there is no beach) until the fishing boats return to shelter of an evening, its older part (the Ville-Haute), still partly fortified, is utterly charming, the windows of the houses around its narrow streets shaded with lace curtains. The Hôtel-Dieu was founded in 1518, and its chapel retains treasures of the next two centuries. It stands opposite the Tour des Anges, part of the former fortifications. From here the tree-lined Avenue du Jeu-de-Battoir leads to a fourteenth-century gateway, the Porte de Nevers, over which a house was built in the sixteenth century. This is one of two gateways in the medieval ramparts which are defended by the powerful Tour Gonzaque and the remains of the château. The Porte Guillaume dates from the twelfth century. Rue de l'Abbaye takes you from here to the eighteenth-century buildings and the ruined thirteenth-century church of the abbey of Saint-Valéry, named after the monk who came here from Luxeuil in 610 and gave the spot its name. The parish church of Saint-Martin, its walls delicately patterned in white sandstone and black flint, is in much better condition and dates from 1335 (though building continued for another couple of centuries). Inside is a Renaissance tryptich and an eighteenth-century reliquary.

Saint-Valéry founded his abbey on the site of a neolithic camp whose remains have been traced on the Mont de la Chapelle. So important was this embarcation point that a fortress was built here certainly as early as the ninth century. And in 1066 William the Conqueror chose Saint-Valéry-sur-Somme as the harbour from which he set sail for England. In later more peaceful times burgundy wine was shipped from here to the British.

Drive westwards from Saint-Valéry-sur-Somme through a

hamlet which surprises the British by bearing the name Brighton-les-Bains, to reach Cayeux-sur-Mer. To the north Cayeux-sur-Mer is protected by the 33 m high lighthouse of Brighton (which you can visit in summer). The 14 km of fine sand which constitute the beach of Cayeux make this spot a tourist trap. A few of the visitors pause to savour the vestiges of a thirteenth-century church in the local cemetery and admire the sixteenth-century carvings in the Town Hall (which were taken from the old church). The nineteenth-century Romanesque church of Saint-Pierre has kept a belfry built in 1602. The woods, chiefly fir-trees, are given over to hikers, campers and hunters, save for the occasional horseman or woman. To preserve the terrain of these woods, a 2 km long wooden walkway has been constructed. Once again you find a casino and, more rarely, a flower festival on the first Sunday in February. You can enjoy the market here three times a week, on Sundays, Tuesdays and Fridays, and each evening the *sauterelliers*, the boats of the shrimp fishers, moor at the quayside.

From Cayeux-sur-Mer take the D102 south-west to Brutelles, whose sixteenth-century church of Notre-Dame-de-l'Assomption shelters a thirteenth-century tomb and a Renaissance font. Here stands the well-preserved manor of Hamel, its half-timbered brick-and-stone buildings and its circular pigeon house dating from the sixteenth century. Yet more evocative are the ruins of the fifteenth-century Château de Poutrincourt, which once belonged to Jean de Poutrincourt, viceroy of Canada from 1604 to 1615. Brutelles is a mere 6 km north-east of the seaside resorts of Ault, Onival and Le Bois-de-Cise, with their superb cliffs dropping sheer to the pebbled sand. At Ault a little Gallo-Roman villa has been excavated, speaking of the antiquity of the town. Its medieval moat and its old mill indicate an age that has passed, for today its beach, part sand, part shingle, its yachts and its cliffs seem as devoted to tourism as its citizens. The church of Saint-Pierre, patterned more strongly than that at Saint-Valéry-sur-Somme and in part thirteenth century, maintains a dignified simple beauty. As for Le Bois-de-Cise, 4 km to the south of the town and shaded by magnificent green holm-oaks, the view out to sea is magnificent. The citizens here have playfully carved ninety-nine steps up the cliff from the beach.

Then, on the border of Normandy, we reach the end of our route. Mers-les-Bains is a charming seaside resort, situated on the nearer side of the River Bresle from Le Tréport. The sandy beach, ample fishing, camping, yachting, horse-riding have combined with the natural shelter offered by the rocky cove to warm the hearts of the holidaymakers. The colourful market of Mers-les-Bains sets itself up on Mondays and Thursdays. And the town is blessed by the statue of Notre Dame des Flots, which was erected on the cliff top in 1878.

Six years earlier the railway had reached Mers-les-Bains, bringing Parisian holidaymakers whose arrival overwhelmed the way of life of this tiny fishing village. Fortunately they built villas in the gracious style of the *belle époque*, indeed the only ones to survive the Second World War intact. Today they are listed buildings. But there is a warning here. The equilibrium between tourism and natural beauty is, I think, a fragile one. These villages are rural havens as well as seaside resorts, some of them protected by the French equivalent of our National Trust. What Victor Hugo wrote in 1837 of the route from Calais to Boulogne remains true of much of the coast I have been describing. The way runs, he judged,

through the most beautiful countryside in the world, hills and valleys rising in magnificent undulations. From the heights you are offered immense views. As far as the eye can see are terraces of fields and meadows stitched together: great russet plains, huge green fields, belfries, villages, woods whose irregular masses present a hundred different facets, and always, at the heart of everything, a beautiful stretch of hills which the sea has filled like a vase.

Should this lovely stretch of coast ever decline into a series of holiday factories, that would destroy the very beauty we come here to enjoy.

2

THE RICHES OF THE PAS-DE-CALAIS

Not only do the fishermen of Boulogne land some 12,000 tonnes of fish a year, the farmers of the Pas-de-Calais also produce more corn and oats than those of any other French *département*, as well as coming only second in cultivating sugar-beet and raising cattle. They live in a deliciously varied region, encompassing the hills of Artois, the plains around Arras, the Houilles basin sloping down to Picardy and the gradual fall of the land into Flanders. In spite of the depredations of the Revolution, the area is still sown with an astonishing number of châteaux, fortified farms and manor-houses, some of them public property, many of them in private hands. The whole region is a patchwork of canals, forests and meandering rivers. The characteristic farmers' houses, long and low, contrast with the later mining villages.

A tumultuous history connects the region with Britain, some-times in friendship, at other times in enmity. Ardres, for instance, a mere 17 km south-east of Calais by the N43, once belonged to the English. The little town had been founded in 1069 as one of the dozen baronies of the count of Guînes. Two centuries later the family sold it to the French crown, and then in 1360 it was given to the English by the Treaty of Brétigny. The English managed to hold on to Ardres for a mere seventeen years, after which Philip the Bold, Duke of Burgundy, took it from them. Louis XI captured the town in 1477, and the English king Henry VIII took it from his son and successor in 1492. Then relations between the two countries improved. In 1520 Henry VIII was at Guînes, 9 km west of Ardres. François I of France was at Ardres. On 7 June in between the two cities, they staged the celebrated encounter known as the Field of the Cloth of Gold.

As Matthew Arnold evoked the scene:

> A thousand knights have rein'd their steeds,
> To look towards Ardres' Golden Field
> Across the wide aërial plain,
> Which glows as if the middle age
> Were gorgeous upon earth again.

The monarchs indulged each other. At Guînes, according to Lord Herbert of Cherbury, Henry VIII and his retinue lodged in 'a square of timber, whereof every side contained three hundred twenty-eight foot, with a Savage before it, carrying bows and arrows'. The building had been prefabricated in England, and was demolished and taken back after the meeting. François I, according to the same source, had planned to house himself and his retinue in a rich pavilion of cloth of gold, until the wind threw it down, after which they had to put up with 'a building rather great than costly, as being erected with such materials as could be gotten in haste'.

On the way south-east from Calais, instead of rushing headlong towards Saint-Omer just beyond Les Attaques take the route signposted left to curl for 8 km into Guînes. Although war has robbed Guînes of most of its ancient parts its tenth-century feudal motte remains, surmounted by a clock-tower of 1763. Its château was destroyed by the duke of Guise who had taken Guînes from the English in 1558. (For his pains he is commemorated with a bronze bust in the Place des Tilleuls.) Its central courtyard can be traced in the modern Place de l'Hôtel-de-Ville, its outer ramifications in the winding of the city walls. Guînes' pretty Town Hall in Place Foch dates from 1864, and the church of Saint-Pierre-aux-Liens, though rebuilt in 1822, houses a lovely pulpit, dated 1706, which came from the church of Sainte-Aldegonde in Saint-Omer. If you are staying in this area and enjoy walking, the forest of Guînes a couple of kilometres south of the town is worth exploring. There you will discover a column set up in honour of two balloonists, the Frenchman Blanchard and the Englishman Jeffries, who crossed the Channel in a balloon in 1785.

On your way east from Guînes to Ardres by the D231 you run alongside the Field of the Cloth of Gold. If the church at Brême-lès-Ardres is open, look inside to admire its late fifteenth-century wooden sculpture of the Deposition. As you approach Ardres you pass by superb lakes, given over to the fishermen, their banks festooned with campers. Ardres itself was fortified by Vauban, but his fortifications were dismantled in the mid-nineteenth century. Today its chief architectural feature is the fourteenth- and fifteenth-century church of Saint-Omer. In past years the statue of Our Lady which it houses was a centre of pilgrimage, but I was told that the cult has lapsed. The church rises in a long cobbled square whose houses curve sweetly. A brick staircase tower embellishes the stone building, which is topped by an extremely squat central tower. If you examine the church more closely you discover that the whole rests on brick foundations. I entirely disapprove of the aisle which is made out of rough concrete. In a grassy square close by it is a bust of the bemedalled, *képi*-clad General de Saint-Just, who lived from 1862 to 1933 and after his glorious military service became mayor of the town.

From Ardres drive 9 km north-east to Audruicq. The road passes through Nortquerke, whose church has a modern brick and concrete tower that I must admit is quite successful. Already the countryside is becoming more attractive and rolling. The long, low farms, built out of brick, have gleaming red-tiled roofs, and the larger ones enclose courtyards. When Audruicq was founded in the ninth century it bore the Anglo-Saxon name Oldwick. For such a little town the Town Hall square and its swashbuckling Hôtel de Ville seem a mite pretentious; but the eighteenth-century château at the end of the same spacious square is elegant and the eighteenth-century church of Saint-Martin, adorned with a Renaissance tower, is a sternly noble sight. Audruicq is a celebrated base for eel-fishing and for canoeists. And for a reason I cannot fathom, at Whitsuntide the town plays host to a concourse of vintage motor cars.

I suggest that you drive south to rejoin the N43 by way of Polincove and Recques-sur-Hem. The Gothic church of Polincove boasts a spiky spire and a classical doorway. At Recques-sur-Hem the church, with a long stone nave and a newly built brick-and-stone tower, dates from the sixteenth century. Its cemetery includes Commonwealth war graves. At the far end of Recques-sur-Hem a signpost directs you to the infamous bunker (or *Blockhaus*) at Éperlecques. This was the first site of the Germans' second ballistic missile in the Second World War, the V2, which

Wernher von Braun had been developing since 1936. Fuelled by alcohol and liquid oxygen, the V2 was the first rocket to crash the sound-barrier and had a range of some 350 km. More than 2,000 were launched on Britain and Belgium, each carrying around 1,000 kg of explosive. The monstrous concrete bunker can be visited between April and November from 10.00 to noon and from 14.00 to 19.00. Audio-visual aids and photographs taken from the archives of the *Wehrmacht* re-create the era of a weapon which nearly won the war for Germany.

From here return to Recques and take the signs in the direction of Saint-Omer to find the mid-eighteenth-century Château de Cocove, a long and elegant stone building. It preserves a glittering moment in history, from the time when Napoleon planned to invade Britain, for Marshal Ney decided to make his headquarters here and in this château followed his customary habit of hosting magnificent parties. Then, before joining the N43, find time to see Nielles-lès-Ardres, which boasts both a twelfth-century church and the eighteenth-century Château de la Cressonière. The church here is worth visiting for its carved capitals alone.

At Nordausques arrives the moment to explore the right-hand side of the main road. The D218 runs south-west to Tournehem-sur-la-Hem, whose Flemish name is matched by the sixteenth-century panels in the church, depicting the Passion of Jesus in a style undoubtedly Flemish. You enter the town through an un-expected fortified gateway. Tournehem's château is in ruins; its forest is luxuriant, part of the regional natural park of the Pas-de-Calais, whose lakes and woodlands are threaded with signposted walks. Our next stop is Guémy. To the right, on the summit of a 121 m high hill, stands the chapel of Saint-Louis, a centre of pilgrimages since it was built in the fifteenth century. Drive on to Clerques, whose Gothic church is saddled with a Romanesque tower. For some reason a massive statue of a sower was erected by the roadside here in 1967. Through undulating country we reach Licques, to find what was once a twelfth-century Premon-stratensian abbey (that is to say, an abbey which belonged to the order of the preaching monks founded by St Norbert in 1120). The nave of the massive abbey church now serves as the parish church of the picturesque town. In spite of its hints of Gothic, this church was built in the 1780s. Other parts of the former abbey have been transformed into the local school and

Hôtel de Ville. Adjoining its church Licques also boasts a seventeenth-century château.

This detour is blessed with wooded hills and forests as well as unlooked for ecclesiastical gems and unusual châteaux. At Sanghem, due west of Licques and a little to the north of the D191, the church dates from the fifteenth century. Further on at Colembert is a huge eighteenth-century château, nestling at the foot of a hill and dubbed the 'Dauphin de Colembert'. As for churches, the most surprising in this part of France is at Le Wast, just beyond Colembert. Saint-Michel at Le Wast was built in the twelfth century, and its crypt remains a rare example of Romanesque art in the gateway to France. St Ide, the mother of Godefroy de Bouillon, founded an abbey here, and after her death in 1113 she was buried in this church. Her relics are still on display here. The Romanesque doorway of the church at Le Wast is extraordinary for its Arabic elements, reflecting the taste of the returning crusaders after their venture into the lands of the Muslims.

Drive back east by way of Colembert and then along the N42 to Saint-Omer. Again the wooded route is dotted with picturesque villages. Nabringhen still preserves its fortified tower. At Surgues the church itself is fortified, standing in the remains of a château. Notre-Dame-des-Ardents (just south of Colembert and Seninghem) is a pilgrimage chapel dedicated to a miraculous cure of a medieval epidemic – a phenomenon we shall again encounter at Arras. Shortly we reach Lumbres. The supposedly thirteenth-century church is a twentieth-century fake. The early sixteenth-century Château d'Acquembrone is authentic.

Wisques, our next stop, remains a centre of Benedictine piety. In the midst of a château the monks built here an abbey dedicated to St Paul. Rising to the right of the N42, the fourteenth-century keep of the château is intact, as are several eighteenth-century abbey buildings. The abbey church is filled with ceramics, and each day at 09.45 the monks sing Mass to a Gregorian chant.

Finally, as we approach Saint-Omer, one of the continual surprises of this part of France appears at Saint-Martin-au-Laërt. In its unpretentious modern church is housed a lovely ceramic relief by Andrea della Robbia, representing the Annunciation. It derives from the tomb of Guillaume Fillastre, abbot of the monastery of Saint-Bertin in nearby Salperwick, who died in the late fifteenth century. If you go to Salperwick, which lies due north, all that you will find of the former abbey is a medieval farm.

Bertin was one of four saints who evangelized this region in the first half of the seventeenth century. They came from the most celebrated monastery of the day, Luxeuil. Bertin's fellow-missionaries were named Momelin, Ébertram and Audomar. Audomar managed to convert a local lord, who gave him land beside the River Aa to found monasteries. Momelin started his at Saint-Momelin, 2 km north of Saint-Omer, and there in the fine late-nineteenth-century church you can see (as well as some sixteenth-century wood carvings) his head, or at least the lovely sixteenth-century reliquary which contains it.

Audomar, from whom the name Saint-Omer derives, set up on the spot a simple chapel dedicated to Our Lady around which the town grew. Bertin founded an abbey nearby. They chose the site well, for Saint-Omer is a well-watered spot. The River Aa on which it lies has been supplemented by the Neufossé canal, which runs from here to the North Sea at Gravelines. One of the bizarre achievements of the navigators of the 1880s was to create on this canal the 'ascensceur des Fontinettes', 4 km south-east of the town near Arques, consisting of a couple of pretty and ingenious hydraulic water lifts capable of raising a 300-tonne barge some 12 m. As one filled with water it sank, in turn raising the other one which emptied sufficiently for the respective weights to differ enough to accomplish this remarkable transaction.

Passing from dynasty to dynasty – the counts of Flanders, the counts of Artois, the dukes of Burgundy, the Austrians and the Spanish – Saint-Omer became part of the kingdom of France only in the reign of Louis XIV. In 1710 it was almost lost when an army commanded both by Prince Eugène and the duke of Marlborough attacked the town, but a local heroine named Jacqueline Robin rallied the citizens and the attack was repulsed. Other illustrious children of Saint-Omer included the Abbé Suger, who was born here in 1082, and became abbot of Saint-Denis near Paris, invented the ogival style of architecture virtually single-handed, was minister and counsellor to both Louis VI and Louis VII, and governed France when the latter set off on the second crusade.

You can usually park in the spacious Place Maréchal-Foch, save on Saturday mornings when it is filled with a market selling flowers and clothing as well as vegetables and fruit. Pining for France I can leave my English home early on a Saturday morning, arrive in time to buy a few garden flowers in the market and then enjoy a leisurely lunch in the restaurant La Belle Époque just around the corner of the square in Place Paul-Painlevé – usually in the company of fellow-Britishers with the same inclinations. The chef serves Flemish specialities: haddock and endives (or rather *tourte au haddock et aux endives*), rabbit (or rather *compote de lapin aux fruits secs*) and its younger brother cooked in prunes (or *lapereaux sauté aux pruneaux*). Saint-Omer lost its late-seventeenth-century ramparts in 1792, replacing them in part with the park to the west of this square, but you can readily trace part of their route and the deep ditch which reinforced the defences by taking Boulevard Vauban to the south. The park is gorgeous, reached by an underpass from the Place Paul-Painlevé, and cooled by an open-air swimming pool.

One side of Place Maréchal-Foch is ranged by a fine classical town hall, built towards the middle of the last century and irreverently known to the locals as the coffee pot. Look out too for the fine late eighteenth-century buildings in the square, particularly that on the north side which is inscribed '*Ludovici XVI Munificentia*'. The former *bailliage* of Saint-Omer (or lower court) dates from 1786 and its statues represent the four cardinal virtues (justice, strength, temperance and prudence). Surrounding the square are cafés, traiteurs, butchers, a *charcuterie*, banks and bakers. The water of the green bronze fountain is softly illuminated in the green light of an evening.

From here you can walk south down one of the narrow cobbled streets of the town, which leads you either to the Musée Henri-Dupuis or further east to Place Victor-Hugo. The museum contains a remarkable collection of stuffed birds as well as examples of Flemish domestic appliances and a beautifully tiled Flemish chimney dated 1633. Both the collection and the eighteenth-century house in which it is displayed were given to the city by the man after whom it is named. As for Place Victor-Hugo, this is the ancient secular centre of Saint-Omer, a long rectangle with a fountain set up in 1757 to honour the birth of a count of Artois. On top of the fountain the two allegorical figures represent the River Aa attended by the River Lys. Three sculpted chubby children were added to the fountain in 1856.

A few paces south is the town's spiritual centre, the former cathedral of Notre-Dame. It remains a superb building, dating almost entirely from the thirteenth to the fifteenth centuries. Its builders clearly relished varying the tracery of the windows of the aisles. The square tower which rises for 50 m at its west end was not finished until 1499. It is the first feature of the cathedral that appears as you walk towards the building up a narrow cobbled street. Delicate windows, a double row of blind arcades and four spiky little towers add to its elegance. Small wonder that its greatest bell, which weighs 8,500 kg, is named 'la Joyeuse'. Of the four entrances to the church, the finest is that of the south side. Built between the thirteenth and fourteenth centuries, its carved porch bears on the tympanum a Last Judgement. A century later a sculpture of the Virgin Mary completed the ensemble. The massive interior (22 m high, 53 m wide and 100 m long) is equally impressive. Abbé Suger would have been proud of the ogival arches of this church. The carvings on the capitals of the pillars are worth enjoying through binoculars. The rose window in the south transept dates from the fourteenth century. That in the north transept was created in the next century.

Although the plethora of later treasures slightly impedes one's appreciation of the overall beauty of this building. I can hardly suppose that any of them ought to be jettisoned. The eighteenth-century high altar came from the church of Saint-Bertin, and the pyx in the sacristy was made six centuries earlier. St Omer's own tomb obviously has a right to be here, though as you can easily see he no longer lies in the stone coffin. Delicately sculpted, the tomb was created to house his bones in the thirteenth century and carries a statue of the saint (though of course the sculptor had no idea what he looked like). It stands between the fifth and sixth of the arches dividing the nave from the left aisle. Between the arches at the opposite side of the church is a much showier tomb, made in marble and alabaster in 1538 by Jacques Dubroeucq for Eustache de Croy, who has provost of Saint-Omer and bishop of Arras. For this tomb Dubroeucq sculpted Eustache in his glory as a bishop and in the lowliness of death.

To list all the treasures of Notre-Dame at Saint-Omer would make this chapter of my book into a catalogue of an exhibition of ecclesiastical art. Mention must however be made of a thirteenth-century group depicting the Christ, seated between the Virgin

Mary and St John the Baptist. Emperor Charles V brought it here from the cathedral of Thérouanne in 1553. In that year he had besieged Saint-Omer from 13 April to 20 June, 3,000 men of Thérouanne defying his army of 60,000. The enraged emperor had personally ordered the complete destruction of Thérouanne, including the demolition of its beautiful thirteenth-century cathedral. The people of Saint-Omer still dub this massive statue (which stands in the north transept) the 'Grand Dieu de Thérouanne'.

Among the beautiful screens, statues, bas-reliefs and funeral monuments of the side chapels and the deambulatory is one (in the deambulatory) sculpted and signed by George Monnoyer in 1554 for Canon Sidrach de Lallaing. The oldest tomb in the church was made out of sandstone in the eighth century for St Erkembode. Two lions hold it up close by the south transept in front of the chapel of Saint-Antoine. Erkembode was a cripple, and has become famed for his ability to heal those similarly afflicted. On St Erkembode's cenotaph I have seen many shoes from crippled children, plus a stocking or two from a sick old lady, with little notes attached to them asking the saint to intercede in heaven for a cure. Beside them is a notice from the clergy of the church, asking people not to place such things on the tomb.

The astrological clock in the same transept, which tells the time, the day in the month, the hours of sunrise and sunset and sundry other useful matters, was made in 1558. In the right transept is an overwrought chapel of Notre-Dame-des-Miracles, housing a beautiful and miracle-working thirteenth-century statue of Our Lady (surrounded by numerous ex-votos). At the west end of the church, beside the north door, faded medieval tiles are roped off. Three alabaster grave-slabs, superbly chiselled in the thirteenth century, line the walls nearby like monumental brasses. The grave-slab of a priest still retains some medieval colour on his stole. A painting of 1612 hanging above the tiles and depicting the Deposition is possibly by Rubens himself. This painting was commissioned from his workshop in 1612 for 260 florins. The dead body of Jesus as it is lowered from the cross is still bleeding, the blood reflected in the red of St John's robe.

The pulpit in this church was fashioned by a Dominican monk named Omer Danvin in 1714. Three years later the impressive organ was installed. This baroque masterpiece is one of the glories of Notre-Dame at Saint-Omer. Designed by Thomas and Jean-Jacques Desfontaines of Douai and sculpted by three local brothers named Piette, from the start this organ was planned not simply as a work of art but also to teach the Christian faith. Statues of the two pillars of the church flank the base of the console – St Peter representing the church as institution, St Paul representing the church as mission. Above them are Faith, Hope with her anchor and Charity represented by a multitude of little cherubic musicians (one of them conducting the rest). The organ case is crowned with a statue of the shepherd-poet King David and a superbly animated St Cecilia playing her own little pipe-organ.

In 1855 the most famous organ-builder of the age, Aristide Cavaillé-Coll, transformed the tones of this magical instrument (comprising 3,300 pipes, four manuals each with fifty-four voices and a pedal with twenty-seven) from their baroque selves to those more suited to his romantic ear. A century and a half later the organ was restored to its baroque original, and on 11 December 1988, the bishop of Arras, Boulogne and Saint-Omer inaugurated a new era of music with the words 'Sacred instrument, awake'.

If you leave Notre-Dame by the door on the north side of the church you will spot the sad sight of the bell from the defunct tower of Saint-Bertin (at least I hope you will, for it was not there when last I visited Saint-Omer). Walk round the apse, noting the former episcopal palace, which is today the Palais de Justice, the Gospel transformed so to speak into the Law. The grand entrance and courtyard of this luxurious building, designed by Jules Hardouin Mansart in 1680 but not finished till 1701, is in Rue des Tribunaux just around the corner. Mansart incorporated part of the twelfth-century canons' houses. His palace was enlarged in the 1840s, no great improvement in my view.

To the south of the cathedral is the Place de Sithieu, in which stands a statue of the composer and violinist Pierre-Alexandre Monsigny, who lived between 1729 and 1817 and was one of the pioneers of French comic opera. His inspiration came from hearing *La serva padrona* by the Italian Giovanni Battista Pergolesi. Monsigny then wrote his own *Les Aveux indiscrets*, which was produced in Paris in 1759, to be followed by a stream of other comic operas until he suddenly stopped composing in 1777. Poor Monsigny lost his entire fortune during the French Revolution, but the Opéra-Comique came to his rescue in 1798 with a pension. I do not know why he stands here in Saint-Omer, for his birth-place was the village of Fauquembergues a good 25 km away. He meditates here elegantly, awaiting inspiration.

Rue Gambetta runs east from the Place de Sithieu. It leads to another of the little-known riches of Saint-Omer, the town library, which contains among its 400,000 volumes nearly 1,700 ancient manuscripts and 212 incunabula. Here is a Gutenberg Bible (probably the first European printed book), and a twelfth-century copy of St Paul's Letter to the Romans which came from the abbey of Saint-Bertin. Just before the library Rue de Lycée runs left off Rue Gambetta. The *lycée* in question turns out to be the former college of Walloon Jesuits, built in the seventeenth century, regularly extended until the nineteenth. Their splendid brick-and-stone chapel with a couple of square towers, built between 1615 and 1629 (and restored in 1775), rises on the right of the street.

Rue du Lycée reaches Rue Saint-Bertin, where you turn right. At the corner is a fountain on which a bronze child plays with a bronze swan (hence the name of the nearby restaurant Le Cygne). As you walk down Rue Saint-Bertin look on the left for the square shaded by the three-storeyed, thirteenth-century tower of the church of Saint-Denis. The interior comes as a surprise, since it was virtually rebuilt in the first two decades of the eighteenth century. The choir, which dates from the fifteenth century, houses a thirteenth-century relief of the earlier church. Another ceramic by Andrea della Robbia, again from the tomb of Abbot Fillastre of Saint-Bertin, depicts the Last Supper and adorns a fifteenth-century tomb. Jacques Dubroeuck made for this church an ala-baster statue of Jesus, which stands in a chapel to the left of the choir along with more bits of St Bertin in an early-nineteenth-century reliquary.

As you walk along Rue Saint-Bertin you encounter first the house in which (according to its plaque) the local painter Alphonse-Marie de Neuville was born in 1836 and revelled in exalting the military exploits of his fellow-countrymen. Next rises a building of 1726 with huge Corinthian pillars, once the home of the Jesuits whose chapel we have already admired. Its inscription declares that the college was founded in 1592 and successively became a military hospital and a royal college. Twice consumed

by fire, it was twice rebuilt, and the last restoration took place in
1845. Its most renowned principal was Alban Butler, the hagiogra-
pher, whose *Lives of the Saints* has remained the daily reading of
Catholics and Protestants alike for more than two centuries. His
most celebrated pupil was Daniel O'Connell, whose campaigns
brought about Catholic emancipation in Britain in 1829. It is
pleasing to know that this English Christian was revered both by
his pupils and their parents. When he died in 1773, hundreds
wept as his body was carried through the streets for burial. 'Dear
Mr Butler, he died like a saint,' wrote the mother of one of his
charges, 'and when his speeches failed ye tears of Devotion
streamed down his face. With his Eyes Lifted up to Heaven he
quitted this miserable world.'

   Rue Saint-Bertin finally crosses a canal to reach a sad spot, the
ruins of the lovely abbey of Saint-Bertin, no more than arcades
and the base of its unfortunate tower. This abbey church, rebuilt
between the early fourteenth and early sixteenth centuries and
dedicated to the saint, prospered here till the Revolution. The
church was almost entirely burnt down in 1820, but its exquisite
tower survived, only to be bombed in the Second World War
(when Saint-Omer lost 600 dwellings). Happily, it did not collapse
under this attack. Unhappily, the authorities did nothing to
repair the damage, and at nine o'clock on the evening of 22 July
1947, the Tour Saint-Bertin gave up the ghost and crumbled into
rubble. The citizens rescued its great bell, '*la Bertine*', and re-
housed her in their basilica of Notre-Dame. Though mutilated
the north doorway of the church remains a beautiful relic. The
wide promenade in front of the ruin is enhanced with a marble
statue of Abbé Suger.

   Walk back from here along Rue Faidherbe, which runs from
the Place Vanquais north of the ruins and joins Rue Carnot. A
curiosity of this second street is the plaque at no. 52, which
records the death here of the British military commander Lord
Roberts, VC, KG on 11 November 1914. The HQ of the
British army had wisely set itself up at Saint-Omer during the
First World War. It must have been more pleasant to die in this
fine home than in the mud of Flanders fields. An exquisite house
on the right of Rue Carnot is ultimately of more interest. Built in
the late eighteenth century by the Viscountess of Fruges, it now is
the home of the city museum. This *musée-hôtel* Sandelin, crammed

as one would expect with local curiosities (including innumerable clay pipes) as well as works by Rubens, Ruysdael, Boucher and Pieter Brueghel, deserves a visit if only for the rooms filled with portraits of some notable figures in French history: Louis XVI, Mme de Pompadour, the daughters of Louis XV.

Saint-Omer's whitewashed houses retain a distinctive charm and its major buildings a particular nobility. Let me mention two others, both in the northern part of the city in Rue Saint-Sépulcre. One is the flamboyant Gothic church of Saint-Sépulcre itself, a fourteenth and fifteenth-century building whose *flèche* rises to 52 m. Taken over at the Revolution to serve as a temple of Reason, Saint-Sépulcre alas lost most of its furnishings. The other fine building, across the street, is the hospital Saint-Louis of 1702, which, like the former Jesuit college, boasts massive Corinthian columns. From Place Maréchal-Foch you reach Rue Saint-Sépulcre by the partly pedestrianized shopping street named Rue de Dunkerque.

Saint-Omer boasts its own brewery (in Rue Édouard-Devaux) which welcomes groups of visitors. This city is also a fine centre for those who enjoy rambling or being taken for a sail in a skiff, especially to the north of the city in the forest of Rihour-Clairmarais or along the amazing network of canals (known here as 'watergangs') created partly to drain the marshlands for cultivation. As Alban Butler of Saint-Omer himself noted, although 'monasteries were anciently built chiefly in uncultivated deserts, rocks or swampy lands ... the monks in many places, with incredible industry, drained their morasses, and converted them into gardens and meadows'. So it was with these 'watergangs'. The monks of Saint-Omer dug no fewer than seven lakes in the forest, and this part of the Pas-de-Calais remains a fisherman's paradise. At Clairmarais itself is a barn devoted to expounding the treasures of the natural park in which it stands and offering ramblers plans and guided tours. The farmers of these marshes sell their produce direct to the general public.

Leave Saint-Omer by the Rue d'Arras, passing on the right a massive and extremely useful supermarket known as Mammouth. Drive south-east to the glass-making town of Arques, situated where the Neuffossé canal links up with the River Aa to join it to the Lys. Arques boasts a church of 1776, and next to it a mid-seventeenth-century château. The apse of the church is pleasingly decorated with 'sandwiches' made of bands of brick and bands of stone. The airy interior is darkened by modern stained glass, which makes it difficult to admire the excellent nineteenth-century stalls in the apse. A little stream defends the Gothic balustrades and minuscule towers of the château. From here a path runs alongside the stream to the public park and tennis courts. Needless to say, the park is washed with lakes and streams.

The Town Hall at Arques is a grandiose brick-and-stone building of 1910. Visitors are made welcome from Monday to Saturday at the famous glass factory (the *Verrerie-Cristallerie d'Arques*). As you are leaving the town (at its very limit) look out for an insignificant sign pointing to the right and to that remarkable piece of nineteenth-century engineering: the *écluse* and *ascenseur des Fontinettes*. Wide canal barges moor at the side of the canal outside the great lock. If you want a guided tour of the amazing hydraulic lift, you can arrange one at Arques Town Hall.

Aire-sur-la-Lys is 19 km further south-east along the N43, the parish church and its powerful belfry soon appearing ahead. The strategic importance of Aire-sur-la-Lys derives from its position at the confluence of no fewer than four rivers, the Melde, the Mardyck and Laquette here joining with the one that is part of the town's name. Four canals also wash the town. As many another town in the Pas-de-Calais, Aire-sur-la-Lys began life as a ninth-century monastery, which the Normans in their pre-Christian days sacked. At the beginning of the next century Count Baudouin IV of Flanders built a château here, and in 1059 his son paid for the construction of the huge church of Saint-Pierre on the site of the ruined monastery.

Aire-sur-la-Lys again and again changed hands throughout the Middle Ages and into the eighteenth century. Philippe-Auguste took it from the counts of Flanders in 1192. Baudouin IX took it back six years later, but in 1200 the Treaty of Péronne forced him to render the town to the French monarchy, along with the whole of southern Flanders. St Louis then declared his newly acquired realms to be the country of Artois. When the duke of Burgundy took control of Artois, he also took Aire-sur-la-Lys. Louis IX captured the strife-torn spot in 1482. Then it passed successively into the hands of the Austrians, the Spanish, Marlborough, and Prince Eugène in 1710, and finally, by the Treaty of Utrecht in 1713, back into the hands of the French.

Its majestic belfry carrying a carillon, the imposing Hôtel de Ville stands at the centre of Aire-sur-la-Lys in the Grand'Place, home of the Friday morning market. Corinthian pilasters and on the portico a carved double-headed eagle amid battle standards add to its grandeur. Though the belfry had to be restored after the First World War, the building basically dates from the second decade of the eighteenth century. Surrounding it are more fine eighteenth-century houses. Contrasting with these houses, the Hôtel du Bailliage across the square at the corner with Rue d'Arras is a Renaissance jewel, built in brick and stone between 1599 and 1603 by a local architect named Pierre Framery. (It is inscribed with the date 1600.) Otherwise known as the guard-house, the building is charmingly irregular in plan and exquisitely regular in detail. Two sides are arcaded, their Doric columns growing more slender as they reach the arcades. Above them even more delicate Ionic columns divide the façade into bays. All the details of this house repay attention. The coats of arms and emblems on the frieze include the symbols of St James the Great and those of the order of the Golden Fleece. The statuary on the west façade also include St James as well as bounty, and the temptation of St Anthony. Those on the east side depict the three theological virtues of faith, hope and charity, those on the north the four cardinal virtues (temperance, strength, prudence and fortitude) and those on the south the four elements of earth, air, fire and water. These alone are not named, but to my mind they are the finest of all the reliefs and readily recognizable.

Rue d'Arras is not without its excellent Renaissance décors, but we really want to travel east along Rue du Bourg and then follow Rue Saint-Pierre to reach the vast collegiate church of Saint-Pierre. As you walk along Rue Saint-Pierre, note the very pretty classical doorway of the Maison des Dévotaries on the right, bearing the date 1602. The massive, pinnacled stone tower of the church, growing ever more elaborate as it rises, contrasts piquantly with the red brick of the aisles. Though the tower remains Gothic, it was not begun until 1559 and finished only in the eighteenth century. (You can read the date 1733 inscribed on it.) The interior, much damaged both by clumsy restoration in the past and the bombs of August 1944, boasts massive arcades, and a balustraded triforium. The arches of the nave bear the date 1864 and are decorated with both classical and Gothic motifs.

The vaults of the apse have been superbly restored since the last war, replacing an intrusive rose window with the original delicate ogival design. The organ with its curly woodwork dates from 1622 and once graced the abbey of Clairmarais. A magnificent pulpit and rood screen were sculpted for the church in 1842.

When Ferrand of Portugal was besieging Aire-sur-la-Lys in 1213 the citizens appealed to a statue of the Blessed Virgin in this church for succour. She miraculously brought them bread, hence her name, Notre-Dame-de-Panetière. Inevitably the Revolutionaries wished to destroy her as an object of superstition, but a baker's boy saved the statue on the pretext that he planned to use it as firewood. When the bombs of 8 August 1944 set alight the sanctuary of the church Notre-Dame-de-Panetière was standing above the high altar and was smashed into pieces. Laboriously the citizens collected every shred of their famous statue and by 1954 she had been put together again, standing once again on a gilded carving of the moon.

The faithful of Aire-sur-la-Lys seem to have been particularly devoted to St James the Great, whom we have already spotted on the Hôtel du Bailliage, for inside the church sixteen paintings depict his legendary life as well as miracles performed in the neighbourhood through his prayers. The first time I visited Aire-sur-la-Lys I could not find them, for the simple reason that they have faded almost beyond recognition. A worshipper took me to them, in a chapel on the right-hand side of the church. We spoke of the problems of raising money for restoration, and when I suggested maybe the authorities in Paris should cough up something, he threw up his hands in mock despair.

Opposite this collegiate church stands the Institution Sainte-Marie (rebuilt in 1926), where the novelist Georges Bernanos was educated between 1904 and 1906. If you look to the right along Rue de Saint-Omer on your way back to the Grand'Place you will find that when the Jesuits came to build their church here in the 1680s (another brick-and-stone building, much restored) they also dedicated it to St James the Great. Its façade is decorated with the cockleshell symbol of the pilgrim saint.

Leaving Aire-sur-la-Lys our route follows the N43 for another 11 km to reach Lillers on the River Nave. On the way we pass through Lambres, with its fifteenth-century church. It is hard to believe that in 575 this humble spot saw the investiture of Sigebert as king of the eastern Franks. Beyond Lumbres the road turns left into Norrent-Fontes, so called because of its celebrated spring, where the Gothic church dates from the sixteenth century.

Following the tree-lined N43 beyond Norrent-Fontes keep a watch for the narrow country road which takes you off to the left for Ham-en-Artois. This part of the Pas-de-Calais is a treasure-trove of fine brick-and-stone churches. That at Ham-en-Artois derives from the former abbey of Saint-Sauveur. Next to it stands a classical brick château with a Gothic stone entrance and jolly little towers. Most of the nave of the church dates back to the twelfth century. The north crossing was rebuilt three centuries after the nave and the south aisle two centuries after that. In 1687 the octagonal brick-and-stone belfry was added. The huge classical choir was finished only in 1695.

The first and most dazzling treasures you see inside the church are the semi-circular retable, made in the seventeenth century, and the eighteenth-century high altar. From the retable God the Father blesses us, while his Son, flanked by the four evangelists, rises triumphantly from the tomb. Now look for the sadly broken funeral statue of Enguerrand de Lillers which was sculpted in 1110. Other treasures include a fourteenth-century Madonna and fifteenth-century statues of St Catherine and St Barbara. The Madonna holds a globe in one hand and her Divine Infant in the other, his red robe matching the dress she wears under her blue mantle. Here too is a fourteenth-century Man of Sorrows.

Drive on through the village and take the D94 (followed by the D188) to reach Lillers 8 km later. Lillers has two main squares, one of them, the Place de la Mairie, hosting a stone-and-brick Flemish house built in the seventeenth century, and, round the corner from the Town Hall, another gabled home built in the next. The pretty, eighteenth-century chapel of Notre-Dame-de-la-Miséricorde should be spared at least a glance before you visit the collegiate church. Once one of the finest Romanesque buildings in northern France, today it seems to me in a mess, yet its venerable self deserves respect. It was built between 1120 and 1150, save for the square central tower which was not added till 1821. The west façade has a humble, attractive rose window, as well as colonnettes and a decorated gable. Inside you are troubled to see a modern roof, though in fact the nave, transepts and choir were never vaulted (save for the crossing and some eighteenth-century ogival vaulting in the north transept). The round pillars are satisfyingly massive. Twin columns, with herring-bone decoration, form a kind of false triforium. To see original twelfth-century arcading you should walk around the de-ambulatory, though here part was replaced in the seventeenth century when the chapels were being rebuilt in the flamboyant style of that era.

Look for the great wooden crucifix, which dates from the twelfth century. Long ago some impious person struck the figure of Christ and according to legend blood miraculously spurted from it. This blood, exhibited in a reliquary, brought countless pilgrims to Lillers, until it was lost sometime in the eighteenth century. All that remains in the church today is its little shrine.

Béthune lies almost equidistant from Lillers and Arras, its brick belfry proudly rising above the market place and combining with the massive church to beckon you into the heart of the town. First built in 1346, like Béthune's Town Hall the belfry had to be rebuilt after the First World War. Risen again, its grey-brown walls supported by yellow stones are topped by a spiky wooden *flèche*, which houses a carillon of thirty-six bells that plays every quarter of an hour. In spite of the sufferings of the two World Wars, the town has saved a good number of Flemish houses, the ornamental balconies of some of their gabled selves overlooking the cobbled Grand'Place. Here too stands the narrow Hôtel de Ville, destroyed in 1918 and rebuilt ten years later, as well as the former Hôtel de Beaulaincourt, built in 1753 and now an art gallery of paintings and sculpture. Look inside the Town Hall to admire its grand staircase, built in a sort of subdued art deco style. The *tartes* of Béthune are justly renowned. I have never tried its celebrated *andouillettes*. Alas, the sixteenth-century church of Saint-Vaast, whose columns were retained from a building three centuries older, was entirely destroyed in the First World War and had to be rebuilt. Its loss was as nothing compared with that of Lens to the south-west, which was virtually eliminated in that war and has risen again as a new town of more than 40,000 inhabitants.

From Béthune the D937 takes us south towards Arras through Noeux-les-Mines, a sizeable and homely town around which still rise a good many slag heaps. The next village is Sains-en-Gohelle, which boasts an extremely pretty flamboyant Gothic church

1. Built for the canons of Noyon in the early sixteenth century, this half-timbered library contains some 3,000 precious volumes.

2. Exquisite thirteenth-century tracery in the cloister of Noyon cathedral.

3. Compiègne's Town Hall was created during the reign of King Louis XII, whose equestrian statue adorns its façade.

4. One of the rare half-timbered houses to have survived in Compiègne.

5. The nineteenth-century architect Viollet-le-Duc described the Town Hall of Compiègne, seen here beyond a statue of Joan of Arc, as the 'finest example of secular architecture in the north of France'.

6. These evocative ruins belong to the Cistercian abbey of Châalis, founded by King Louis VI in 1136.

7. Two superb Romanesque belfries guard the west end of the former Benedictine abbey church at Morienval.

8. Symbol of civic pride: the Flemish belfry of Arras Town Hall is topped by the lion of Arras and supports a carillon of thirty-eight bells.

9. Late-Gothic spikery: the central façade of Arras Town Hall, built between 1502 and 1505.

10. The eighteenth-century delicacy of Château Bagatelle, Abbeville.

11. Old Testament prophets flank the west portal of Senlis cathedral.

12. At Senlis polygonal towers and elaborate balustrades enshrine the flamboyant Gothic south porch of the cathedral.

13. Seven chapels radiate around the resplendent thirteenth-century Gothic apse of Amiens cathedral.

14. The Golden Virgin of Amiens cathedral.

15. The decoration of the left porch of the cathedral at Amiens includes sculpted quatrefoils depicting the signs of the zodiac and the corresponding tasks of the months.

16. Ruined yet magical: the abbey of Saint-Jean-des-Vignes, Soissons, its southern spire dating from 1495, its northern one from 1520.

17. The flamboyant south porch of Beauvais cathedral, built by Michel Laye in the first half of the sixteenth century.

18. This half-Gothic, half-Renaissance palace which a bishop of Beauvais built in 1500 is now the departmental museum.

19. Château de Chantilly rises above its shimmering reflection.

(save for its modern Romanesque tower). Further on we reach the village of Aix-Noulette, the delicate Gothic vaults of whose parish church are supported by round stone pillars. In the tiny apse are a couple of fine keystones.

As you continue south, keep an eye open for the signpost directing you right along the D58E, in order to wind bleakly up to the sanctuary of Notre-Dame-de-Lorette, set on a ridge which saw some of the bloodiest fighting of the First World War. A pilgrimage chapel was first built here in 1727, but it perished during the First World War and was rebuilt in the 1920s as a memorial to the French soldiers who died in the war. Thousands of their graves spread around the chapel, their white crosses reminding one of that final harrowing scene in the film *All Quiet on the Western Front*. In the cemetery of Notre-Dame-de-Lorette lie some 18,000 identified men and the remains of another 16,000 soldiers whose bodies could not be identified. A lantern-tower shelters an eternal flame, up to which you can climb. The inscriptions on the tower cry out on behalf of the mute voices of the dead, begging the nations to be united and men and women to remember their humanity. The obelisk shelters the remains of unknown warriors as well as the coffins of eight unknown soldiers, while another inscription declares that God will recognize their dust.

The Latin inscription on the plinth outside the chapel of Notre-Dame-de-Lorette laments in biblical terms the slaying of the glory of Israel on these high places. The chapel itself, by Louis-Marie Cordonnier, is a Byzantine pastiche. A huge mosaic of Jesus in glory fills the apse. To the right of the apse is a statue of Notre Dame de Lorette and a tryptich from Poland of Notre Dame de Czestochowa. To the left of the choir is a touching symbol, the broken crucifix from the former Calvary at Carency, mutilated during the battles of 1915.

At the edge of the ridge is an orientation table directing your gaze to the scenes of the battles of October 1914 to September 1915. Over to the left across the industrial landscape you can see Vimy Ridge and the Canadian war memorial. The obelisk and chapel of Notre-Dame-de-Lorette are open each day from 08.30 to 12.00 and from 14.00 to 16.30 and there is a restaurant and souvenir shop at hand.

The graves of French soldiers are conventionally marked with white crosses. Since the British and Commonwealth warriors in the First and Second World Wars were by no means all Christian, their graves are marked with a simple memorial slab. Such graves are found at the village of Souchez, which lies on the D937 east of Notre-Dame-de-Lorette, the graveyard entrance sheltered by a gateway designed, I think, by Edwin Lutyens. Tucked away in the wall, as in many such gateways, is a little visitors' book. I feel that I have signed too many of them.

Yet the tragic number of war graves spread across this region should prevent no one from visiting the Canadian memorial of Vimy Ridge. If you have time I suggest first a visit to the medieval Château d'Olhain at Fresnicourt-le-Dolmen. You will reach it by way of the D57, which runs west from Souchez. Although the Pas-de-Calais is speckled with châteaux, this is one of the most delightful. Though in private hands, you can visit Château d'Olhain between April and the end of October on Sundays and holiday afternoons. Its walls were built by Hugues d'Olhain around 1200 and rise from a lake formed by the waters of the River Lawe. Partly destroyed by fire during the Hundred Years War, the château was rebuilt in the early fifteenth century by Jean de Nielles, governor of Arras and chamberlain to the duke of Burgundy. He died in 1423, and you can see his tomb in the château he restored, one of the last such fortified castles to be built in northern France. Jean de Nielles must have been a man who needed security, for his moat is 80 m wide and crossed by no fewer than three bridges while the fortified pepperpot towers must have seemed an anachronism when he built them. Nevertheless these towers, the drawbridge and a nineteenth-century chapel (built to enshrine the relics of a Roman martyr whose bones now lie in Fresnicourt church) complete an enchanting ensemble. And as the full name of the village indicates, Fresnicourt possesses an ancient dolmen.

To reach Vimy Ridge from Souchez, drive a little further south along the D937 to turn left at Neuville-Saint-Vaast, where you can see a German war cemetery, its graves as usual marked with black crosses. Here too is a military museum devoted to the First World War. The road to the Vimy memorial park is well sign-posted, situated on what was known as Hill 145 during that war. The Moroccans took it from the Germans in May 1915, but lost it again. The Canadians stormed the ridge on 9 April 1917, taking Hill 145 three days later.

Designed by the Canadian architect Walter Seymour Allward, the memorial salutes some 64,000 Canadian war dead who are buried in France as well as another 11,285 whose bodies have never been found but whose names are inscribed on the monument. The twenty sculpted figures represent such moving themes as Canada mourning her young, peace and justice, gallantry and sympathy, and the spirit of sacrifice throwing a torch to his comrades. Canadian trees and shrubs have been planted in the surrounding park. The pock-marked land on either side of the road is littered with undetonated mines, and you can explore reconstructed trenches and tunnels in which the soldiers on both sides lived in heroic squalor.

While we are exploring the neighbourhood between Béthune and Arras it would be sad to miss Mont-Saint-Éloi. On your return to Neuville-Saint-Vaast from the memorial of Vimy Ridge cross over the D937 and continue along the D49. Mont-Saint-Éloi is a more approachable spot than Vimy Ridge and is in fact more of a hillock than a mountain. Here in the year 640 St Éloi made his home. Long after his death, during a medieval plague, Éloi appeared to two citizens of the region commanding them to set up a charity which would bury the dead and nurse the sick. The *Charitables de Béthune* still exist, annually parading through the town at the end of September. (I also saw them one February as they emerged from the church of Saint-Vaast at Béthune. Clad in their quaint black hats and cloaks they were, alas, accompanying the coffin of one of their confraternity to his grave.) The monastery which St Éloi and his followers built was rebuilt in the eighteenth century. The Revolution and the German artillery of May and June 1915 converted it into an evocative ruin.

From here the D341 runs for eight undulating kilometres to Arras. Exceedingly straight, the road virtually follows that which the Romans built between Cologne and Boulogne. Staying with his uncle near Arras, the poet Paul Verlaine conceived an intense desire to visit the city. The railway had already reached Arras, but he preferred to sail along the River Scarpe. Arras is where the Scarpe becomes navigable, its waters swollen by the River Crinche. By Verlaine's time the river had also been partly enlarged as a canal. The journey entranced the poet. 'Along the richly varied banks grew seemingly endless fields of cereals, oats, wheat, rye and winter fodder,' he recalled. 'In virtually bottomless pools pike slept, and eels swam amidst the stems of bullrushes and water-lillies. Black poplars, white willows and the tall grey grass shaded the river.' Just before it reached the ramparts of the city the Scarpe became filled with an underwater vegetation which the poet declared to be as beautiful as the oriental glamour of an Arabian night.

As he sailed, Verlaine thought of the ruddy-faced women who ran the whitewashed inns in the villages on either side. Though they spoke dialect most of the time, he found them far from unattractive. In fact he was sailing to Arras not so much to taste its architectural beauties but rather to visit its taverns and houses of ill repute. Fishing and hunting in the calm and lonely fields and rivers of Artois, Verlaine had become bored. He had, as he later recalled, brought some of his former Parisian life with him: 'alcohol, women, the wicked yet tempting memory of my empty, licentious past.' So on that day he visited almost every café in Arras. Next he found himself in eight or ten or even more taverns. Finally he reached a brothel. At midnight Verlaine caught the train back to his uncle's home. 'I awoke the next day with a headache, not only physically but also morally sick,' he wrote.

The restaurants and *bistros* of Arras remain as charming as they were in Verlaine's day. They serve local delicacies, especially the spicy cakes known as *'coeur d'Arras'* which I adore and the equally spicy chitterling sausages which I find inedible unless served hot. What Verlaine ignored on this particular visit was its remarkable architectural legacy. Arras is a city which has cherished and restored some outstanding treats from its rich past.

History has created at Arras not so much one city as three, and this curious development is recognized in the nomenclature of the place. Today the earliest of the three is known as Arras-Cité. Rising on the slopes of Mount Baudouin, it occupies the site of ancient Nemetacum, which developed into a Gaulish capital, was taken by Julius Caesar, became the seat of a Christian bishop and was completely destroyed by Alaric's barbarians, in AD 407. Arras-Cité rose again in the next century under the inspiration of St Vaast. Arras became a free commune, enriched from the eleventh century by trading in cloth. Mount Baudouin itself derives its name from the son-in-law of Charles the Bald, Baudouin Bras-de-Fer, who established the city as an independent countship. On the ruins of the first cathedral rose a new one. Soon the kings of France were casting envious eyes on the commune. They finally acquired dominion over it by marriage when Isabella of Hainaut became the wife of King Philippe-Auguste in 1180. Arras continued to prosper, its tapestries gradually becoming another valuable source of income. As these became increasingly renowned the Italians even adopted the word '*Arazzi*' to mean tapestry.

Outside Arras-Cité the Benedictines built an abbey, dedicated to St Vaast, above whose tomb they built their church. Around the abbey of Saint-Vaast grew another quarter, distinguishing itself from Arras-Cité by its name, La Ville. For centuries La Ville belonged to the counts of Flanders. Only in 1749 was it formally united with Arras-Cité. And by this time a third part of Arras was rising to the south-west of La Ville, an orderly eighteenth-century town with streets set at right angles to each other. It took the name of La Basse-Ville.

Today a drive into Arras will almost certainly bring you to the Place du Maréchal-Foch which fronts the main railway station. On this station in 1872, waiting for a train to take them to England, the drunken Paul Verlaine and his equally intoxicated fellow-poet Arthur Rimbaud, decided to terrify their fellow-passengers by pretending to be criminals. Talking of murder, robbery and other such mayhem, they went too far and were arrested – a prelude to the more serious occasion in Brussels when Verlaine shot at and wounded Rimbaud and was jailed.

Two wide boulevards running north and north-east from the square follow the path of the ancient ramparts of the city. The square houses a proud memorial to the dead heroes of France, designed by F. Desruelles. Inevitably Arras is replete with such memorials. The brick building, Flemish in style, beyond the monument is the headquarters of the British War Graves Commission. In Rue Chanzy to its right stands an Augustinian convent on whose wall is a plaque commemorating the bravery of those members of the British 56th division who gave their lives in the First World War. Equally inevitably, I suppose, we remember the literary figures before these other brave patriots who also gave their lives. Here in 1917 died the poet Edward Thomas. His wife Helen described their last leave-taking. 'A thick mist hung everywhere, and there was no sound except far away in the valley, a train shunting. I stood at the gate watching him go; he turned back to wave until the mist and the hill hid him.' Edward Thomas called out 'Coo-ee' to his wife. 'Coo-ee,' Helen answered back. 'Panic seized me,' she recalled, 'and I ran through the mist and the snow to the top of the hill, and stood there a moment dumbly, with straining eyes and ears. There was nothing but the mist and the snow and the silence of death.' Posthumously her husband's poems were acclaimed. As Helen put it, 'Death came leading Fame by the hand.'

Small wonder that after the war Siegfried Sassoon, in his brilliantly vicious poem 'The General', remembered this city:

> 'He's a cheery old card,' grunted Harry to Jack.
> As they slogged up to Arras with rifle and pack.
>
> But he did for them all with his plan of attack.

During the war the enemy continually bombarded the city from the neighbouring hills, causing terrifying destruction virtually till the armistice. In the inter-war years the city strenuously restored itself, only to be bombed yet again in 1940. During the Second World War Arras also witnessed some heroic tales of derring-do. In 1943 a British secret agent code-named the White Rabbit (no doubt partly because his real name, Wing-Commander Forest Frederick Edward Yeo-Thomas, was too much of a mouthful) was smuggled out of France with a suitcase crammed with information about the German V1 and V2 weapons. His aide was a Frenchwoman, Mme Berthe Fraser. The two identified themselves when the White Rabbit went into her shop and, by prior arrangement by the Resistance, asked for an outsize brassière. To escape discovery by the guards of a nearby German camp Mme Fraser hired undertakers, a hearse and a coffin, inside which the wing-commander hid his precious documents, concealing himself under a mass of flowers in the hearse. Though the Germans stopped the cortège, the ruse worked and they were allowed through. Mme Fraser was later awarded the Légion d'honneur, the George Medal and the Croix de Guerre. Alas, the enemy captured and tortured this heroine, sentencing her to death. The allied victory of 1944 saved her life, but her health had been ruined and she died in 1956 in her sixtieth year.

These dangerous years seemed only to be repeating past history at Arras. The Normans pillaged the city as early as the late ninth

century. Walk along Rue Gambetta across Boulevard de Strasbourg and you find another plaque, this one on the post office,
recording that in 1430 the English imprisoned Joan of Arc in this
city. Shortly afterwards Arras was of consequence in bringing
peace to Europe, for here in 1435 King Charles VII of France
and Duke Philippe the Good of Burgundy formed an alliance
against the British which led to the end of the Hundred Years
War. It did not bring an end to the sufferings of Arras. Louis XI
took the city in 1479 only after a savage siege. The king proceeded
to expel every citizen, replacing them with more tractable subjects, brought here from the Loire valley.

Throughout the centuries the people of Arras developed the
habit of hiding from their tormentors in the deep cellars, subterranean caverns which you can still visit, arranging your tour at
the Hôtel de Ville. (In the First World War these also sheltered
British soldiers.) Created as early as the Romanesque era, some of
these caverns boast Gothic vaulting. During the Wars of Religion
the Prince of Orange took the city. Then the Spanish captured it.
In 1640 Richelieu took it back. Fifteen years later Turenne
decisively defeated a Spanish army here led by the French traitor
Louis, Prince of Condé. The citizens hold a festival each August
to celebrate Turenne's victory. They also hold a more peaceful
rose festival in June, and a bizarre festival of rats in the second
fortnight of May. From time to time the giants of Arras, Cloas
and Jacqueline, who were born in 1891, parade the streets.

From 1655 until the Revolution, the citizens of Arras lived
in comparative peace, prospering on the cloth trade and creating a magnificent city centre. Notwithstanding the fact that
none other than Maximilien Robespierre was a son of Arras,
the Revolution inaugurated yet another era of destruction here.
Another native of the city, Joseph Lebon, even directed the
Terror throughout Artois. Virtually every parish church was
destroyed by anti-clerical fanatics. The Catholic church has
seen fit to beatify four devout daughters of the Charity of St
Vincent de Paul who were martyred in 1794. In 1793 Lebon
secularized their house, changing its name to the 'House of
Humanity' and imposing a lay director. Marie-Madeleine
Fontaine, who was superior of the community, and her fellow-
martyrs Marie-Françoise Lanel, Marie-Thérèse Fontou and
Jeanne Gérard, refused to take an oath to 'Liberty and Equality'.

Brought to Cambrai they were condemned and guillotined.

As Victor Hugo complained when he visited the city in the following century, although he found two fascinating squares whose gabled houses seemed to him half-Flemish, half-Spanish, the only religious building he managed to discover was a belfry that resembled an ugly woman – and a prudish one too, since (as he observed) when he tried to get inside he found the door triple-locked. In 1795 the Revolutionaries had even sold the cathedral of Notre-Dame. Begun in 1160, the cathedral was not finished until 1484. In 1812 the owners of this Gothic masterpiece tired of its upkeep and demolished the building. Only the church of Saint-Jean-Baptiste was saved from this revolutionary vandalism, to be left in ruins in 1914. Built between 1565 and 1584, it has been well restored. Carved leaves and plants writhe up its doorways. Its stained glass was of course irreplaceable, and I derive little joy from the modernist glass of Max Ingrand. A couple of fine works of religious art did survive the conflagration of 1914: a fifteenth-century statue of the Virgin enshrined in an eighteenth-century altar, and a painting of the Descent from the Cross from the workshop of Rubens.

You find the church on the way to what is the most character-istic piece of Flemish urban planning in the whole of France, the ensemble of the cobbled Grand'Place, the Rue de la Taillerie and the huge Place des Héros (paradoxically known as the Petite-Place). All three consist of tall, virtually identical, slender houses, built out of brick and stone, their lower storeys serving as modern shops. Arcaded galleries resting on powerful sandstone columns run along their lower storeys, while the top of each house is en-livened by a decorated gable. Those in the Petite-Place still carry their ancient names: *Le Limaçon* (the snail), *Les Coquelets* (the cock-erels), *Le Peigne d'Or* (the golden comb), *La Baleine* (the whale), *Le Paon* (the peacock), *La Sirène* (the mermaid), *L'Amiral* (the ad-miral), *La Grappe d'Or* (the golden cluster). Because the shops have encroached on the pavements, most of the arcades in the Grand'-Place are too narrow to walk under comfortably (unlike those in the Rue de la Taillerie and the Petite-Place). The contrast of red brick, stone, and a hint of pink sandstone is entrancing. The cobbled sets in these squares glow blue and pink. Each Wednesday and Saturday a market spreads into both of them.

Most of the 155 houses date from the eighteenth century

(though they nearly all needed restoration after the First World War). By contrast the flamboyant Gothic Town Hall at the north-west corner of the Petite-Place was built between 1502 and 1505 by the architect Jacques Le Caron. Seventy years later it acquired an exceedingly attractive Renaissance wing. The central building has an arcaded lower storey, part of whose charm derives from the fact that the arcades are not at all regular. From it rise eight tall windows, their tracery in the style known as Flemish flamboyant. Above these windows are pierced little round ones, with inventively varied tracery. Three rows of dormer windows illuminate the lofty roof. Behind it rises the belfry, 75 m high, begun in 1463 and finished by Jacques Le Caron in 1554. Square at first, the belfry becomes a round tower and ends in a little spiky crown. Topped by the lion of Arras, it holds a carillon of thirty-eight bells which usually plays at noon. Visitors are welcome to ascend to its summit.

The interior of the Hôtel de Ville is equally fine. From the large vaulted hall a staircase of honour leads into the Marriage Chamber, whose walls are decorated with eighteenth-century murals. By way of the Council Chamber you reach the Festival Hall. It runs the whole length of the Gothic front of the Town Hall with its eight windows. Oak panelling, a massive chimney and paintings depicting Arras at the beginning of the sixteenth century (by Charles Hoffbauer, who produced a passable imitation of Brueghel) decorate the room.

Behind the Hôtel de Ville its Renaissance wings extend to enclose a gracious courtyard. From the Place de la Vacquerie here signposts direct the tourist down the Rue des Grands-Véziers to the former abbey church of Saint-Vaast, which was consecrated as a cathedral in 1833 to replace the one destroyed after the Revolution. Constant d'Ivry, whose chief claim to architectural fame is the church of the Madeleine in Paris, began building Saint-Vaast. A massive, buttressed classical building, Saint-Vaast could not be used for worship again after the frightful damage of 1914–18 until 1934. The restoration was impeccable, and the cathedral today rises to its height of 32 m and its *flèche* stretches for 102 m. As with the Madeleine, the west façade is a most impressive affair, forty-five steps leading up to its double set of Corinthian columns. The interior is startlingly white. Eight huge baroque statues stand in the nave, brought here from the

Panthéon in Paris. As we have come to expect, a pillar bears a plaque in tribute to a million British dead of the First World War.

It is worth seeking out a goodly number of treasures from the earlier church which are still sheltered here. A terracotta statue of the eighteenth century depicts the Deposition. An abbot of Saint-Vaast lies in a sixteenth-century alabaster tomb. Other fine tombs date from the following century, including the statues of a seventeenth-century governor of the city (Philippe de Torcy) and his charming-looking wife. In the north aisle is a copy of a fragmentary head of Jesus, dating from the seventeenth century, all that remains of the once famous Calvary of Arras. The Saviour's eyes are closed, his mouth open in suffering, his locks of hair almost palpably greasy with the sweat of his death. In the same chapel has been placed a savagely depicted sculpture of the Man of Sorrows.

Adjoining the cathedral is the former Benedictine abbey of Saint-Vaast, today called the Palais Saint-Vaast. Fronting the abbey buildings is a little park, with children's swings and a slide. Another vast classical building, its little dormer windows matching those of the cathedral, the abbey had just been rebuilt, between 1746 and 1783, when the monks were thrown out by the Revolutionaries. Today it serves in part as the cathedral treasury, a museum of fine art and also a Musée de la Résistance et des Déportations de la Deuxième Guerre Mondiale. The beautifully panelled refectory, where the monks used to eat and warm themselves before a sculpted chimney, is now used for civic receptions and festivities.

You enter the museum from the Place de la Madeleine through a splendid gateway surmounted by a pediment bearing the abbey's coat of arms. Incorporating a couple of cloisters and a courtyard with a well, the museum itself occupies the most beautiful part of an extremely graceful building. Elegant swags and garlands decorate the columns and graceful arches of the corridors. Its finest paintings include those of the Flemish masters, particularly Jordaens and the Brueghels. Its most important treasures are the statues housed on the ground and first floors. They include a marble funeral mask of a young woman, dating from the fourteenth century, and the funeral monument of Gilles Lefranchois, sculpted in 1446. Whereas the first exudes peace, her eyes half-shut, her mouth held closed by cloth, two curls protruding from her headdress, the latter work seems calculated to bring the fear of death to the most sanguine, since it depicts Gilles's corpse half-eaten by maggots. Rustic paintings by Corot and a rare fifteenth-century Arras tapestry add to the riches. Here too are displayed a couple of triptychs, one representing the Adoration of the Magi, the other the Crucifixion, painted respectively in 1528 and 1530 by Jean Bellagambe, both still in their original frames.

Walk south-west from the Palais by way of the Rue de la Gouvernance and the Rue Robespierre, named after the *Arrageois* who was born at no. 9 in 1758, to reach the centre of La Ville, the Place du Théâtre. In 1783 the citizens decided to build their theatre on the site of the former fish market. Opposite this elegant building the sirens and fishes sculpted in 1710 on the baroque 'Ostel des Poissonyers' recall the ancient market.

Our visit has so far entirely occupied that part of Arras known as La Ville. North-west along Rue Saint-Aubert rises Arras-Cité. The street takes us through Place du Wetz-d'Aman. The statue in the centre is that of Abbé Halluin, who lived from 1820 to 1895 and whose charitable life earned him the praiseworthy title of 'Saint Vincent de Paul d'Arras'. The Hôtel de Chauines has survived in this square since 1583. Continue as far as the Place Terrée-de-la-Cité, with its monumental, Renaissance-style fountain, and take Rue Baudimont to reach the Place de la Préfecture and the church of Saint-Nicolas-en-Cité. Although it dates only from 1846, it stands on the site of the demolished cathedral of Notre-Dame. Inside you should look out for the sixteenth-century triptych by the Bruges painter Pierre Clasessens, as well as the statues of the Virgin Mary and eight saints in the choir. As for the prefecture itself, it was once the bishop's palace, finished at the precise moment that France was about to be convulsed by the Revolution.

If your legs and taste for military cemeteries will stand the walk, Rue d'Amiens leads south-west to the British military cemetery, where no fewer than 2,642 soldiers lie buried. A memorial, in the form of an obelisk surrounded by a massive semi-circular portico, commemorates 35,942 British soldiers whose bodies were never found after 1918. Whatever your feelings and whether you decide not to visit this cemetery, half-way down Rue d'Amiens turn left along Rue Sainte-Claire, which becomes the Boulevard Crespel. It reaches a splendid park, the Promenade des Allées. On the right, flanking this park, the Avenue des Fusillés warns by its name that we are close by a spot made sacred by the blood of twentieth-century martyrs. Follow it as far as the citadel which Vauban built here in the late seventeenth century. Behind it is the '*mur des fusillés*', a wall against which the Nazis shot civilian resisters during the Second World War.

To the west of the Promenade des Allées is the Basse-Ville of Arras. Its centre is an octagonal square, dedicated to Victor Hugo but deriving like the rest of the Basse-Ville from the eighteenth-century plans of the civil architect Beffara. The stone pyramid at its centre was erected in 1779. Walk on along Rue R. Courtin to find across Rue Aristide-Briand the church of Notre-Dame-des-Ardents. Normally I would not recommend anyone to look twice at a modern brick building in a pseudo-Romanesque style, but this one commemorates an amazing series of miracles which occurred in twelfth-century Arras. The citizens were dying of an epidemic which they dubbed the sickness of the Ardents. Since recourse to doctors failed, they appealed to the Blessed Virgin Mary, who revealed to a couple of supplicants the where-abouts of a miraculous candle. A morsel of its burning wax, dropped in water, was sufficient to effect a cure. Inside Notre-Dame-des-Ardents, on the left of the choir, is a thirteenth-century reliquary in which several pieces of this holy candle are still pre-served.

Two excursions from Arras are historically resonant. One simply takes us 22 km south to Bapaume. The town lies on the great plateau which separates the Somme and the Escaut. Here in 1180 Philippe-Auguste took Isabella of Hainaut as his bride. Here too was one of the few places where the French army could hold up its head during the Franco-Prussian war, for on 3 January 1871 troops commanded by General Faidherbe forced the enemy back beyond the Somme. The citizens proudly erected a statue in his honour, sculpted by Louis Noël. The one we see today is a replica, for during the Occupation after the collapse of France in the Second World War the Germans dismantled the statue of their old enemy.

Bapaume suffered more during the First World War. The Germans took it in September 1914. When the allies forced them to retreat three years later they set fire to much of the town. Two melancholy mementoes of this episode are the medallions of deputies Briquet and Taillander which adorn the new,

Renaissance Town Hall, which was built with a fine new belfry. They perished inside the old one when the Germans' mine exploded. The late-sixteenth-century church of Saint-Nicolas was also damaged, but is now restored and still houses its fifteenth-century *pietà*. In 1917 the Germans did not give up easily. Recovering their strength they forced out the British army and held Bapaume till the end of August 1918. The battle provoked one of Siegfried Sassoon's most vicious stanzas:

> I'd like to see a tank come down the stall,
> Lurching to rag-time tunes, of 'Home, sweet Home',
> And there'd be no more jokes in Music-halls
> To mock the riddled corpses round Bapaume.

The second, much longer excursion would follow the N39 north-west to Saint-Pol-sur-Ternoise. *En route* we cross a tributary of the Scarpe at Pont-du-Gy, close by which are the remains of a Roman camp. The villages are all as usual nestling round churches, that at Berlette built in the fifteenth century (with a fourteenth-century tower), that at Tincques in the sixteenth. For the most part they lie just away from the road, which runs through wide green fields. Little Ligny-Saint-Flochel boasts both a medieval church with eighteenth-century choir stalls and an early-seventeenth-century château. Saint-Michel-sur-Ternoise soon appears, its fourteenth-century church carrying an octagonal Renaissance tower added in 1621. The church of Saint-Pol-sur-Ternoise was rebuilt in 1682; its Town Hall of 1767 was once a convent; its former château is now a few crumbled stones.

The River Ternoise now makes a great loop, and if we follow its valley north-west as far as its confluence with the River Faulx at Anvin we can pause for a moment at its little fifteenth-century church, before crossing the river to admire the château at Petit-Anvin. Then drive on north-west along the D343 to Crépy. Turning left here along the D71 will bring us first to Ambricourt and then to the tiny village of Azincourt. At the first Georges Bernanos wrote his most popular novel, the *Journal d'un curé de campagne*. Just outside the second, on St Crispin's day, 25 October 1415, Henry V led an English force of 6,000 men to victory over perhaps 60,000 French, leaving 12,000 of the latter dead, among them above a hundred princes and lords.

From Azincourt the D71 leads to the D928, which runs speedily south-west to Hesdin. On the way look out for the signs for Fressin to the right. They lead you to a town whose church has a magical fifteenth-century choir and whose ruined château, boasting eight cylindrical towers, rises on a hill in the woods and is defended by deep ditches. Then drive on to Hesdin, a town lying amid green forests at the confluence of the rivers Canche and Ternoise.

Whereas, for some reason, the final 's' of Arras is voiced, that of Hesdin is silent. The town did not exist before 1554, when Emperor Charles V founded it having destroyed Vieil-Hesdin the previous year. The Town Hall in the Place d'Armes was begun in the sixteenth century and was enriched with a sumptuously decorated balcony in 1629. Its belfry was not built until 1875. Inside are some rare seventeenth-century Flemish tapestries. On Thursday mornings the building gazes benignly on the weekly market. Other treasures of the town include numerous elegant seventeenth- and eighteenth-century houses, including the one at no. 11 Rue Daniel-Lereuil in which the Abbé Prévost, author of *Manon Lescaut*, was born in 1697. His bust is in the churchyard. The Gothic collegiate church of Notre-Dame, standing beside the little River Canche, was built in brick in the second half of the sixteenth century. Notre-Dame at Hesdin was given a magical Renaissance doorway (in stone) in 1582 (and another little classical porch in 1887), the former an ensemble of swags, Corinthian capitals, coats of arms, little towers and angels. The interior is richly furnished with a sinuous pulpit and baroque confessionals. The baroque retable is beautiful, and its eighteenth-century stalls incorporate misericords which I wish could be better made out in the gloom caused by the stained-glass windows. The church is also the venue of excellent free concerts, and its carillon rings out local tunes. The hospital chapel too at Hesdin is an exceedingly quaint Gothic treat.

Auxi-le-Château south-east of Hesdin is another town with a splendid flamboyant church, this time with some sixteenth-century stained glass, and the remains of a château, built in the twelfth century. From here our way back to Arras should undoubtedly take in Frévent 18 km north-east of Auxi-le-Château. The road runs through the Auxi forest. Frévent has two sixteenth-century churches, Saint-Vaast, which is fine, and Saint-Hilaire which, by reason of its furnishings and vaulting, is I think finer.

The most pictureseqe way back from here to Arras is undoubtedly by way of the D339. On the outskirts of Frévent it leads by the superb eighteenth-century château of Cercamp, set in a huge park designed by Le Nôtre and approached by an avenue of lime trees. Now a rest home for the retired, the château once belonged to a Cistercian monastery founded in 1137 and suppressed at the Revolution. Over the main pediment is the coat of arms of Bardon de Fourmet, who bought the building in 1822. This was the building in which Marshal Foch set up his headquarters before the Artois offensive of 1915. Our route then runs alongside the River Canche, passing a couple of Renaissance churches at Rebreuve and Rebreuviette. At Estrée-Wamin we leave the valley of the Canche to reach 9 km later Avesnes-le-Comte on its hill above the left bank of the River Gy, a town 20 km from Arras and sporting a delicious flamboyant Gothic church with a pretty thirteenth-century choir and a massive square tower and porch that were fortified in the twelfth century. Further on at Agnez-lès-Duisans is another church with an early-fourteenth-century fortified tower and an unpretentious mid-eighteenth-century château.

The remarkable writings of Georges Bernanos seem to me to give a curiously unpleasant picture of the Artois which he loved. His novels obviously demanded a setting that reflected the drama between good and evil being played out in the villages where the priests he depicted grapple with their own dilemmas and the souls of their parishioners. At Ambricourt in *Journal d'un curé de campagne* his parish priest is not only an alcoholic but also suffering from cancer. It rains a lot, 'that thin incessant rain which you suck in with every breath', as the *curé* puts it. Damp steams desolately from every side. Along the road to Saint-Vaast the little houses seem to him to huddle together in misery. He describes a world 'consumed by boredom', a world of sodden fields and mud. I hope my readers will agree that this is nothing like the Pas-de-Calais I have been describing – a land of lush valleys, of varied skies, of noble châteaux and churches, of elegant cities and contented villages, and of hills and forests whose aspect changes at almost every bend in the road.

3

THE POETRY OF THE SOMME

The Somme, a *département* created in 1790 out of the ancient Generality of Picardy, is a land of rivers, marshes and lakes, taking its name from one of these great rivers, all of them gouged out of the land when the sea made its inroads into the heart of Picardy. As we have already seen, parts of the *département*, such as the cliffs as Le Bois-de-Cise and the Somme estuary itself, are visually stunning. So are the 5,000 hectares which constitute the forest of Crécy. The Somme is littered with Stone Age remains (the finest outside Abbeville, at Saint-Acheul-lès-Amiens and at Montières-lès-Amiens), while Amiens itself has excavated a prehistoric village in the suburb of Saint-Acheul. Wherever you see the phrase '*camp de César*' you are beside a Gallo-Roman camp, for Julius Caesar established his legions beside the River Somme to subdue the Belgians and to invade Britain.

Caesar's *Gallic Wars* describes the chief city of the *département*, Amiens, under the name Samarobriva, which means 'bridge across the Somme'. Although the first Christian bishop of the city was St Firmin, his fame was eclipsed by the Roman soldier Martin. Alban Butler tells the tale:

One day, in the midst of a very hard winter, and severe frost, when many perished with cold, as he was marching with other officers and soldiers, he met at the gate of the city of Amiens a poor man, almost naked, trembling and shaking for cold, and begging alms off those that passed by. Martin, seeing those that went before him take no notice of this miserable object, thought he was reserved for himself. By his charities to others he had nothing left but his arms and clothes upon his back; when, drawing his sword, he cut his cloak in two pieces, gave one to the beggar, and wrapped himself in the other half.

Some of the bystanders laughed as they saw the soldier ride on wearing only half a cloak, but that night in a dream Martin saw Jesus his Lord wearing the other half.

Just above Amiens the River Somme is swollen by the waters of the Avre. It gently washes the city, once the capital of Picardy and today the prefecture of the *département* of the Somme. The Avre waters a section of the market gardens known as the *Hortillonages*. The Somme itself divides into numerous tributaries as it flows through the lower part of the industrial section of Quartier Saint-Leu, while a canal circles the northern section of the same sector of the city. Yet another river, the Selle, runs through the huge promenade known as La Hotoie, not far from an unexpected zoological garden.

On the left bank of the Somme the boulevards of Amiens follow the line of the ancient fortifications of the city. Once these ramparts enclosed an equally ancient city centre, alas almost completely destroyed in 1940. Rebuilding has inevitably resulted in modern suburbs that are scarcely enchanting. No visitor should be put off by them. At the heart of the city I have looked out of my bedroom window in the Hôtel Postillon and gazed on the entrancingly illuminated cathedral and beyond it to the Tour Perret. The same hotel is flanked by the flamboyant Gothic church of Saint-Germain, built in the fifteenth and sixteenth centuries, its doors carved at the Renaissance. The hotel bar warms the heart of the British simply by being dedicated to the saviour of our country in the Second World War, Winston Churchill. And I venture the suggestion that a further British trait at Amiens is that this is one of the few French cities whose citizens blithely jay-walk.

To the north-east of the Hôtel Postillon and the church of Saint-Germain is the lovely Quartier Saint-Leu, well-watered by the Somme and its attendant canals. It takes its name from its church. Saint-Leu was begun in the fifteenth and finished in the eighteenth centuries, its hammerbeam roof sheltering today sixteenth- and seventeenth-century statues. Rue Saint-Leu takes you from the church past a ruined brick-and-stone church as far as a powerful citadel which was built on the orders of Henri IV after he had taken Amiens from the Spaniards in 1597. Finished in 1606, it occupies the site of a Renaissance gateway which the builders happily decided to incorporate rather than destroy.

To the east of the church of Saint-Leu is the most picturesque quarter of Amiens. Crumbling gabled houses with steep roofs and dormer windows flank the canals of the Quartier Saint-Leu. These little houses were the homes of the market gardeners of yesteryear. In narrow cobbled Rue Granville some are half-timbered, some wholly boarded. Others overhang the streets, rising alongside streams, sometimes with their own little bridge crossing a canal to the doorway. Rue des Granges is equally lovely, with another stream bordered by more gabled homes. South of the quarter runs Place Parmentier, whose country market sells fruit, vegetables and flowers and is washed by one of the tributaries of the Somme. The Port d'Amont to the west offers a view of the market gardens themselves, the remarkable *Hortillonages* of Amiens. They cover some 300 hectares of land, criss-crossed by canals navigable by flat-bottomed boats with curiously high prows. Guided tours are naturally available throughout the spring and summer months.

To reach the cathedral of Amiens from the Quartier Saint-Leu you cross a bridge (whose stream divides itself round a gabled house) and walk towards the fountain in the cathedral square. To the left rises the handsome pale brick-and-stone classical façade of the seventeenth-century episcopal palace. Across the cathedral square to the west rises a pleasing ensemble of a half-timbered seventeenth-century houses, a classical façade and a nineteenth-century Romanesque mansion. As you climb the steps to the square, the cathedral itself seems to rise higher and higher. Of the five major cathedrals which chart the evolution of French Gothic, three are found in the region covered by this book. Laon begins the sequence in the mid-twelfth century, followed by Paris some fifteen years later. Chartres dates from 1195. Next comes Amiens, an almost perfectly unified Gothic building, begun in the 1220s, followed by the never-to-be-finished cathedral of Beauvais.

The superb cathedral of Notre-Dame at Amiens survived the Second World War completely intact. This magical building, the largest Gothic cathedral in Christendom, should draw the discerning tourist to Amiens above all its other treasures. Fittingly, the present cathedral of Notre-Dame derives its magnificence chiefly because of the wealth poured into its coffers by earlier tourists, in the thirteenth century, devout men and women drawn here by a remarkable curiosity.

Already Amiens was rich, reviving from the devastations of the Franks and the Normans by obtaining a charter as a commune in 1117 and developing the cloth trade. The chalky ground was conducive to the cultivation of woad, whose leaves supplied a coveted blue dye. By the Middle Ages Amiens boasted some 30,000 citizens. Now the wealth brought by tourists was to be suddenly multiplied. In 1206 knights returning from the fourth crusade brought from Constantinople what purported to be the head of St John the Baptist. Beheaded by King Herod at the whim of his wife and daughter, the Baptist had been buried in a tomb by his followers. Mysteriously, as the craze for relics gathered momentum over the Christian centuries, parts of his body had found their way to Byzantium. French pilgrims were enthralled at their good fortune at being able to venerate such a holy object which was reputed to work miracles for those who deserved them. They thronged the Romanesque cathedral in which the grisly head was enshrined.

Six years later this cathedral was burnt to the ground, enabling Bishop Évrard de Fouilloy to set in motion the construction of a new one in the pure Gothic style of the thirteenth century. His master mason was Robert de Luzarches. By 1238 the new nave and the façade were complete. Under successive master masons, chief of whom were Thomas and Renaud de Cormont, building continued for the next half-century, until all the cathedral lacked of its present form were the upper structures of its towers and the two rose windows that pierce the transepts. These were finished by the fifteenth century. Until the sixteenth century sculptors continued to enrich the building. Apart from the inspired restorations of Viollet-le-Duc in the nineteenth century, what we see today is what these medieval and Renaissance geniuses created.

The three entrances of the west façade exquisitely illustrate the skills of the earliest of these masters. Statues and carvings dating from the late 1220s cover the porches. Even some of the ironwork of the massive doors is thirteenth century, and the rest but a century later. Powerful towers between the doorways buttress the masonry. Then you read the history of the building as your eye rises. The towers reach as far as the second storey of the façade, the celebrated gallery of kings which derives its name from the twenty-two colossal statues sculpted here. Admittedly at this point Viollet-le-Duc considerably modified the arches, as he restored the gallery of bell-ringers above it. Then two massive square towers make their weight felt, flanking a rose window which is more than 11 m in diameter and, created in the sixteenth century, dates from the very last moment of medieval Gothic.

Part of the loveliness of Amiens cathedral derives from the inequality of its towers. That on the south side rises to a height of 62 m, that on the north 5 m higher. In the third quarter of the fourteenth century a buttress was added to reinforce the left side of the taller tower. Cardinal Jean de la Grange took the opportunity of commissioning the sculptor André Beauneveu to create nine masterly statues to enhance this buttress. He also was vain enough to have himself sculpted among the lower row of these statues.

But ultimately the statuary of the thirteenth century entrances most, above all the superb Christ between the doorways of the central porch. In one hand he holds the Gospels, while the other blesses us. 'Sculptured tenderness', said John Ruskin of this statue, ignoring the fact that underneath the foot of Jesus lie a helpless dragon and a trampled lion. Apostles, indeed all the major members of the heavenly band (150 of them in all), attend this statue, while the tympanum of the porch portrays the Last Judgement. The carvings enlivening the left entrance are devoted to the patroness of the cathedral, depicting the Annunciation to the Virgin Mary, the events surrounding the birth of her Son, his Presentation in the Jerusalem Temple. Adam and Eve and the three Magi put in their appearance, along with King Herod, who would have killed the infant Jesus, King Solomon and the Queen of Sheba, who though great and glamorous (so the Psalmist sang) would be found inferior to the Christchild. Mary's death, assumption and heavenly coronation complete this outstanding execution of traditional Christian iconography. A pigeon settles nonchalantly on the head of one of the Magi, while others coo, hidden among the rest of the statuary.

The sculptures of the west door are homelier, though no less enchanting, depicting the saints of Picardy, among them St Firmin who, having brought Christianity to this region from Spain, became the first bishop of Amiens and in 301 or thereabouts was martyred for his pains. The scene in the tympanum shows the discovery of his relics. 'Provincial,' Ruskin appositely dubbed these statues, 'as it were, personal friends of the Amienois.' Finally, as if the thirteenth-century masters had not presented us with enough delights on this façade, they filled it up with quatrefoils sculpted with virtues and vices, fables, traditional tales, signs of the zodiac, and what most of all transports us back into the daily life of the thirteenth century, the occupations of the months. All of these sculptures are blackened with soot, but when I asked M. Jean-Marie Lasblais of the Somme regional tourist board why they were not cleaned he was adamant that they must stay as they are. 'In the past paint protected them, just as gold-leaf protected the golden Virgin,' he said. 'Today only the black covering protects these priceless statues.'

Instead of entering the cathedral by any of these three doors, I suggest we walk around it, past the Porte de l'Horloge on the right just round the corner from the doorway of the Blessed Virgin Mary into Rue Cormont, so as to admire the statue of St Christopher which adorns it. The saint has rolled his trousers up to wade across the river with Jesus on his back. The transepts of Notre-Dame at Amiens are pierced not only by rose windows but also by massive doorways, and we are approaching the finest, dedicated to the Virgin Mary. Once this doorway honoured St Honoré, but in the early fourteenth century his statue was replaced by a gilded (and in my view simpering) Madonna and Child. The same masons sculpted the twelve Apostles who decorated the bottom of the tympanum, while poor St Honoré was taken to the less glamorous doorway of the north transept, which in any case was already dedicated to St Firmin. The rose window, on closer inspection, represents the wheel of fortune. As you walk around the apse of Notre-Dame to the north doorway, with yet more statues to dazzle the eye on the radiating chapels, the *flèche* of the cathedral adds its 122 m of elegance to the ensemble. Although in a moment we shall enter the cathedral, to wander north from the cathedral apse, across waterways and among little, sometimes tortuous, streets, is rewarding. The apse shades Place Saint-Michel, which houses a mid-nineteenth-century statue of Peter the Hermit, who was born here and preached the first crusade in the early twelfth century. Rue de Metz-l'Évêque, which runs north, is still sprinkled with some ancient buildings.

Winding our way around the north side of the cathedral we at last find ourselves inside the building by way of the Porte de Saint-Firmin-le-Martyr. So be it that parts of the décor date from

the eighteenth and nineteenth centuries, particularly those of the
chapels which surround the whole cathedral: the effect is one of
utter Gothic delicacy, 126 slender pillars upholding a masterpiece
whose vault rises to over 42 m, whose length stretches for 143 m
and whose transepts spread themselves for another 42 m and a
little more. Trying to work out how this effect of extreme lightness
was created, I have worked out that the arcades reach almost
half-way up the cathedral, seeming to push the roof yet higher
towards heaven. The columns taper as they reach the roof, which
thus appears bizzarely wider than the lower part of the nave. The
slender tracery of the windows adds a further illusion of height
and grace. Another quality is that (save for the lierne vaulting of
the crossing), the vaults of the cathedral are uniformly and
elegantly ogival. But in the end I simply acknowledge the brilli-
ance of the medieval architects and do not try to uncover all their
secrets. We should walk down towards the rose window of the
west façade to pay homage at the bronze tombs of Bishop Évrard
de Fouilloy, who inaugurated the whole building, and of Bishop
Geoffroy d'Eu who continued the work after Évrard's death in
1222. They lie virtually side by side across the nave in a cathedral
which is surely as much their shrine as that of the head of John
the Baptist. Six lions support each tomb. A couple of playful
mythical beasts support the feet of Bishop Geoffroy on his
thirteenth-century tomb, as do two different monsters the feet of
Bishop Évrard opposite.

Then it is time to explore the other outstanding masterpieces of
this cathedral, including the wooden pulpit which a local sculptor
(Jean-Baptiste Dupuis) created in 1773, setting it on statues representing faith, hope and charity, as well as the oak organ loft of
1452 with an organ originally built three years later. Dupuis also
sculpted the fine tomb of Monsignor Sabatier. In the south
transept are early-sixteenth-century statues exuberantly depicting
the life of St James the Great, the cockleshell saint, wearing
prominent boots (for he is the patron saint of pilgrims). The
carvings here begin to burst out of their canopies. The stone
sculptures of the life of St Firmin are the work of Adrien de
Hénencourt, one of the finest of those who gloried in the French
flamboyant style and loved to paint and gild his work. Adrien
intended them as a tribute to his late uncle Ferry de Beauvoir,
who was bishop here. As you walk around this deambulatory you

find the story of Firmin's life continued in stone by another sculptor working forty years later. The muscles of an executioner flex as he prepares to decapitate the saint. On a nearby pillar is a tribute to the Australian soldiers killed in the First World War, another to the men of the Royal Canadian Dragoons and a third remembering some 600,000 dead of Great Britain and Northern Ireland. Other treats include a Byzantine crucifix in the chapel of Saint-Sauveur on the north side of the nave. The Christ on the cross bows his head, a fact legendarily attributed not to its unknown painter but to Jesus's courteous nod as the relics of St Honoré were carried past this crucifix in the Middle Ages.

When Adrien de Hénencourt died in 1530 he was rightly buried close by and given a fine monument. Other benefactors of this cathedral lie not far away, such as Cardinal Jean de la Grange, who died in 1402 having no doubt exulted in the statues he commissioned for the outside buttress of Notre-Dame. His sculpted portrait lies on his tomb against the choir wall opposite the chapel of the Virgin. This chapel, which Viollet-le-Duc redecorated in 1855, stands at the easternmost part of the apse.

None of these magnificent treasures measures up in my view to the choir stalls, altogether 110 of them, made for Amiens cathedral in the second decade of the sixteenth century in the workshop of Alexandre Huet and Arnould Boulin. Our British architecture never fully incorporated the style which the French call flamboyant. These stalls, in which more than 3,500 figures are brought into play in some 400 separate scenes, are masterpieces of the genre. John Ruskin rightly adored them. On the eighty-sixth stall on the left one of the sculptors proudly signed his name: Jean Turpin. Each scene is a masterpiece, my favourite perhaps that depicting the coming of the Holy Spirit on Jesus's followers, the spirit depicted as if it consisted of flaming bags of gold.

Because much of the glass of Notre-Dame has been lost, it is worthwhile tracing what remains from the thirteenth century in this part of the cathedral – a little in the third chapel to the right of that dedicated to the Virgin; more in the one just beyond the Virgin's chapel; and some colourful depictions of the lives of St Leonard and of Our Lady in the chapel of Saint-Quentin further on. Then walk on to find that the sculpted life of St Firmin which we have already seen is matched in skill at the north side of the choir stalls by statues representing the life of St John the Baptist. They date from 1531.

It is surely time we venerated his grisly head. It is enshrined in the south transept, which is virtually an art gallery of medieval and Renaissance art, with its fourteenth-century rose window gleaming blue (whereas that in the south transept blooms predominantly green and red), the late-thirteenth-century tomb of Canon Jehan de Wytz, the mid-sixteenth-century tomb of Cardinal Charles Hémard de Denonville and above all Jesus throwing the money-changers out of the Jerusalem Temple, a group sculpted around 1520. Opposite this group is the reliquary containing most of the head of St John the Baptist. The shrine is carved with a depiction of the swordsman-executioner, the headless corpse and Salome handing over the Baptist's head on a platter. Alas, someone has knocked the carved head off the platter. No matter, for here perhaps is the real thing. 'STE JOANNES-BAPTISTA, ORA PRO NOBIS', reads the inscription.

Leaving the cathedral by way of the door opposite to that by which we came in, spare a glance for the wide and handsome Rue Robert-de-Luzerches which honours the builder of this mighty church and then turn right to reach Place Dusevel in which is a fountain decorated by the decorously dressed statue of a lady known in Amiens as Marie-sans-Chemise. Representing Spring and designed by Albert Roze, she once adorned a monumental clock in Place Gambetta which was destroyed in the Second World War.

Further west you reach the market square (also known as Place Maurice-Vast) which lives up to its name when the market arrives on Thursdays and Saturdays. Here rises the belfry of Amiens, decidedly squat and defensive and built in the twelfth century – apart from its eighteenth-century hat. It markedly contrasts with the airy church of Saint-Germain nearby, separated from here only by the Rue du Chapeau-de-Violettes. Some 45 m west of the church you reach the evocative ruins of the cloister of the Soeurs-Grises, decently shored up and kitted out with benches. Look back from here towards Saint-Germain to discover that its tower has been leaning precariously to the left from the time it was built. Beyond this church you can spy across the rooftops the beautifully proportioned west front of the cathedral, with its two quite dissimilar towers and the long slender *flèche*.

The brick-and-stone building further west from the ruined cloister bears the date (in metal characters) 1658. Next to it stands a mock-Gothic edifice built 310 years later, yet admirably complementing the older house. Follow Rue de Général-Leclerc south from here and turn right into Rue Jean-Calvin to reach the church of Saint-Jacques. In this city of Gothic wonders to see a church with its elegant Corinthian capitals and portico, built in that style in 1827, comes as a sweet surprise.

Although something in the region of 60 per cent of old Amiens was destroyed in 1940, the city magnificently pulled itself together after the war, utilizing wherever possible what remained from the architectural carnage. Its inspired architect was Auguste Perret, responsible for the enormous Place Alphonse-Fiquet fronted by the modern Gare du Nord and sporting the equally megalomaniac Tour Perret which rises for 104 m. You reach it from the church off Saint-Jacques by walking south-east along Rue Jean-Catelas, across Place Léon-Gontier and along Rue Gresset. To your left rises the Town Hall of Amiens. On 15 March 1802, the Peace of Amiens, between Britain, France, Holland and Spain, was signed in its predecessor. Peace did not last long. Today's building is a successfully grandiose example of late-nineteenth-century municipal pride, built between 1876 and 1885. Behind it is the Cour du Bailli, whose Renaissance façade still glitters with pride.

Further on you discover bustling shops and restaurants still offering the traditional goodies of Amiens. Rue des Trois-Cailloux is the most celebrated, blessed with an eighteenth-century theatre whose façade survived the last war. The goodies include macaroons and chocolates whose special recipes are said to derive from the kitchens of eighteenth-century convents. They include the even older pastries which both Rabelais (who loved Amiens duck pie) and Mme de Sévigné relished. On the left, just beyond the theatre, stands the House of Sagittarius, built in 1593 and so called because of the sign of the zodiac which adorns its richly decorated façade. It sits alongside another sixteenth-century survival, known as the Logis du Roi, which was built for King François I.

Shortly you reach the railway station and the Tour Perret. I dislike both of them and habitually walk speedily from here south-west to the Jules Verne monument. The visionary bust of this adopted son of Amiens (for he was in truth born at Nantes) dreams of new science-fiction masterpieces, while youngsters lounge around him, inspired by his works. Across the flowery green Place du Maréchal-Foch and along the tree-lined boulevard you can find his red-brick house, which overlooks the railway track and is now a Jules Verne museum. The legendary novelist lived here for the last fourteen years of his life until his death on 24 March 1905. Then walk on to the quaint Cirque, built in 1889 like a circus tent. This is to my mind an exceedingly jolly effort, with a ravishingly ornate cupola. At times a genuine circus sets itself up here, but the Cirque d'Amiens, with its splendid acoustics, is mostly used for political rallies and for jazz and classical concerts. I looked up the menu of the Restaurant du Cirque last time I was in Amiens and found it serving a *gratin de moules aux poireaux*, a *pâté des Hortillons*, and an *escalope Bellovaque* – in short a succulently Picardy meal.

Make your way from the Cirque up Rue de la République. This is a most elegant street. The prefecture stands on the right, the Musée de Picardie on the left, preceded by the municipal library which is dedicated to the surrealist novelist Louis Aragon. This library dates from 1826, a Greek classical building surrounding a grassy courtyard. I much prefer it to the late-nineteenth-century baroque Banque de France on the other side of the road, but the Musée de Picardie next along the street captivates by its very vulgarity. Its inscriptions give its dates, 1854 to 1862, and glorify Napoleon III as a 'liberal patron of the arts'. No visitor should miss this Picardie art gallery and museum, which was frescoed by Puvis de Chavannes. By a remarkable chance Amiens was blessed with a confraternity called 'du Puy de Notre Dame' which, based on the cathedral, was dedicated from 1388 to 1730 to extolling the Virgin Mary. Each year the members elected a Master, who judged poems in honour of Our Lady and in return for this honour donated a painting praising her life and virtues to the cathedral. Although much of this unique collection was destroyed in the eighteenth century, nearly twenty pictures remain, some of them in their original frames and dating from the mid-fifteenth to the mid-seventeenth centuries. In 1906 they came into the possession of the gallery, adding a remarkable flavour to its already important international and local collection, whose eighteenth-century paintings – especially those of Jean-Honoré Fragonard – are renowned.

Escaping from culture, one reaches the Galerie des Jacobins, an arcaded shopping complex, not so lavish but quite as elegant as the street we have been enjoying, with cafés and restaurants.

Walking on to Place Gambetta you reach a sad and ugly sight: the church of Saint-Rémi, a pathetic memory of senseless destruction. The choir and transepts have been rebuilt in the Gothic style. They house some imposing sixteenth-century monuments, and the fine seventeenth-century mausoleum of the Constable de Lannoy. Yet only a shell remains of the rest of the fourteenth- and fifteenth-century church, which was ruined in the First World War. To cheer yourself up return to your car and drive to the cemetery of the Madeleine. As you park and walk through the main entrance, continue directly onwards (right of the administrative building) until you reach a crossroads and turn left. Instantly you arrive at the tomb of Jules Verne. It was sculpted by Albert Roze, the master who created Marie-sans-Chemise. Jules is also *sans chemise*, half-way out of his shroud. What is more, he is also half-way out of his tomb, the visionary already fighting his way to resurrection, or maybe simply wanting to make another trip around the world in eighty days.

Running north-west from Amiens, the N235 takes you along the left bank of the River Somme to reach Picquigny 13 km later. Nondescript villages soon give way to rolling green countryside, with woodlands on the left and fishing lakes to the right. Picquigny merits a pause for its riverside walk alone. The townscape is enhanced by several half-timbered, overhanging houses. A green sign will direct you to the British military cemetery, and another to Poix-de-Picardie. Unless you are staying in the vicinity of Picquigny, this is not the speediest way to Poix-de-Picardie, for there is a much more direct route from Amiens. Nevertheless, one way or another do not miss visiting its unusually beautiful church of Saint-Denis. An older building had been ravaged first by the English in 1346, then by the *jacquerie* (or peasants in revolt) twelve years later, and finally left in ruins by Charles the Bold and the Burgundians in 1472. The church was rebuilt in 1540. Paradoxically one is grateful for the savage marauders who progressively destroyed the previous building, for its successor is a masterpiece of vaulting and statuary. The sculpted hanging keystones are supported by delicately carved arches. The overall purpose of the decoration of the choir is to illustrate the themes of the Holy Trinity and the redemption of humankind. As for the patron of this church, Denis is also regarded as one of the patron saints of France herself. He was beheaded at Montmartre (the

'martyrs' hill') in Paris in the mid-third century. Legend has it
that he picked up his severed head and carried it to the spot
where he was to be buried, the site of the present cathedral of
Saint-Denis. You can see him doing so, sculpted outside Saint-Denis
at Poix-de-Picardie, his mitred head looking decidedly irritated.

The whole town is set amid greenery, and on summer evenings
its church is softly illuminated. Poix-de-Picardie is a perfect base
for a little tour of sweet villages: Blangy-sous-Poix with its Romanesque church dominating a little hill; Famechon, clustered
around its sixteenth-century flamboyant church; Bergicourt, with
another partly Romanesque church housing a thirteenth-century
font; Guizancourt, boasting an ancient mill; Méreaucourt, with
an early-eighteenth-century chapel and a medieval farm which
once belonged to the Knights of Malta; Agnières, whose church,
built between the twelfth and the sixteenth centuries, lies at the
foot of its feudal mound; and Saulchy-sous-Poix whose stone
chapel dates from the sixteenth century.

Whether or not you are planning a journey from Picquigny to
Poix-de-Picardie, the signpost to the latter also takes you to
Picquigny's finest ensemble, its church and château. You cannot
drive up to them but the little climb is well rewarded. Saint-
Martin, her pointed tiled roof rising above the bastion of the
sixteenth- and seventeenth-century château, was founded in 1066.
Her present transept dates from the twelfth century, her nave
from the thirteenth and the choir from the sixteenth. Inside are a
late-fifteenth-century font and Louis XV furnishings. As for the
remains of the château with its powerful walls, you can still see
what was once the kitchen (vast, Gothic and built in 1583) and
the seventeenth-century pavilion now named after Mme de
Sévigné since she stayed there in 1689 (presenting the church
with its present pulpit fall and a couple of vestments). This
formidable bastion also preserves its insalubrious prisons.

At Picquigny in August 1475 King Louis XI of France and
King Edward IV of England met on an island in the river to
negotiate an end to the Hundred Years War. Another sign points
you from here across the river to a decided curiosity, the fortified
Gaulish camp of Samara. The authorities have successfully gone
to town to make this a centre of prehistoric studies, which opens
daily from 09.00 to 17.00. The fortified *oppidum* itself is the most
important of its kind in northern France. What the Gauls have

left us has been supplemented by reconstructed neolithic and Bronze Age houses, and by an Iron Age barn. Prehistoric crafts (pottery, jewellery, weaving and the rest) are demonstrated in another part of the complex. A botanical garden and arboretum have been created. The exhibition halls are an exceedingly comical set of buildings designed to resemble igloos. The tourist office here also offers motorists details of rewarding little tours of the surrounding area – to Prouzel, for example, with its sixteenth-century church and château; to Pissy, whose brick-and-stone château has a classical eighteenth-century façade; to Long and Vauchelles-lès-Domart which respectively boast an eighteenth- and an early seventeenth-century château.

North-west of Samara is Belloy-sur-Somme, where (in the Hostellerie de Belloy) I have eaten extremely well. Here in fact I first tasted the local delicacy known as *ficelle picarde*. Very hot and tasty, *ficelle picarde* is classically a thin pancake or *crêpe* wrapped around a slice of ham or several pieces of ham and enlivened with mushrooms and maybe also some grated cheese. The chefs of the Somme brilliantly utilize apparently unpromising vegetables of their region, producing a succulent peasant cuisine which relies much more on spices than on sauces. I remember following my *ficelle picarde* at the Hostellerie de Belloy with a duck steaklet served with a purée of turnips and endives (*magret de canard à la purée de navets et à l'endive*). Alas, this is not wine country. It could have been. Legend has it that King François I ordered every vine to be grubbed up after falling ill when he had drunk some wine of the region. In consequence, where the beverage is not beer, the ciders of neighbouring Normandy have infiltrated this region, and the phrase '*au vinaigre de cidre*' frequently appears on local menus. So do the fish of the rivers and lakes, landed at this *hostellerie* from a lake in which its fishing guests can sport themselves.

From the Hostellerie de Belloy (which lies beside the N235) you should retrace your steps as far as Picquigny and drive north-west along the D3 to see the abbey of Gard. The eighteenth-century church, which appears quite suddenly on the right, fell into ruins after being sold at the Revolution, along with the rest of the abbey buildings. In our own century a group of monks have taken over the Cistercian monastery and set about a meticulous restoration. The long eighteenth-century abbey building has risen anew, its two storeys, tall windows, mansard roof and classical loggia now in pristine condition.

We are driving through a region of villages which enfold huge walled farms. At the next one, Crouy-en-Somme, is a signpost to yet another British military cemetery. Beyond Crouy lies the village of Hangest-sur-Somme. Its church of Sainte-Marguerite boasts a belfry that is in part Romanesque and a decorated Gothic west porch. Not long ago the furnishings of its choir included lovely carved woodwork, eighteenth-century work from the former abbey of Gard. This region, however, is one of locked churches, and I cannot say whether they have been taken away as a result of the laudable restoration of the abbey.

Just beyond Hangest-sur-Somme is a village with the intriguing name Longpré-les-Corps-Saints (where there is another British military cemetery). The name derives from the bones of Christian saints brought here from the Holy Land by Alleaume de Fontaine in the early thirteenth century. In 1190 he had already founded a church to house them. It stands at the end of the Grand'Rue, much renewed as you can judge from its machine-cut stones. The first reconstruction of this church took place in the eighteenth century (hence the gay balustrade of its tower), when a little row of thirteenth-century pillars was placed in the church grounds, where they stand to this day. The thirteenth-century porch, sculpted with scenes from the life of the Blessed Virgin Mary, has been in a sorry state since the Revolutionaries mutilated it in 1793. Happily, they failed to destroy two angels, sculpted in the fifteenth century to support the lintel.

Look out for the signs directing you to the right to the eighteenth-century château of Long at Le Catelet. The Gothic church at Le Catelet is modern, apart from its belfry and porch which date from the sixteenth century. Then return to the D3 and drive on to Fontaine-sur-Somme, whose church boasts exquisite hanging keystones in the chapel of the Virgin and whose porch carries statues of St Peter (with the keys of heaven), mitred St Riquier and St Adrian with the anvil on which he was crushed to death around AD 304. The font dates from 1590 and the belfry is elaborately decorated – indeed the church seems altogether too elaborate for such a little spot. The last time I was there a lady came out of the house opposite the church and told me what I had already guessed: that these days the church is open only when the priest is celebrating Mass, and that this major Christian celebration no longer occurs here every Sunday.

Next you arrive at Liercourt, once a Gaulish *oppidum*, then a Roman camp and now enriched with a church dedicated to St Riquier. The patron saint is sculpted over the doorway, and inside, among the figures carved in the early-sixteenth-century medallions of the nave appear both Louis XII and François I. The design of the hanging pediments of the choir and of the chapel of Notre-Dame are Renaissance. Why the windows of the apse are bricked up I do not know.

Shortly after Liercourt you reach a T-junction. Poix-de-Picardie lies due south 34 km distant by way of Airaines, where monks from Cluny founded the priory of Notre-Dame in the early twelfth century. The Burgundians destroyed the priory, save for its church which still stands, its nave basically twelfth century, its crossing built a hundred years later, its sanctuary modern. Inside is a large twelfth-century font, sculpted with wild-looking people, as well as a couple of tomb-slabs dating from the thirteenth century and commemorating Henri and Catherine d'Airaines. Airaines boasts a parish church of Saint-Denis, built in the fifteenth and sixteenth centuries. Its treasures include some Renaissance stained glass, a sixteenth-century statue of the beheaded Bishop Denis, and an entombment and a crucifix of the same date. The ruined château of the dukes of Luynes is guarded by a couple of hexagonal towers and the half-ruined Porte de la Châtelleine, which dates from 1620.

To see a fifteenth-century feudal stronghold which has been inhabited by the same family since it was built, make your way west from Airaines to Oisement (where there is a church with a sculpted Romanesque doorway) and follow the sign for Rambures. Château de Rambures can be visited from March till October every day (save Wednesdays) and during the rest of the year on Sundays and public holidays. The family was famous long before building the present château, for when King Charles VI went mad in 1392 David de Rambures was one of the twelve knights who ruled France in his stead. The family fought valiantly for France against the English. Twenty-three years later David and three of his sons died at the Battle of Agincourt. His sole surviving heir, André, was captured by the enemy in 1430 and spent the next ten years imprisoned in England. From the family château, which preceded the present one at Rambures, a champion of France named Charles Desmarets now took up the struggle so successfully that in 1435 he took back first Rue, then Abbeville and Saint-Valéry-sur-Somme and finally Dieppe from the English.

During the struggle of Louis XI against Charles the Bold, Jacques, son of André de Rambures, remained consistently loyal to his sovereign, meanwhile rebuilding the family seat. Its convex walls were designed to deflect the most powerful cannonball. The new château was finished in 1472, just two years before Jacques de Rambures was forced to surrender it to Charles the Bold, the convex walls notwithstanding. The enraged Louis XI was to confiscate the château for three years as punishment for Jacques' capitulation. In the next century the family regained its laurels, Charles de Rambures bravely serving Henri IV and Louis XIII alike. (He saved Henri's life at the Battle of Ivry.) His successor, the last of the Rambures, was killed in Alsace in 1676 aged only eighteen. When his sister married her cousin, the Marquis de la Rochefontenilles, he took on the title Marquis de Rambures.

This is the oldest brick-and-stone château in Picardy. The five fifteenth-century pink-and-white defensive towers of Château de Rambures were built high enough to make it impossible to scale them but deliberately positioned low enough as to make it difficult for enemies to shoot at them. Even the curtain wall that joins them together is curved. In case they were hit, the walls were built 7 m thick. In the early seventeenth century Charles de Rambures replaced the drawbridge with the present stone bridge that crosses the moat. The outhouses date from the seventeeth and the eighteenth centuries and the chapel from the nineteenth. Cellars, a nineteenth-century Gothic hall and an ancient forest with a park landscaped in the English fashion complete the ensemble. The park is so beguiling that you almost forget how formidable is the château.

If instead of making your way towards Rambures or Poix-de-Picardie you turn right at the Liercourt T-junction, the D901 winds its way to Abbeville, which lies 46 km from Amiens. You cross the Somme at Pont-Rémy, whose fifteenth-century château is washed by a couple of meanders of the river. As you make your way towards Abbeville, spot at Eaucourt the remains of a château half-demolished in the early fifteenth century and be ready at

Épagne for its eighteenth-century château and outhouses which suddenly appear on the left as you pass through the village.

Approaching Abbeville, also look out for the sign 'Quartier Saint-Gilles', where you turn right to find Château Bagatelle. This sophisticated mid-eighteenth-century brick-and-stone residence stands in long cool woods of holly and pine, enhanced by a sunken lawn. The massive ancient trees surrounding it have given its park protected status. Visitors are welcome in July and August in the afternoons (save on Tuesdays). Château Bagatelle was built in the 1750s by Abraham van Robais, who had grown rich as director of the royal tapestry and curtain factory at Abbeville. Garlands of leaves decorate its lower windows, swags of simulated curtains its upper 'bull's eye' openings. The interior is as delicate as the exterior.

Abbeville had flourished long before the time of Abraham van Robais, in part because the navigable Somme and its many tributaries which dissect the town helped trade to burgeon. It began life as an abbey (hence *Abbaye-ville*) founded by the monks of nearby Saint-Riquier. After the marriage of Eleanor of Aquitaine to Edward I in 1272, Abbeville became English for over half a century before reverting to the French monarchy. Here in 1527 Cardinal Wolsey and François I concluded an alliance against the Emperor Charles V.

As you leave Château Bagatelle, ahead of you rises the chunky, decorated square tower of the flamboyant Gothic church of Saint-Gilles, majestic in spite of the depredations of war and at last in the process of being restored to its former glory. Saint-Gilles stands just inside the city ramparts first created under Hugues Capet, their ditch still traceable across the road. Its sculpted double doorway dates from 1485, a riot of varied tracery. In the middle the Virgin Mary, standing on the moon, crushes a coiled serpent underfoot. Beautiful balustrades, carved heads, birds, mythical beasts, an elephant, a queen's head, a fish and grotesque corbels embellish the church. Two of the little sculpted figures beneath the east-end balustrade are behaving in an extremely vulgar fashion.

Drive on along Rue Saint-Gilles, whose Hôtel de Gaillon has a fine eighteenth-century porchway. You pass the neatly embellished modern Palais de Justice and the less attractive modern Town Hall to turn left and park in front of the magnificent church of Saint-Vulfram. Its first stone was laid in 1488; work stopped in 1539; the choir was finished in the 1660s. If you look to the left at the octagonal tower of St Firmin, you see that it remains slightly leaning, an aspect it took on shortly after being built. The façade of this church, topped by a couple of merry towers each 53 m high, is a treat. We owe it to Louis XII and Cardinal d'Amboise, who paid for the work. Over the main doorway is the sculpted representation of the Trinity. The carved doors are one of the glories of the Somme. The top row of sculptures depicts in parallel the lives of Jesus and his Mother, each given equal status. On the left the Virgin's mother, St Anne, meets her husband St Joachim. Next Mary is born and presented in the Jerusalem Temple. Matching these scenes are those of the Annunciation, the Birth of Jesus and his own Presentation in the Temple. Beneath these carvings is a frieze of knights, and then the motto of Jehan Mourette, president of the confraternity of the Puy, who gave these doors: *Vierge aux humains la porte d'amour estez.* Finally, below this motto are carved the four evangelists, flanked by the Apostles Peter and Paul.

In spite of the bombardments of 1940, Abbeville offers other delights, in particular the façade of the chapel of its mid-seventeenth-century Ursuline monastery and the ancient belfry of the mid-nineteenth-century church of Saint-Sépulcre. A thirteenth-century belfry in Rue du Beffroi announces the Musée Boucher de Perthes, a collection of a decidedly specialized interest. Jacques Boucher de Crèvecoeur de Perthes, who founded it in 1826, was a distinguished local prehistorian, and the museum has built itself around his collection of the palaeontology of the Somme valley.

The occasionally tree-lined D925 which takes us 9 km northeast from Abbeville to Saint-Riquier passes through golden, undulating meadows and cultivated fields, with the occasional little vineyard skirting woodlands. Then the great abbey rises ahead in its village. Its superb flamboyant Gothic façade dominates the houses in its cobbled square. Saint-Riquier takes its name from a Benedictine monk named Ricarius, who died here in 645. The monastery arose around his tomb. Sacked by the Normans and set on fire by Count Hugues of Saint-Pol in 1131, it rose again under plans devised by Abbot Gilles de Machemond in the second half of the thirteenth century. Gilles transformed his

Carolingian foundation into a church based on a Latin cross, adding a deambulatory with radiating chapels. With his death in 1292 the impulse to rebuild ceased, to be recharged when Pierre Le Prestre became abbot in 1457. Pierre's successors shared his vision. Today we look on a sixteenth-century façade surmounted by a mosaic and a richly decorated square tower. A couple of hexagonal staircase towers flank the main doorway. The treasures inside include colossal stone statues of St Peter and St James the Great, as well as the seventeenth-century woodwork of the choir and the fifteenth-century alabaster statues in the left transept.

Virtually every symbolic figure of the medieval Christian mind crams the carvings of the main doorway. The lives of St Riquier and St Angilbert are given their due prominence, along with the triumph of the Virgin Mary, Adam and Eve after the Fall, and Moses and Elijah. The tympanum is decorated with a tree of Jesse. Most amusing of all, to my mind, are the intrusive little statues of two abbots, Eustache de Quieux and Thibaut de Bayencourt. Their presence has forced two of the twelve Apostles offstage, so to speak. Yet what ultimately counts at Saint-Riquier is not such details but the ensemble: the façade of the church; the adjoining monastic buildings, created in the late seventeenth century; the fortified wall of the cloister; the little square and across it the thirteenth-century belfry (with a line of trees taking your eyes and interest around the corner), a belfry with four little turrets and a central higher one, yet still menacing. Drive on to see the Hôtel-Dieu, its present form deriving from the rebuilding which took place between 1688 and 1704, against which rises its buttressed chapel.

From Saint-Riquier follow the D925 east for 32 km to Doullens. The hamlet of Les Quatre-Saisons seems unprepossessing, until you realize that it stands where the old Roman road crosses our route on its way from Amiens to Boulogne. You pass by Longvillers, whose former château retains its twelfth-century keep. At Beaumetz, half-way to Doullens, take a detour south to enjoy the long, classical, brick-and-stone château at Ribeaucourt, which – though private property – is readily visible from the road. The next village along the D925 is Bernaville, with its sixteenth-century church. If you have time at Bernaville, follow the signpost that winds you north to Château de Remaisnic just outside the village of Le Meillard. Though of the same epoch as that at Ribeaucourt,

its feel is completely different as it is constructed wholly of brick
and is really a glamorized farmhouse. The wealth of châteaux here
depended upon riches derived from the land, and if you are in
this region in January you will find the farmers replenishing this
source, liberally spreading the earth with dung in the gentle misty
rain.

Doullens is a much more complex spot than Saint-Riquier, but
its ensemble still adds up to a charming if busy town. Its former
Town Hall begins on the ground floor in brick, continues higher
in brick-and-stone and the whole is embellished with a slate-and-
brick belfry built in 1426. Much of Doullens was smashed to
pieces in the wars of the fifteenth and sixteenth centuries, with the
consequence that many of its older houses date from the seventeenth. Its flamboyant Gothic church of Notre-Dame survived
these conflicts and the Second World War partially intact. Go
inside to find a magnificent entombment, sculpted in stone in
1583, the participants (especially dead Jesus) all seemingly at
peace in spite of their sad task. The church of Saint-Pierre, which
dates back to the thirteenth century, was less fortunate, though it
remains an entrancing ruin. As for the citadel, for once this was
not inaugurated by Vauban (for François I decided that Doullens
needed a defensive barracks), but in its present form he is the
master hand that created it.

Doullens is 30 km due north of Amiens. Following the N25
south by way of Beauval (whose church has a Gothic belfry
topped with a sixteenth-century spire) you reach a crossroads
which directs you 3 km west along the D60 for a bizarre treat, the
subterranean village at Naours. Dug into malleable chalk by
peasant farmers longing to escape the countless invaders of this
succulent region, whose neighbouring coastline brought the ships
of their enemies and where dynastic rivalries shed warm blood on
quiet hamlets, these caves comprise the most extensive network of
underground habitations yet discovered. Up to 3,000 villagers
could find refuge here. Guided tours take place throughout the
year, save in December.

Then return to the N25 and drive on south for 3 km to Villers-
Bocage, which boasts a church built in the thirteenth and sixteenth centuries. Here you turn south-east to follow the extremely
winding D30 through beautiful rolling countryside, dotted with
clumps of trees and coppices, through villages with tumbledown

wattle-and-daub barns, until you reach Corbie. At sleepy Pont-Noyelles, where the road takes a sharp turn right, you would scarcely believe that a bloody and indecisive battle took place here in 1870 during the Franco-Prussian war. It is also hard to believe that Corbie was once one of Europe's most powerful spiritual centres. Monks flocked here to join the Benedictine monastery founded in 657 by St Bathilde, the wife of King Clovis II. A century and a half later they founded the celebrated monastery of Corvey on the River Weser, a monastery which sent forth monks to evangelize most of pagan Europe.

What remains? At La Neuville-sous-Corbie, which we reach first, stands a forlorn and beautiful church, Notre-Dame-de-l'Assomption, built in the fifteenth and sixteenth centuries. Its glory is its carved west portal whose tympanum bears a bas-relief of Jesus's triumphal entry into Jerusalem. He rides a huge donkey. Men clamber into trees. Another man lays down his cloak in awe for the beast to walk over. Meanwhile in the city Jesus's enemies are waiting for him, while keepers squat in the battlemented, portcullised gate of the Holy City. Because the sculptors imagined that Jerusalem must have resembled a city in Picardy, they included in the tympanum a windmill.

La Neuville-sous-Corbie is 2 km from Corbie proper and as you approach, suddenly you are greeted ahead by the thrilling sight of the rose window and double tower of the abbey church of Saint-Pierre, rising above a perfectly simple Picardy town. Saint-Pierre was begun in 1502 but finished only in 1740, with the result that its Gothic upper storeys contrast piquantly with the classical interlacing and motifs of its three main doorways. In 1928 its south tower was equipped with five bells, weighing altogether 7,400 kg. Although only the nave remains of the earliest building, the church houses some exquisite treasures, such as the early Byzantine painting of the holy face of Jesus and a fragment of the True Cross, both brought here in 1242 after the first crusade, as well as religious statues dating from the fourteenth to the sixteenth centuries. They include a thirteenth-century statue of a wild-eyed St Peter, the keys of heaven pinned on to his hat for safe-keeping, and a lovely fourteenth-century statue of St Bathilde.

Saint-Pierre stands in a quiet square, opposite a horse butcher and the bar-hôtel-restaurant L'Abbatiale, which serves *andouillettes* and chips, *ficelle picarde* and *pâté de campagne*. If you perilously stand on the wall outside the post office you can just make out, over the wall of the local private school, the remarkable mutilated porch of the former collegiate church of Saint-Étienne, whose pride is a statue of the Blessed Virgin Mary based on Byzantine models and carved in the early thirteenth century.

Drive on to Moreuil, taking the road out of Corbie which passes its jolly brick Hôtel de Ville whose pepperpot towers and nineteenth-century crenellations are delightful. To your left presently rises the monumental Australian war cemetery. Its memorial, set up in 1938, bears the names of 10,866 Australian combatants who died in the First World War. Not far away is a Canadian military cemetery of the same war. Moreuil, washed by the waters of the River Avre, has a château which, though rebuilt in 1785, retains its ancient feudal towers and a Town Hall with a brick belfry. Its church is huge, a modern building of brick and concrete with a massive spire.

From Moreuil the D14 runs through the valley of the Avre and south-west to Folleville. The route passes through Mailly-Raine-bal, with its ruined fifteenth-century château and a church which, though rebuilt in the 1920s, houses a sixteenth-century statue, a thirteenth-century font and three ancient slabs of tombs. Over Folleville brood the ruins of its late-fifteenth-century château with its feudal keep. The *jacquerie* set fire to this château in 1358, and the English captured it in 1440. In part rebuilt in the seventeenth century, its owner demolished most of the building in 1789.

But this is not the treasure of the little town. In the sixteenth-century Folleville belonged to the lords of Poix, passing into the hands of Raoul de Lannoy when he married Jeanne de Poix in the late sixteenth century. Raoul was an impetuous soldier. After the Battle of Le Quesnoy in 1477 Louis XI placed a chain around his neck with the words, 'Dear God, my friend, you fight too furiously. I want to chain you down to moderate your ardour, for I do not wish to lose you, desiring you to serve me more than once.' Raoul went on to serve both Louis XI and his successors. In 1507 Louis XII made him governor of Genoa. Knowing that his death was approaching, Raoul took the opportunity of employing two Milanese masters, Antonio della Porta and Pace Gaggini, to sculpt a tomb out of Carrara marble for himself and his wife. When he died in 1513 his will directed that a new sanctuary be built to house it. Jeanne oversaw the work, and the new, half-flamboyant-Gothic, half-Renaissance sanctuary at the end of the church of Folleville was consecrated in 1524. She and Raoul lie there together, he wearing the chain given him by Louis XI, she sweetly turning to her husband. The Milanese have signed their work. Incorporated into their tomb is an astoundingly beautiful medallion of the Madonna and Child, emerging from a fleur-de-lys, surrounded by a garland of daisies.

The simple exterior of the church (whose façade carries only the statue of its patron, St James the Great) does not prepare you for the riches that are inside. They include a Carrara marble font bearing the symbols of Raoul and Jeanne de Lannoy, as well as the saints and the Madonna who decorate Jeanne's sanctuary. Among the carved foliage look for the peas (*pois*), the rebus of Jeanne de Poix. Peas and chains decorate the ribs of the church, as another memento of Jeanne and her husband. Their son François died in 1548, and his Renaissance tomb bears the kneeling effigies of himself and his wife, Marie de Hangest.

The church at Folleville still rejoices that St Vincent de Paul preached a celebrated sermon from its pulpit on 25 January 1617. He had come here to oversee the education of the sons of the then lord of Folleville, Philippe-Emmanuel de Gondi. (One of them became famous as the intriguer, enemy of Mazarin and finally bankrupt, Cardinal de Retz.) This sermon was the impetus leading to the foundation of the Lazarists, an order which became celebrated for its charity and its dedication to preaching the Gospel to poor country folk.

Drive on to Breteuil-sur-Noye and then take the D930 east to Montdidier, some 21 km away to discover another huge spire, this one belonging to the church of Saint-Pierre. Saint-Pierre dates from the sixteenth century, though as its eleventh-century font and thirteenth-century tombs indicate, a church was first built here much earlier. Its porch is beautiful, though all the Christian statues which once adorned it have gone (presumably destroyed at the Revolution) and only gargoyles and evil beasts remain. The excellent brick Town Hall of Montdidier, rebuilt in the 1920s after the devastation of the First World War, boasts a 45 m high belfry which carries what we British call Westminster chimes. The bells are conducted by the *jacquemart* (or mannikin) known as Jean Duquesnes, which was placed here in 1640.

Further south Rue Parmentier (named after the philanthropist Antoine-Augustin Parmentier, who was born at Montdidier in 1737 and introduced the potato to France) leads to the partially rebuilt fifteenth-century church of Saint-Sépulcre. In spite of the damages it sustained in 1918, Saint-Sépulcre has preserved several of its Renaissance treasures, including a font of 1539, a sixteenth-century group depicting the entombment of Jesus, and six mid-sixteenth-century statues of the Apostles in the choir.

Tilloloy, 14 km due east of Montdidier and reached by the D931 and the D133, boasts both a Renaissance church and a seventeenth-century château. Louis XIV provided funds for this château and is said to have coveted the building when it was completed. The splendid doorway decorated with deer and hunting dogs bears the coat of arms of Charles-Maximilien de Belleforière, one of the most fanatical huntsmen in eighteenth-century France.

From here Roye is but 4 km to the north, by way of Laucourt whose sixteenth-century church has preserved some stained glass of the same era. The present city of Roye was founded on what had been a Roman township, Rodium, which was destroyed by the Normans in the ninth century. Traces of the Roman camp can still be made out a couple of kilometres west of modern Roye, its importance deriving from its position on the road from Lyon to Bordeaux. Sacking by the Normans was not the last of her sufferings. The English pillaged Roye in 1373, as did the imperial forces in the sixteenth century. As you drive into Roye along Rue de Paris you pass the remains of its fifteenth- and sixteenth-century ramparts (of which two fifteenth-century round towers remain intact) to reach the Place de l'Hôtel-de-Ville. From here Rue Saint-Pierre leads the church of Saint-Pierre which, though it had to be restored after 1918, has preserved a lovely sixteenth-century choir and some contemporary stained glass.

Nesle lies north-east of Roye, its former château now a ruin, its collegiate church of Notre-Dame much damaged in the First World War but still boasting a Romanesque crypt and fine capitals. Then the D930 winds east to Ham. Ham was defended by a mighty medieval fortress until the Germans blew it up in 1917. Today all that remains are its postern on the bank of the Canal de la Somme and an entrance on the esplanade of Ham. In this fortress were incarcerated such notables as Charles the Simple, the orator and revolutionary count of Mirabeau, the ministers of Charles X in 1830, and the future Napoleon III after his disastrous attempted *coup d'état* at Boulogne in August 1840. Six years later Napoleon managed to escape, in the clothing of a mason called Badinguet – a name which stuck to the future emperor ever after.

The thirteenth-century church of the Assumption proved easier to restore after 1918. Its façade dates from its origins, though the arched bays flanking the nave were added in the eighteenth century, as were the present remains of the monastery which it once served. The late-twelfth-century crypt of the church of the Assomption rises on monolithic columns. Here are the tombs of Isabelle de Berthencourt, wife of Odon IV de Ham who rebuilt the château in the thirteenth century.

From Ham drive north-west to Péronne, passing through Sancourt with its very early Gothic church and certainly pausing to admire the thirteenth-century façade of the church at Athies. Radegonde, the captured daughter of a king of Thuringia and unwilling wife of King Clotaire I, lived at Péronne in the sixth century after she managed to persuade her husband to let her lead the life of a nun. Next, Péronne was given by King Clovis II to Erkinoald, his mayor of the palace. Soon Irish monks were living here under the rule of St Fursy, who died in 650. In the ninth century the counts of Vermandois chose Péronne as their capital. They built here the keep in which Count Herbert imprisoned his king, Charles the Simple, a first time between 924 and 927 and again between 928 and 929 when Charles died. Five and a half centuries later Charles the Bold performed the same feat when in 1468 he received King Louis XI at Péronne and promptly imprisoned him in the château until in October Louis gave way and signed the humiliating Treaty of Péronne.

In 1536 the army of Emperor Charles V would have taken the town had not its citizens been rallied by the feminine bravery of Catherine de Poix – who is for some reason also known as Marie Fouré and celebrated by a feast and procession each July. Far less fortunate during the Franco-Prussian war and the First World War, Péronne was bombarded for thirteen days in the former conflict and in the latter occupied by the Germans from August 1914 to March 1917 and again from March 1918 to the end of the war.

The heart of the town is Place Louis-Daudré, where you can

park save during the animated Saturday market. At one end is the Town Hall, faithfully rebuilt by G. Debat-Ponson to replace the one dynamited by the Germans in 1917. Beyond it Rue Saint-Sauveur leads to a fine vestige of the former fortifications, the Porte de Bretagne, which was built in 1602. Its brick pavilions, roofed in slate, are still intact, as are its drawbridge and the remains of the moat that once defended the town. The coat of arms of Péronne on the Porte de Bretagne bears its prescient motto *'URBS NESCIA VINCI'* ('city that knows not defeat').

At the opposite corner of Place Louis-Daudré from the Hôtel de Ville and at the other side of the road that cuts through Péronne, rises the sole church in the town to have survived the wars, the sixteenth-century Gothic Saint-Jean-Baptiste. Its white stones are none the less scarred. Finally walk to the other corner of the square at the same end as the church, and make your way past the Hôtel Saint-Claude to admire what remains of the thirteenth-century château of the counts of Vermandois. Three towers joined by a curtain wall rise from lush green lawns. The château has long sheltered a museum of local history and prehistory. The *département* of the Somme has recently decided to establish behind the château a museum of everyday life during the First World War, to try to explain for instance how men were persuaded to go to their deaths singing. Alongside the witness of great poets such as Guillaume Apollinaire the museum aims – through recordings and slides as well as photographs and film – to re-evoke the sometimes sordid, sometimes humorous, sometimes magnificent experiences of those four years. The decision to set it up came only just in time, for authentic memories are dying as old soldiers fade away. M. Jean-Marie Lasblais of the Amiens tourist board told me that one British veteran, crossing the Channel to visit the scenes of his war years, had such an important story to tell that it was deemed worthwhile recording what he had to say on television. By the time the crew had been brought together, the old soldier had died.

Péronne is surrounded by excellent hunting country and above all the many lakes of the upper Somme offer plenty of opportunities for fishing. They cover some 2,000 hectares, and we pass by some of them on our way west to Bray-sur-Somme. We meander by and through ancient villages, in particular Cappy, which boasts a brick-and-stone château set on a hill. Its church was built in the twelfth and fifteenth centuries, with a majestic tower added in 1654. The Town Hall was built in 1863, while the environs include two Gallo-Roman villas. When not sampling its eel pâté or terrines of fresh-water fish, summer tourists can ride in the sightseeing train that the townsfolk have thoughtfully provided.

Cappy was initially founded to control the river, and here we cross the Somme to reach Bray-sur-Somme, whose church was begun in the thirteenth century. Its apse and some of the chapels, with their conical heads and leafy capitals, may be even earlier. The ribs of the choir are flamboyant Gothic, and the huge square belfry was added at the beginning of the eighteenth century. The vaulting of the nave was constructed only in the nineteenth century. The name of Bray-sur-Somme derives from a Celtic word meaning marshland, and archaeologists have traced a Roman villa and a Merovingian cemetery here. Today the citizens promote fishing, camping, swimming and horse-riding, and there is even a little aerodrome.

Make your way back to Amiens by way of Albert, which lies 9 km north-west of Bray-sur-Somme, for a totally different aesthetic experience. Albert was called Ancre until Charles d'Albert, Duke of Luynes, inherited the town in the early seventeenth century and changed its name to his. In the eleventh century a shepherd discovered a miracle-working statue of the Virgin Mary which over the centuries became such an object of veneration that between 1885 and 1895 the architect Edmond Duthoit was commissioned to build as its home an astonishing neo-Byzantine basilica. Constructed out of brick and white stone, its massive 70 m high tower carried a gilded statue of the Madonna by Albert Roze, itself 5 m high.

This church, like most of Albert, was destroyed in the First World War, though the miraculous (and black) Virgin was saved. Between 1926 and 1929 the architect's son Louis rebuilt it according to his father's plans. Today Notre-Dame-de-Brebières at Albert is again topped by a massive golden statue of the Virgin Mary and once more houses the eleventh-century statue of Notre Dame de Brebières (Our Lady of the Lost Sheep). Beginning on 8 September each year pilgrims still flock to venerate her. The celebrations last for ten days.

In 1932 Albert also rebuilt its Town Hall, another brick-and-

stone building, this time in the Flemish style with a splendid
belfry, gables and a tall roof pierced with dormer windows. The
town also profits from the fact that its public garden is enlivened
by the cascades of a tributary of the River Ancre. The Saturday
market, and a much more elaborate one on the second Wednesday
of every month, are both practical affairs and treats for the
tourist, as are the annual fête (on the first Sunday in August)
and the countless walks and lakes of the pretty surrounding
countryside. From here the old Roman road runs directly south-
west for 27 km to Amiens, passing through the hamlet of Layhos-
soye with its eighteenth-century church, and through Querrieu
which is blessed with a nineteeth-century château that preserves
some restored medieval towers, a church with a seventeenth-
century belfry, the waters of the Halleu and the remains of three
Gallo-Roman villas.

If you wish to meditate more on the bloodshed of the First
World War, pause at Albert to follow some 25 km of signposted
roads which are known as Circuit du Souvenir. The route
includes two superb memorials, that at Thiepval designed for the
British by Sir Edwin Lutyens, and the majestic statue of a caribou
which presides over the Canadian memorial park near
Beaumont-Hamel.

The war memorials of the Somme are so tragically abundant
that each of us can find a spot of particularly personal interest on
Circuit du Souvenir or in its environs. I remember visiting Paris
with my late father when the president of the USA also chose
to arrive there, so that for reasons of security most of the finest
streets were blocked off. We decideed to leave the city and visit
the war memorial of the Manchester Regiment at the hamlet of
Riencourt-lès-Bapaume, a regiment with which we were both connected. The inscriptions on the gravestones remain indescribably
moving:

NOT DEAD TO THOSE WHO LOVED HIM,
NOT LOST BUT GONE BEFORE

are the words over the grave of Private N. Greaves, who died on
2 September 1918, aged nineteen. On the tombstone of 2nd
Lieutenent L. J. Stafford, who died twenty years later, aged
twenty-nine, is inscribed:

ONLY GOOD NIGHT LEO,

NOT FAREWELL.

YOUR TRUE WIFE EDITH.

REV. 21–4

Revelations 21:4, reads, 'And God shall wipe away all tears from their eyes: and there shall be no more death, neither sorrow, nor crying, neither shall there be any more pain: for the former things are passed away.'

An army chaplain named Stacy Waddy, working with a British field ambulance in France in 1916, wrote:

It is piteous work to see men who were so keen and strong when you said goodbye to them a few hours before, come back so helpless, weary and in such pain. There is no glamour about war. Just a hateful hideous business, but the comfort is that the whole world realizes it now; . . . The surest preventative of future war is the fact that if two nations start, others know they cannot help being drawn in; and all are so utterly sick and sad that they would do anything to prevent it.

Alas, he was completely wrong.

4

EXPLORING THE CHARMS OF THE AISNE

Whereas the great cities of Amiens and Arras are washed by rivers, Laon rises 181 m high on its hill. Inescapably entrancing, you drive around it noting its treasures unfolding above you. The suburbs which form today's lower city can scarcely encroach on the older part of Laon, set securely on the triangular summit of the hill. As you drive up around the ramparts, magnificent views of the surrounding plain open up.

Such a magnificent position did not render Laon impregnable over the centuries. Partly its problems arose because of the different factions who inhabited the city. At first the clergy, successors of St Rémi, a native of the city, who in the late fifth century established an episcopate here, ruled unopposed. Charlemagne's mother had been born here, but when the later Carolingians decided that Laon would form an excellent capital city and built here a palace, their intrusion was enormously resented by the bishops. Their eventual response was to side with Hugues Capet, Duke of France, against the sovereigns.

The bishops, by now dukes and peers of France, also became increasingly at odds with the bourgeoisie of Laon. The consequence in 1111 was bloodshed. While Bishop Gaudry was away from his see, the leading laymen bought their freedom from the cathedral canons. The enraged Gaudry persuaded King Louis VII to annul the deal. Enraged in return, the citizens murdered him, set fire to his palace and also accidentally burnt down the cathedral. Many of them then sought refuge in the stronghold of Thomas Marle, Lord of Coucy, but then the troops of Louis VII besieged and took it, and most of the insurgents were hanged.

Thenceforth the bishops ruled more or less supreme until the

Revolution suppressed them. During the war which brought about the downfall of Napoleon Laon displayed its independent spirit by siding with his enemies. In February 1814 and again in July and August 1815 Blücher succeeded in fending off the forces loyal to Bonaparte. Laon was less fortunate in the Franco-Prussian war. In September 1870 when the Prussians moved into the city an imaginative guard sought to repulse them by setting off the arsenal of the citadel. Unfortunately the resultant explosion killed 500 more French than Germans. The First World War was less disastrous, since Laon was taken in 1914 and remained occupied by the Germans until the end of the war. The Second World War was a far more serious affair for the city, especially in 1944 when the air-attacks of the invading allies smashed down 800 houses, destroyed the Hôtel-Dieu and left in ruins the neighbouring church of Saint-Martin.

Laon consists of narrow, bustling streets, many of them cobbled, some of them still with water-channels in the middle. The heart of the city is Place du Général-Leclerc. Place du Général-Leclerc is, not surprisingly, oddly shaped in view of its site on top of an oddly shaped hill. The Town Hall here dates from 1838 and 1864, as you can see from the dates inscribed on its pediment. When it had to be restored after 1918, the opportunity was taken to adorn its staircase with a portrait of General Mangin, who liberated Laon in that year. So high is this square from the Ville-Basse that you can descend precipitously by cable-car. The Town Hall annex which also stands here is imaginatively installed in an eighteenth-century building which turns out to be the former church of Saint-Rémi-au-Velours. Delicious Renaissance streets lead from the square eastwards into the old city and the cathedral square.

The British, who rightly regard Durham cathedral as one of the pre-eminent houses of God in Europe, inevitably feel at home as they approach the west façade of Durham's sister-cathedral in Laon. By contrast the nineteenth-century Gothic architect Viollet-le-Duc said that from a distance Laon cathedral resembled more a château than a cathedral. I disagree. Three deep porches, roofed and gabled, pierce the lower part. Above them is the great rose window, flanked by two others and topped by a row of three arcades. Above the central arcade a sculpted Madonna, flanked by two angels, blesses the city from the façade. Mary and her

Child have been much mutilated over the centuries, but the sculptures in the sheltered porches remain magnificent. In the centre is depicted the life of the Blessed Virgin: crowned she stands on a dragon; above she falls asleep and rises from the dead to be enthroned in heaven alongside her Son. Around these scenes are sculpted saints, patriarchs and prophets. The statue of Abraham (the first on the left) touches me most. He holds his son Isaac by his head, about to slaughter the boy, supposedly on God's orders, with a cleaver. Isaac looks understandably miserable. Both are standing on the ram which will eventually be substituted for the human sacrifice. As for the right-hand porch, its sculptures depict Jesus reigning in heaven. The sculpted left-hand porch again glorifies the Virgin Mary.

From the third storey two of the seven towers which crown Laon cathedral rise to a height of 56 m. Peering from the corners of these turreted towers are carved oxen, a tribute to the beasts which dragged up this mighty hill the stones which built this cathedral. Statues ornament the porches, restored versions of those mutilated at the time of the Revolution.

The five other towers are also justly famed – for their gracefulness, as well as the skills by which their masons have increased their complexity and embellishment as they rise. Those at the corners of the transept reach 60 m on the north side and 75 m on the south side. That at the crossing, a squat square lantern, is clearly quite content to be the smallest of all. Walk round the apse to see its rose window, pierced above three slender windows, guarded by a couple of little spires.

Gautier de Mortagne was the bishop who in the mid-twelfth century begun building this cathedral on the site of the one burnt down fifty or so years earlier. He envisaged a cathedral 118 m long, whose vault should rise to 24 m. Inside his cathedral you hardly notice the classical doorways of the side chapels which are overwhelmed by the Gothic immensity of the rest. Even the ornate wooden pulpit, made by Michel Ducastel of Laon in 1681, virtually disappears. The three bays of the four-storeyed church are supported by massive cylindrical pillars. From their varied capitals slender columns take your eyes up to the vaulting, slicing upwards through the tribune, triforium and clerestory. The thirteenth-century stained glass at the west end glows even pinker by contrast with the criss-crossed patterns of the marble floor of the apse. To stand under the crossing and gaze up at the square lantern is thrilling and slightly unnerving.

In the thirteenth-century stained glass at the centre of the great round east window, Jesus, carried by his mother, is heralded by the prophet Isaiah and by John the Baptist. The twelve Apostles fill the medallions of the first circle, and the twenty-four elders of the Apocalypse the medallions of the second circle. The central lancet depicts the Passion and Resurrection of Jesus. The lancet on the right is filled with glass illustrating his birth and infancy, while the lancet on the left depicts St Stephen and St Theophile. Beneath is a carving of Christ crucified, mourned by his mother Mary and his disciple St John.

The rose window of the north transept is fascinating. Fired around 1190 to the designs of Pierre d'Arras, it depicts the nine liberal arts as taught in Laon. Clockwise from the top the roundels represent rhetoric, grammar, dialectic, astronomy, arithmetic, medicine, geometry and music. In the centre is the crowning science: theology. The non-figurative glass below, designed by L. Chevalier in 1972, makes a valiant, vain attempt to match its predecessor.

Spare time to look at the Romanesque font in the south transept, lovely swirling patterns embellishing four mutilated heads which represent the four evangelists. This Romanesque font, a sixteenth-century wooden retable depicting the Descent from the Cross and a Louis XIV wrought-iron choir screen add a humbler charm to the power of this cathedral. So does the long thirteenth-century cloister and chapter house.

Laon cathedral is flanked by other elegant ecclesiastical buildings. On the same side as the cloister rise the houses in which the canons used to live. On the north side stands the former bishop's palace, which now serves as the Palais de Justice. Part of it dates from the thirteenth century. Its garden is reached from the north side by a powerful arcade. Alas, except on business no one is allowed into the courtyard, so that you must peer through the railings at the arcades as well as the flying buttresses and Gothic tracery of the cathedral apse.

The Gothic windows and three unassuming round towers of the former episcopal palace overlook the northern rampart of Laon. The bishop's apartments were rebuilt in the eighteenth century and stand in the courtyard, abutting on to an unusually complex little chapel dating from the twelfth century. The little square itself has been named after Giselle and Nicole Aubey and their mother, who were executed here by the Nazis.

If you have strong enough leg muscles you should certainly make at least a partial tour of Laon's thirteenth-century ramparts, which remain remarkably well preserved, their fortified gates, their square and round towers still intact. Taking the route east from the Palais de Justice you can follow the rampart as far as the citadel of Laon, profiting from superb panoramas. As for the citadel, it was built in 1594 by Henri IV in his Protestant days in order to wean Laon from its affection for the Catholic League. You reach it by steps leading down from the end of the northern rampart. Then walk back under the plane trees along the south side of the city, skirting the Rampart du Midi, huge, buttressed and set with round bastions, until you reach the thirteenth-century Porte d'Ardon.

Set perilously on the edge of the hill, the Porte d'Ardon clearly intends to tolerate no nonsense from any unwelcome visitor. A cobbled street runs under its round arch which is flanked by a couple of round pepperpot towers and topped by a steep, red-tiled roof. The portcullis is gone, though its slits remain. The room above the gateway is supported by ancient wooden beams. Above the main archway is a blind arch designed to allow defenders of the city to drop missiles on the heads of would-be attackers, while narrow openings in the towers enabled archers to rain arrows on them. For some reason in 1978 the citizens fixed a plaque on the gateway commemorating Roland, the hero of the Battle of Roncesvalles which took place 1,200 years earlier.

As you re-enter the city by this gate, ahead of you the oxen of the cathedral tower gaze placidly down. Turn left along Rue de Signier, passing the elegant eighteenth-century doorway of the *Trésor public* to reach the prefecture. It occupies the seventeenth-century buildings which once were the royal abbey of Saint-Jean. Otherwise from the Porte d'Ardon you can readily find the municipal museum, signposted 100 m or so north-east along Rue Georges-Ermant. On the way the charming antiquity of Laon is revealed as you pass a stone house whose plaque informs you that this was once the thirteenth-century chapel of St Corneille and St Cyprien. The museum stands further on where the Knights Templars in 1160 built their headquarters. Their octagonal funeral chapel still stands in the garden, extended by a porch and an apse decorated with pig faces and staring human heads. This is another remarkable feature of Romanesque Laon, dating from the very beginning of the twelfth century. The civic fathers have taken the excellent decision to shelter inside it two statues of prophets, sculpted in the twelfth or thirteenth century, which once graced the cathedral façade. Among the other tombal sculptures is a funeral effigy depicting the sculpted skeleton of the doctor of King Charles VI, Guillaume d'Harcigny, who died aged ninety in 1393. The doctor himself was responsible for this grotesquery, for he stipulated that his corpse be exhumed after a year in the grave and a copy made. Apparently his hair had continued to grow after death. It lies in curls beneath his cadaverous head. His hands delicately conceal his private parts. His mouth has fallen open.

As for the museum itself, it contains to my mind too many paintings 'attributed' to such masters as Rubens and Perugino (especially sad in view of the fact that the three brothers Le Nain all came from Laon), as well as some soppy works by the local artist Jean-Simon Barthélémy (1793–1813); but two authentic treasures make up for all this: a marble head of Alexander the Great, sculpted in the first century BC and slightly knocked about, and a head of Zeus, sculpted around 150 BC, his hair far wilder than that of Dr Guillaume d'Harcigny. The sports of long-forgotten Gauls are recalled in ancient bronzes of wrestlers. Another Gallo-Roman bronze found near to Laon depicts a charioteer balanced precariously between a couple of wheels pulled by two proudly prancing steeds. The rest of the collection consists of pre-Christian jewellery, swords, Roman and Attic finds and yet more noble Greek heads.

On the way west from Place du Général-Leclerc in Rue Saint-Jean-du-Bourg you pass the city library, a collection remarkable not only for its medieval manuscripts and miniatures but also for a splendid Roman mosaic, found at Blanzy-lès-Firmes, whose artist, working around 50 BC, has portrayed Orpheus playing his lyre and charming a wild boar, a peacock, a fox, a leopard, a horse, a stag and an elephant. The next street, Rue Saint-Martin, still boasts some picturesque houses of yesteryear, such as that known as the Little St Vincent (no. 1) since the monks of Saint-Vincent-de-Laon built it in 1529, and a couple of others (nos. 16

and 24) built in the eighteenth century. The streets of Laon are
blessed with many such houses, the earlier ones often boasting
little towers.

The church of Saint-Martin, in part restored since the Second
World War, originally belonged to a Premonstratensian abbey.
Building began on the present Saint-Martin in 1124. By the end
of the thirteenth century its second range of windows had been
finished, as well as the west façade. Two delicately crocketed
spires rise from either side of the façade, and flying buttresses
support the nave. A squatter, square tower rises over the crossing.
Over a little arcade on the façade is a triangular gable, decorated
with a roundel containing a relief of the patron saint slicing his
cloak in two in order to clothe a naked beggar (an event which as
we have seen actually took place a few kilometres north-west of
Laon just outside Arras). In the form of a Latin cross, the interior
derives much of its elegance from the ogival vaulting, created
around the mid-thirteenth century. Scarcely any architectural
feature of this church, including its rose window, dates from
another era. Most of the statues on the façade have lost their
heads, and the Annunciation above the porch has almost completely disappeared. The wood carvings in the church date mostly
from the seventeenth century, and the choir stalls were made in
1740.

The Hôtel-Dieu to the north of this church, also left in a sorry
state in 1944 though today in much better condition, was built in
the late nineteenth century within the walls of the former abbey
of Saint-Martin. Not everything was rebuilt, and you can still
visit the Gothic *salle des Malades* and see the early-seventeenth-
century abbot's lodgings and the eighteenth-century cloister.

Rue de la Libération leads from the church down some steps to
the early-thirteenth-century Porte de Soissons, which opens in the
ramparts to the west of the city. The city wall adjoins a gateway,
with a thirteenth-century tower which used to be called Tour de
Dame Ève. Since a minor landslide caused it to start leaning, it
changed its name to '*Tour penchée*'. Beside it is a statue to one of
Laon's most famous sons. Born here in 1637, Jacques Marquette
died in Canada in 1675 having discovered the River Mississippi.
His memorial depicts him in clerical costume, a crucifix tucked in
his girdle, while Redskins behind paddle a canoe. Two lines from
Longfellow's *Hiawatha* are quoted in French:

Que le soleil est beau, Français,
Quand tu nous viens visiter.

[The sun is so beautiful, Frenchman,
When you come and visit us]

Did the Redskins really think the sun began to shine when the Frenchmen arrived?

Whenever I see this monument, I am reminded of a far less complimentary poem written by Victor Hugo, after he had dined and lodged execrably at Laon. 'Everything is lovely at Laon, the churches, the houses, the environs, everything save the horrible *Auberge de la Hure* where I slept, on whose wall I wrote this little good-bye:

'TO THE INNKEEPER OF "LA HURE":
Salesman of adulterated dishes,
Hôtelier who serves a fricassee
Of filthy muck;
Eating-house where one collects
Thin soup in a greasy dish
And all the lice of the city,
Your inn, like your face,
Is a boar's head by God's good grace
And desperate for cleanliness!'

After describing Victor Hugo's devilment, I feel I must add that at Laon I have never eaten or slept badly. I remember for instance eating here a superbly bleeding *filet de boeuf à la ficelle*, i.e. cooked hanging from a piece of string (*une ficelle*) by lowering the fillet into a pot of boiling carrots, turnips, onions, tomatoes and leeks – with no doubt a few secret spices that the chef was not keen to reveal. Entranced by such delights as well as by the architectural enchantments of the upper city at Laon, it would be easy to neglect those of the Ville-Basse, which include the church of Saint-Jean-Baptiste-de-Vaux whose nave is pre-Romanesque, and the former church of Saint-Lazaire, once devoted to caring for lepers.

Then the so-called Route de Charlemagne (which here is really the more prosaically named N2) runs north-east for 18 km to Marle, which lies just off the road to the right. Its mighty church carries over the porch a smiling Madonna. A tiny doorway to the

left of this porch gives access to a most powerful building, supported by great round pillars, the chancel arch cunningly widening as it rises to give an impression of yet more height. Pendent
bosses, a splendid organ adorned with angels, a triforium, wooden
choir stalls sculpted with saints in bas-relief and a delicate Renaissance pulpit enliven the church. On the left as you enter is the
tomb of a balding knight, his remaining hair elegantly shorn, a
lion rampant on his shield. On the opposite side of the church is
its Romanesque font.

Turn left beyond the church and drive back to the N2 with the
town ramparts high on your left. This is Thiérache, frontier
country near the Belgian border and a land of fortified churches.
The people who built them had countless reasons for fearing the
worst. From 1515, when François I came to the throne of France,
this region was a sporadic battlefield for virtually 200 years. In
1542 the Emperor Charles V was ravaging Picardy and Cham-
pagne. A year later François invaded the Hainaut at the head of
an army numbering no fewer than 40,000 men. Far from improving, the second half of the sixteenth century experienced strife
exacerbated by religious passion that was often vicious. A brief
period of peace inaugurated by Henri IV was savagely interrupted
by the Thirty Years War, which had scarcely ended when the
Frondeurs rose against the power of the monarchy, creating
misery and chaos in Thiérache. Finally Louis XIV's determina-
tion to oust the Spanish from France brought new terror to this
region. Significant dates in these epochs continually recur in the
architectural history of the fortified churches of Thiérache.

So the people transformed their churches into places of not
simply spiritual but also physical refuge, into stables, kitchens,
garrisons and communal homes. The house of God became a
defensive château, with slits in the walls through which a defender
could fire in safety, with holes for raining debris on the enemy,
with machicolations, massive turrets and powerfully reinforced
doors.

That at Vervins is no exception, an enormous affair of brick
and stone. To one's delight, most of these churches are unlocked
during the day (save those around Amiens in my experience).
Built over centuries, the church at Vervins has massy columns
supporting its arched roof, with a far more delicate thirteenth-
century apse (in spite of its nineteenth-century modifications) at

the far end. In 1553 Jacques II of Coucy-Vervins gave this basically Romanesque church its huge fortified tower. Inside it remains a house of God, and the dark and horrible stained glass should be thrown away, for its murky light prevents one enjoying the huge 1699 painting of Jesus dining with Simon the Pharisee.

For another 19 km our way follows Route de Charlemagne north-east to Hirson. On the way we pass the extraordinarily huge church at La Bouteille, which one might readily mistake for a château as its four pepperpot towers approach, two of them built of brick, the other two of stone. The church walls are strengthened by alternating bands of brick and stone. To reach it you have to pass through a further defence of an arch set in a solid brick wall. La Bouteille's church was fortified by the monks of Foigny in 1547. The next village but one, skirted by our route, is Origny-en-Thiérache. As well as possessing an extremely neat Town Hall built of brick and faced with stone, Origny-en-Thiérache boasts a church equally impressive as that at La Bouteille. Almost entirely constructed out of brick, its huge round towers, built in the sixteenth century, flank the main doorway and seem to threaten to shoot down anyone who dares venture inside for worship.

Though surrounded by the splendid hilly and wooded walking country of the Hirson forest, and in spite of its campsites, lakes and concrete church, the industrial town of Hirson is not to my taste. Three kilometres east in the forest of Saint-Michel is a lovely abbey of the same name. But I prefer to turn west at Hirson along the D31 and make my way by the extremely scenic route which takes us as far as Guise by way of several more of these altogether amazing fortified churches of Thiérache. As we drive, the River Oise appears and disappears from view. At Luzoir are campsites and caravan resorts. You can canoe down the river from Étréaupont. Sorbais is a village given over to camping and hikers, yet its villagers in the fifteenth century decided that its little twelfth-century church lacked a machicolated keep and promptly supplied one. At Autreppes the church boasts not only a defensive keep over its porch but also a couple of chimneys, once belonging to fireplaces where refugees could cook for themselves and their families. The church at Saint-Algis – beautifully situated over the valley of the Oise – added at the beginning of the Thirty Years War an even more powerful keep than that at Autreppes, while its nave and choir, built in the 1680s, form a huge defensive rectangle. Further along the valley the church at Marly-Gomont is flanked by four defensive towers. At Faty (where the little church still carries a keep, inscribed with the date 1676) turn north-west to reach Monceau-sur-Oise where a couple of tall towers guard the belfry. Then make your way back to Beaurain, whose isolated church is defended not only by its massive and square half-brick, half-stone keep, but also by four brooding cylindrical towers.

These are but a few of the multitude of fortified churches – well over fifty of them – in this tiny part of France. From Beaurain the D31 drives into the camping and canoeing centre which is also the citadel of Guise. Here a curving cobbled street leads past the brick-and-stone monster of a church as far as the fortified château. In the Place d'Armes is a fish shop entertainingly dubbed 'Poissonerie Thalassa', as well as a statue of Camille Desmoulins, who was born here in 1760 and looks every inch a romantic hero.

In fact (if Thomas Carlyle's *French Revolution* is authentic history on this point) while Desmoulins may have lived as a romantic hero, he scarcely died as one. Initially able to take on anyone with his sarcastic journalism, he endeared himself to Robespierre with whom he had studied law in Paris. But Desmoulins' friendship with Danton and his noble belief in clemency turned Robespierre against him. Both he and Danton were arrested on 30 March 1794. Five days later they mounted the guillotine. Carlyle contrasted the mien of the two men as they faced execution:

Danton carried a high-look in the death-cart. Not so Camille: it is but one week, and all is so topsyturvied; angel wife left weeping; love, riches, Revolutionary fame, left all at the Prison-gate; carnivorous rabble now howling round. Palpable and yet incredible; like a madman's dream! Camille struggles and writhes; his shoulders shuffle the loose coat off them, which hangs knotted, the hands tied: 'Calm, my friend,' said Danton, 'heed not that vile *canaille*'.

Desmoulins died aged thirty-four, the same age, he told his accusers, as '*le bon sans-culotte Jésus*'. Two weeks later his angel wife Lucille Duplessis shared his fate, with immensely greater courage.

The road from Guise south-west towards Saint-Quentin runs absolutely straight and lined with trees until it crosses the canal at Mont-d'Origny. Within a few moments we reach Origny-Sainte-

Benoîte. Now the rows of single trees disappear from the roadside, replaced by more distant woods and coppices on either side. Fifteen kilometres further west by way of Homblières we reach Saint-Quentin. A busy modern city, Saint-Quentin is dominated by its basilica and its ornate nineteenth-century Chamber of Commerce, both larger than life. The latter houses a butterfly museum, the exquisite creatures pinned inside glass cabinets.

Although its magical Porche Lamoureux is one of the masterpieces of flamboyant Gothic art and its partly Romanesque west tower is delightful, the basilica at Saint-Quentin has its faults, chiefly in my view the nasty glass doors which threaten to burst the noses of the elderly faithful as we make our short-sighted way to Mass. Though dark, the building soars beautifully, built between the early thirteenth and the fifteenth centuries. In the deambulatory is ancient glass, some of it six centuries old, and the organ case is a late seventeenth-century oaken masterpiece by Jean Bérain. A curious maze has been created by the tiled floor at the entry to the nave, but take care not to overstay your welcome in trying to solve it: the verger once locked me inside at ten minutes past five in the afternoon.

You can park in the cathedral square. Traffic-free Rue Saint-André leads from here to the Place de l'Hôtel-de-Ville. The Town Hall, a Flemish *tour de force* chiefly designed by Colard Noël and (though begun in 1330) not finished until 1509, boasts sweet Gothic arcades from which rises a most delicate second storey topped by three equally delicate gables. In its belfry you can see the bells ranged in order, ready to chime a ditty for a couple of minutes before each hour. I have noticed that only tourists pause to hear them, whilst the regular citizens of Saint-Quentin hurry about their business. After the ditties chimed by the carillon, the bell that rings the hours offers only a disappointing clunk. In the same square rises the classical municipal theatre and behind the Town Hall a suitably pompous Palais de Justice, a building completed in 1908. As for the city art gallery, the Musée Antoine Lécuyer, few connoisseurs would want to miss the splendid collection of portraits by Maurice Quentin de La Tour, who was born here in 1704 and died here eighty-four years later. More stamina, in my view, is needed to come safely through the huge cut-price and second-hand fair, held at Saint-Quentin on the first weekend of September, when the citizens tuck in to vast platefuls of tripe and chips.

Drive south to La Fère. Eight kilometres west is Tergnier, whose modestly attractive Town Hall square (Place Doumer) is bordered by a school which is dedicated to André Malraux, minister of culture under Charles de Gaulle. Malraux would have looked quizzically at the rebuilt church and belfry of Tergnier, which rely on concrete to offset their red bricks. From here the N32 runs south-west to Chauny, passing by patterned and unpretentious brick houses. Chauny too is unassuming, having rebuilt its centre attractively, hanging in the belfry of its Town Hall a gentle glockenspiel. But these towns are really displaying to us the results of industrial success brought by the trade along the Canal de Saint-Quentin, and I prefer to speed away south, threading my way to the altogether delightful Coucy-le-Château. Amid its grandeur it is easy enough to neglect the fine Gothic church of Saint-Sauveur, built from the fourteenth to the sixteenth centuries. The mere drive up to the Ville-Haute, by way of its fortifications as far as the feudal château, is exhilarating. Continue as far as the belfried Town Hall in the main square. Opposite, trees and a well front the seventeenth-century gateway which gives access to the park (and hidden children's swings) of the former Domaine de la Grangère, where a notice tells you that in 1594 was born the son of Henry IV and Gabrielle d'Estrées, Duchess of Beaufort. The notice neglects to inform you of his name, which was César, or that he was dubbed Duke of Vendôme.

You can walk around the medieval fortifications of Coucy-le Château. Built by Enguerrand III between 1230 and 1242, they once rivalled the greatest in France, until retreating Nazis wickedly blew them up. The ensemble must have been superb, virtually intact on its height. What survived remains breathtaking, especially when a goat leaps up above you and peers uncertainly down at the intruder. The Hôtel Belle-Vue in the Place du Marché must be one of the most delightful in which to stay or eat, though I confess that as yet I have never done either. Just past the hotel rises the massive ancient city gate, through which the D5 runs into the forest of Saint-Gobain. In the midst of this forest is a historically redolent spot, Prémontré. At this leafy spot in 1120 St Norbert of Xanten founded an order whose monks became known as Premonstratensians, men in white habits whose aim was to combine an austere contemplative life (including a total abstention from meat) with a life of active charity in the world.

Running west from Coucy-le-Château the D934 takes you for 14 km across the D1 and the Canal de l'Oise by way of Guny, with its sixteenth-century church, to the delightful town of Blérancourt. The gabled, medieval stone church has a twelfth-century tower with a tall pointed spire that holds up a weathercock. Its unusual Renaissance porch, given by Guillaume de Lanvin in 1537, is decorated with cherubs, a winged horse and bizarre angels in roundels. The coats of arms of two sad knights also decorate the doorway. We know they are sad from their effigies, both of them bareheaded and in prayer. Three other religious effigies have I regret to say disappeared, only their niches remaining.

Nearby is a mini-château, the Moulin-Vert, which some claim as the oldest hospice in France. It was set up in 1661 by Bernard Poitier, Duke of Gesvres, though the building dates from the fifteenth century. Its classical chapel is adorned with four massive Doric pillars. On the wall of this hospice a sundial warns us:

> *Nous ne sommes rien en ce monde*
> *Toi sans soleil et moi sans Dieu*

[We are nothing in this world,
You without sun and me without God]

Should it not be the other way round? The legend ends '*sine illo sumus nihil*' ('without you we are nothing'). In case the sun lets the sundial down, its work is supplemented by a chiming clock in the belfry above.

The classical Town Hall of Blérancourt, built in 1850, rises above an arcaded market and is enhanced by a wrought-iron balcony and a decorated pediment. Walk round it to admire the bronze statue of the three Graces on a fountain, the ladies only slightly *déshabillées*. The entrance to the Town Hall is on the far side, up a flight of steps that leads to an impressive pedimented portico. This portico looks across the wide and long Place du Général-Leclerc, bordered by plane trees which lead as far as the château built for Bernard Poitier at the beginning of the seventeenth century. Alongside it is a three-star hotel. This unusual opulence derives from the fact that at Blérancourt in June 1917 two Americans, Anne Murray Dicke and Anne Morgan, established here the HQ of the American voluntary ambulance brigade of the Great War. In consequence the château of

Blérancourt (which you can visit daily, save on Tuesdays) became twelve years later a major centre for Franco-American co-operation.

The Revolutionary Louis-Antoine de Saint-Just was born at Blérancourt. You can find the tumbledown house of his family at no. 2 Rue de la Chouette on the south side of the town, at the corner with Rue Saint-Just. A plaque declares, 'In this house lived Louis-Antoine de Saint-Just, celebrated revolutionary tribune, deputy for the Aisne, president of the National Convention, born August 25, 1757, guillotined the 10 Thermidor year II.' Whereas Danton and Desmoulins perished on the scaffold because they turned against Robespierre, Saint-Just stayed loyal to his master and was executed with him on the same day, 18 July 1794. I parked my car to muse on this historic spot, and a farmer driving a tractor nearly demolished it with his harrow. It seemed a suitable moment to drive lazily and picturesquely along the D6 south-east to Soissons.

At Soissons I gratefully sat down in the restaurant of the *Lion Rouge* and ordered a *carbonnade de boeuf picarde*, first asking the waitress what the word *picarde* signified. 'It's cooked in beer,' she answered. This was one of those waitresses displaying the delicious wit of the region, for as I left my car in the hotel parking I noticed that a radio was playing in a locked and empty Renault. I thought it wise to alert the waitress to this, at which she replied, 'That's normal; the car doesn't like to be bored.' The *carbonnade* sizzled in its cooking pot on my table. Though delicious, its huge chunks of beef were too much for me, and I must have left nearly half of it, so as to make way for a dessert. As the warmth enveloped me I took off my jacket, noticing that virtually everyone else in the dining room had done the same.

At one end of Rue Gustave-Alliaume in which the hotel stands rises the skeleton of Saint-Jean-des-Vignes, its rose window a gaping hole, the twin spires intact, the right one far more elaborate than the one on the left. At the other end is the dangerous roundabout that constitutes the Place de la République, with its swaggering memorial to the dead of the 1870 war. ('A soldier dies on his cannon, *La France* holds aloft her flag, while a bronze angel tops the ensemble with a halbard and torch.') From here runs the tree-lined, prosperous Avenue Thiers, its boutiques selling shoes, handbags and clothing and occasionally interspersed with a

butcher or a *pâtisserie*. We are making our way to the cathedral,
though ahead towers the church of Saint-Léger. On the right
appears the cold-looking Palais de Justice, which was built in
1933. I prefer to avoid looking at it by turning instantly left past
the jolly *Palais du Vêtement*, whose upper storey is decorated with
merry mosaics, to arrive at the covered market, its stalls spilling
out on to the square. The covered and the open markets divide
themselves respectively into meats (beef, *charcuterie*) and eggs and
cheese indoors, with clothing, fruit and vegetables outside.

Soissons market is twice blessed, a cathedral at one end and a
ruined church at the other. At the east end stands the church of
Saint-Pierre. At the west end rises the apse of the cathedral of
Saint-Gervais-et-Saint-Protais, with its double buttresses, chapels
and narrow windows. Once a cloister stretched on the north side.
Its sole memorial is the name of the Place du Cloître. Walk
around the pock-marked walls and half-ruined north side of the
cathedral. Its west façade is best seen from across the street.
Soissons cathedral is a great might-have-been. Its left-hand tower
was never finished, for when the Armagnacs sacked the city in
1414 the materials designated for building it were sold on the
orders of Charles VI. In 1567 the Huguenots took the city and
held on to it for a year, taking the opportunity to destroy the
Catholic relics and shrines, shooting at the stained-glass windows
and mutilating statues. Other statues disappeared when the
façade was rebuilt in the eighteenth century. Most of what
remained was lost during the sometimes daily bombardments of
the First World War.

Saint-Gervais-et-Saint-Protais does retain some thirteenth-
century glass in the windows at the east end. A notice sadly
explains that other glass has been stolen – some exhibited in the
Pitcairn Collection in Pennsylvania, in the Isabella Stewart Gard-
ner Museum, Boston, and in the Corcoran Gallery, Washington.
That looted by the Germans in 1918 was taken to Berlin and
perished during the Second World War.

Yet this remains a moving example of twelfth-century Gothic
architecture. Standing in the nave we are enclosed by walls built
between 1220 and 1240, looking towards a choir that dates from
1192 to 1215. Simple round arches become more complex as they
rise and at the crossing, the earlier ones the more delicate. The
glass at the east end glows purplish-red. Of its themes, the story of

Adam and Eve is the easiest to make out, but of course what counts most of all is the overall warmth. The north transept, constructed in the two decades after 1250, rises on massy round pillars, and its rose window has preserved its fourteenth-century stained glass. Rubens painted the Adoration of the Shepherds here. He had fallen ill on a visit to Soissons, and the painting was a thank-offering for his recovery. Alas, it is very difficult to see in the gloom. The chapels opposite this transept constitute the earliest and I think the most entrancing part of the cathedral. The arcades and slender columns, and the delicious polygonal chapel were built between 1170 and 1190.

Cross the market square, passing the war memorial in the middle with its vast rows of names, to reach what remains of the twelfth-century church of Saint-Pierre. Beside it is another sweet ruin, part of the Romanesque church of the former abbey of Notre-Dame. Then walk north along Rue du Commerce towards the church of Saint-Léger. An impressive eighteenth-century palace, now the Hôtel de Ville, stands on the right just before the church. No longer used for worship Saint-Léger is in mint condition. The first curiosity you notice is an odd addition on the south side, the fourteenth-century doorway of the abbey of Notre-Dame, which was destroyed in the 1790s. The choir and transept of this church date from the thirteenth century, the nave from the late sixteenth and the porch from the seventeenth. Outside the church is a memorial to 108 men who died on 6 June 1972, when the Vierzy railway tunnel collapsed and two trains crashed. The memorial uncompromisingly observes that they died *'par la faute des hommes'*, that is through human folly.

Walk around the church to its still intact little cloister, which dates from around 1300. Saint-Léger now serves as an intimate museum, and an attendant will take you round on any day save Tuesdays. Its eleventh-century crypt houses a couple of tombs, its vaults still fragmentarily painted. The main body of the church houses treasures brought from other religious buildings in the region, among the finest in my view being capitals from the former abbey of Saint-Yves-de-Braine. From the tympanum of the abbey church came a marvellous thirteenth-century carving of the harrowing of hell – the damned grimacing in a cooking pot warmed by flames from a dragon's mouth, while pardoned sinners joyfully leap from limbo towards Jesus. Here are ancient Christian sarcophagi, carved with the $\chi\rho$ sign, Renaissance chests and a finely chiselled monumental brass of the heart of Enguerrand VII de Coucy, who died in 1397. He had been count of Soissons for thirty years, having bought the position from Louis de Châtillon who had been captured by the English at the Battle of Crécy and desperately needed cash to pay his own ransom. I like too the funeral statue of Catherine de Bourbon-Vendôme, abbess of Notre-Dame-de-Soissons till her death in 1594, even though she has lost both her hands.

A further treat is the art gallery and museum of local history in the eighteenth-century abbey buildings. That entertaining nineteenth-century traveller Augustus J. C. Hare, writing of this very part of France, once enunciated the superb dictum that 'in a town where galleries exist, there is no weariness so weary as that caused by seeing too many pictures; no dreariness so dreary as that which too many pictures themselves convey'. Judged by that standard, this gallery at Soissons is exactly the right size. Two masterly rococo works by the eighteenth-century Venetian Giovanni Antonio Pellegrini depict Alexander viewing the corpse of Darius and then showing mercy to the widow and weeping children of the Persian king. (Alexander has taken off his helmet in the presence of the corpse and replaced it in the presence of the supplicants.) Close by is an ethereal Venus. Here too is a remarkably realistic painting of St Sebastian by Honoré Daumier, all pearly white skin and red blood. Eugène-Louis Boudin has contributed a couple of nineteenth-century seascapes. I also warm to an early seventeenth-century picture of the Flight to Egypt by Benjamin Cuyp, the Holy Family a very Dutch-looking group, the landscape fearfully dark. The local history section I find less entrancing, but those who are fascinated by fragments of Gallo-Roman mosaics and ceramics will find much to interest them here.

Behind the Town Hall of Soissons is a little formal garden, shaded with trees and furnished with seats. Beyond it is a riverside walk, with barges moored beside the River Aisne and across the water the spire of Saint-Waast rising over the rooftops. Signs point you across the river to the former abbey of Saint-Médard. Though little remains save its ninth-century crypt, this abbey speaks much of the history of Soissons. Once it housed the tombs of kings Clotaire and Sigebert, the sons of Clovis. In 486 Clovis gained a celebrated victory over the Gallo-Romans just outside Soissons and set up here his capital, from which he ruled the whole of the territory encompassed by the Somme and the Loire. On the eve of the battle, so the historian Gregory of Tours tells us, St Rémi, who had baptized Clovis, asked him to give back a beautiful vase which one of the Franks had stolen from a church. Before Clovis could respond, the soldier who had stolen it smashed the vase. Next year, reviewing his troops, Clovis spotted that the arms of the same soldier were in a horrible state. Clovis seized them and flung them to the ground. When the soldier bent down to pick them up, Clovis sliced off his head with the words, 'That is what you did to the vase of Soissons.' As Gregory of Tours commented, 'So he managed to inspire a great fear in everyone.'

Soissons has known other great ones. After being condemned at the Council of Soissons in 1121 for teaching heresy, Abelard was imprisoned in the abbey of Saint-Médard, as in the early ninth century was the Emperor Louis the Debonair by his treacherous sons. Returning across the river by the Pont Gambetta, look out on the right for a sweet, early-seventeenth-century brick-and-stone building which is known as the Pavillon de l'Arquebuse and was given a most unsuitably massive monumental doorway by Marshal d'Estrées in 1658.

Then it is time to visit the most spectacular building in Soissons, the ruined abbey of Saint-Jean-des-Vignes. Walk up the Avenue Thiers, turn left along Rue Carnot and right up Boulevard Jeanne-d'Arc until you reach the barracks. Founded in 1076, the abbey had survived the Revolution, indeed housing the assemblies of the Third Estate in March 1789. Then the monks were expelled. Between 1805 and 1825, by imperial decree and incredibly with the consent of the bishop of Soissons, most of the abbey was demolished, its stones used for refurbishing the cathedral. Enough remains to evoke a vanished world. The sculpted decorations of the abbey include medicinal plants – ground ivy, buttercup, and so on – utilized by the monks who also served as local doctors. On the broken spires you can still see an exquisite fourteenth-century statue of the Blessed Virgin and a sixteenth-century Crucifixion, unusually set at the centre of a rose window. The most delicate tower was finished in 1495, the mightiest in 1520. Statues of the Blessed Virgin Mary and the twelve Apostles flank the blank rose window. Christ's Passion is depicted on the taller spire and on the smaller one is sculpted Cardinal Jean de Dormans, along with his family. A monk of Soissons, he became chancellor of France under Charles V and remained a generous benefactor of the abbey.

Two wings of the cloister exist and the foundations of the rest are being excavated. The ogival vaults of the thirteenth-century refectory and cellar remain intact. No vines grow these days in this part of France, for as we believe François I grubbed them up; but a reminder of happier times are the vine-leaves sculpted on a capital of one of the slender pillars supporting the roof of the cellar. From this cellar the monks arranged an escape of water outside the city walls and used it themselves to escape marauding Huguenots in the sixteenth century. You can still see a hole in the refectory wall where once was a pulpit for the monk who read to his fellows as they ate, a little staircase leading up to it. For some reason a curious so-called Merovingian house has been re-created in the abbey grounds.

South of Soissons the D1 winds and climbs and gently falls through fields and woods. After 5½ km, at Noyant-et-Aconin where the sixteenth-century château has been reduced to a farmstead and the choir of the church dates from the same century, make a very brief diversion left to see the romantic fourteenth-century keep of the château of Septmonts, once the summer retreat of the bishops of Soissons (and open for visits on Sundays). Although much else remains – parts of the walls and the Renaissance pavilion where the bishops rested – this astonishing and elegant 43 m high keep has no parallel, a keep built at a seemingly unique moment when military architecture was suddenly embellished by the refinement of the Renaissance. Septmonts village also boasts a fine, impressively sculpted fifteenth-century church.

Return west from here to Berzy-le-Sec, a village guarded by a ruined fortress and hallowed by a church dating from the twelfth century. Drive along the D1 to the village of Hartennes, with its campsites and German military cemetery. The next village is Oulchy-le-Château, where an eighteenth-century priory abuts on to the finest Romanesque church of this region. Park here in front of the quiet brick-and-stone Town Hall, which was built in 1883, and climb up to the church on the left. Usually it is locked. If you could break your way into the church you would enjoy its primitive capitals, its fifteenth-century stalls and its seventeenth-century

pulpit. Locked out, from the graveyard you can still relish the
Romanesque arches of its three-storeyed tower, admire the blind
arcades and walk around the apse to revel in the comical creatures
carved thereon. Is one of them a merman? Another couple of
fearsome beasts have caught a terrified man. From the graveyard
you can see through the church windows the partly Gothicized
north aisle. To the left of the church stands the classical former
priory, with fortunate children running through its Renaissance
doorways for today it serves as a school.

It is time to wander through more open countryside, finding
villages and towns that keep themselves spruce and to themselves.
Take the D803 from the right-hand side of the Town Hall to
discover the thirteenth- and fourteenth-century Château d'Armentières, with its keep and double-towered doorway. Four kilometres further on you reach Coincy. Whereas Château
d'Armentières, though partly ruined, still survives outside the
village over whose peasants and fortified farms its lords once ruled,
Coincy by contrast is dominated by its church, which was begun
in the twelfth and finished in the fifteenth centuries, apart from
the little classical doorway at the north side. A chunky tower with
a pointed tiled roof squats over the crossing. Inside is a fine
eighteenth-century pulpit, matched by some lovely Renaissance
and classical statues. The stained-glass depiction of the Crucifixion
over the high altar was fired in the sixteenth century.

Here youngsters lean over the little river and fish. The D803
leads due south to Brécy, at whose heart is a walled and fortified
village on a little eminence, with its own fortified Romanesque
church. The D470 and D80 then take you east from here towards
the communal forest and the hamlet of Beauvardes, which was
once simply an agglomeration of fairly massive farms. Just before
you reach the forest you pass by another huge fortified farm – a
phenomenon often repeated in Picardy. From here a signpost
speeds you south-west towards Épieds (whose sturdy walled
church is further defended by a powerful tower which gives place
to delicacy only in its upper openings) and then along the picturesquely winding route into Château-Thierry.

As you wind down into Château-Thierry the cool, pseudo-
Greek and extremely impressive American war memorial appears
in the distance on its slopes beyond the town. We are in the
Marne valley, and once inside the town I recommend making a

swift turn right at the traffic-lights half-way down the hill in order to park in the square of the church of Saint-Crépin opposite the subprefecture. The flamboyant Gothic church of Saint-Crépin is defined above all by its massive single tower, a smaller staircase tower running up to the top. Inside its choir is a lovely example of eighteenth-century ostentation, and the church has retained its elegant Renaissance organ console.

The name Château-Thierry derives from a fortified Gaulish camp beside the River Marne where Charles Martel, ruler of the Franks, built a château around the year 710 – ostensibly on behalf of King Thierry IV. In reality Charles Martel exercised complete power from here. In this château the count of Vermandois imprisoned Charles III of France, known as the Simple, after his deposition in 922. Around the same powerful fortress the town of Château-Thierry slowly grew, while the various rulers of the region continued to strengthen its defences.

Walk down the cobbled pavements of Rue Saint-Crépin and cross the Avenue de Soissons into the Grand'Rue. It runs into Rue Jean-de-La-Fontaine, named after the most famous son of Château-Thierry who was baptized in Saint-Crépin in 1621. La Fontaine's father was master of the waterways and forests of the region, his mother had been a rich widow. The fabulist was educated in Paris, but returned to the family home in 1647 when his father was widowed. Eventually he took over his father's old post, supervising the sluices, locks, mills and fishermen of the Marne while also caring for the neighbouring forests. La Fontaine was never rich. He married Marie Héricourt of La Ferté-Milon, who brought a substantial dowry of 30,000 *livres* and proved unfaithful to her husband. Nor was he faithful to her. When rumours of her friendship at Château-Thierry with a retired captain of the dragoons proved publicly insupportable, La Fontaine was unwillingly obliged to fight a duel with his rival. The captain, knowing that his opponent was no swordsman, politely defeated La Fontaine, and then promised never to enter the poet's house again. La Fontaine was aghast. Taking the captain by the hand he declared, 'On the contrary. We have now performed what everyone expected. If you will not now visit my house every day, I shall have to fight you again.'

In his story '*La Coupe*' La Fontaine elaborated the notion that a man is blessed when cuckolded by his wife, since it leaves him free to pursue his own ways. Jealousy had no part in his scheme of life, for, as he wrote:

> *Pour songer il faut dormir,*
> *Et les jaloux ne dorment guère.*

> [To have a dream one must sleep,
> And the jealous scarcely sleep at all.]

Eventually he and Marie amicably separated. To visit their home, turn left along Rue Jean-de-La-Fontaine and wind up a narrow street between ancient houses to reach his former home, the house in which he was born, which now serves as a museum in his memory. It was built in the Renaissance style (with the date 1559 engraved on a pilaster to the right of the doorway). A band of fleurs-de-lys runs above the doorway. An old well graces the courtyard. La Fontaine lived here until he sold the house in 1676. It remains as homely as in his own day. I was failing to open the gate properly when a lad appeared and turned the lock for me, adding, 'I live here.' His mother was sitting at the door. In his portraits the quirky, long-nosed face of La Fontaine is sharply etched. Here are portraits of his friends and patrons, as well as original manuscripts and countless translations of his fables. Engraved on silver, fired on plates, scratched on buttons, and created out of terracotta are scenes from the same celebrated works, alongside illustrations of them – ranging from those of his own time to the twentieth-century interpretations of Marc Chagall.

Walk back along Rue Jean-de-La Fontaine and wind down the Grand'Rue as far as the Place de l'Hôtel-de-Ville. The cobbled Grand'Rue is here pedestrianized, lit by elegant lanterns and crammed with shops. I find this whole town human in size. Opposite the Town Hall, just around a corner, pokes the Tour Bahlan, built in the fifteenth and sixteenth centuries as part of the town defences. Once it served as the keep of Fort-Saint-Jacques, whose chapel and hostelry was a staging post on the pilgrimage route to Santiago de Compostela. Today its steep spires and pepperpot hat humbly serve as a belfry. Finally, explore the château by taking Rue du Château across the Town Hall square. As you climb on the right appears the mighty Hôtel-Dieu, which was founded by Jeanne de Navarre in 1304 but mostly rebuilt in brick and stone in 1878. You can still visit the eighteenth-century chapel. Rue du Château is lined with lovely eighteenth-century houses, some of them with jolly, irregular courtyards behind their arched entrances. Scarcely one modern house intrudes.

At the top of the hill you look down at the fourteenth-century Porte Saint-Pierre, on top of which perches the tourist office of Château-Thierry. Turn left to encounter a more formidable gate-way, the fourteenth-century Porte Saint-Jean. Little slits once allowed archers to menace visitors. Its double entrance boasted two portcullises. Through it you reach the former château, whose concrete seats enable you to rest and gaze across the town and the slightly industrialized Marne valley. Surrounded by five rings of walls and fifteen towers, the château rises on what was a first Gaulish *oppidum* and then a Merovingian fort. An enterprising restaurant has provided children's slides and more shaded seats. You can walk from the Porte Saint-Jean between two outer ramparts which have been planted with plane trees, noting how the medieval architects designed slits in the formidable walls to allow water to escape rather than washing everything down. The route brings you back to a point above the Town Hall where you can descend steep steps to the Place de l'Hôtel-de-Ville.

From Château-Thierry take the D1 back towards Soissons, turning left after 11 km along the D973 towards Villers-Cotterêts. Our route is lined by wide open fields and passes through charm-ing little villages made up of white-walled homes with red-tiled roofs. We run through the sizeable town of Neuilly-Saint-Front. On a rise to the left stands the white, classical Château de Maucreux, before you reach a proud memorial to the French 128th division (the Division of the Wolves), who stopped the enemy here in June 1918 and sent him retreating a month later. A pyramid flanked by three shells, this monument is decorated with a savage wolf's head. Soon the D17 takes us on an excursion left for La Ferté-Milon, through woods, past farms which seem more like fortified manor-houses, through Silly-la-Poterie and its château.

France's superb playwright (to my mind her finest), Jean Racine, was born at La Ferté-Milon in 1639. Orphaned four years later, he was brought up by his grandmother, Marie Des-moulins, whose house is singled out by a plaque at no. 14 Rue de Reims. Racine naturally became a friend of La Fontaine. The dramatist himself is commemorated here by a marble statue sculpted by David d'Angers. The effect of La Ferté-Milon, its narrow streets lounging along the valley of the Ourcq, is utterly enchanting. Above the town towers the ruined château, rebuilt at the end of the fourteenth century for Louis d'Orléans (who was assassinated in 1407). Its façade still stretches for a 100 m or so. Nearby, up a cobbled street, rises the church of Notre-Dame. Ever, it seems, in danger of sliding down the steep incline, this church boasts a late-twelfth-century portal and a mighty square tower added in the sixteenth century. The choir dates from the mid-sixteenth century, as do the aisles. Warm Renaissance stained glass fills some of the windows. But for this magnificent building, another church, the fifteenth- and sixteenth-century Saint-Nicolas, would draw every discerning tourist, and even now it takes an honourable second place to Notre-Dame.

Crossing the river, you drive on to Villers-Cotterêts through the Retz forest. A signposted diversion right will take you to see the fifteenth-century Château d'Oigny-en-Valois. The approach to Villers-Cotterêts is disappointing, but not the town itself. Park in the long Place du Docteur-Henri-Mouflier. Here a stern lady sculpted on the war memorial looks towards the post office. Walk towards it and turn left to reach the church of Saint-Nicolas, whose bulbous dome supports a long thin spire. Next to the church is a former Premonstratensian abbey, now the eighteenth-century Town Hall. The neat church doorway with its statue of Bishop Nicolas was added in the seventeenth century. The rest of the church dates from the thirteenth to the sixteenth centuries. Inside a groaning Samson holds up an Italianate Renaissance pulpit. The fifteenth-century woodwork around the high altar is lusciously carved with swags and fruit. As for the stained-glass windows, those on the south wall were fired in 1934 by L. Billotey. The only one I like is that of St Hubert. The rest depict the history of Christianity in these parts – the earliest missionaries; Parisian clerics fleeing the Normans and carrying the relics of St Clothilde and St Geneviève to Pisselieu; Charles and Philippe de Valois dedicating the charter-house at Bourgfontaine to St Louis. At the other side of the church, in a theologically suspect window of 1924, an apparition of St Joan of Arc comforts weary French soldiers in 1918. The rest of the stained glass is yet more cloying: the master woodcarver of Naza-reth inspiring twentieth-century craftsmen, and so forth.

Do the farmers and sturdy peasants who appear each Thursday at the market of Villers-Cotterêts pay the remotest attention to such feeble attempts to make the Christian faith relevant to our own times? The Renaissance château of François I performs a more useful act of contemporary charity by serving today as an old folks' sheltered home. Though the elderly deserve their privacy, the concierge let me in with a nod. A couple of staggering and happy dotards gave me a cheery wave. Vast and elegant, enhanced by trees and green shrubs, the ranges on either side of their home are topped with rows of brick-and-stone dormers, some of them still decorated with urns. The far end has a marvellous Renaissance façade, decorated with salamanders, shells and a wrought-iron balcony.

Rue Demoustier runs to the right from where we are parked, away from the church and incorporating what was once the home of the two greatest members of the Dumas family and is now their museum. They evidently lived in a grander house than most modern authors can manage. The poet Charles-Albert Demoustier, in whose street this house rises, has long been forgotten, but Alexander Dumas père, born here in 1802, was pleased to begin his memoirs with the proud observation,

I was born at Villers-Cotterêts, a small town in the *département* of the Aisne, situated on the road between Paris and Laon, about 200 paces from the Rue de la Noue where Demoustier died, two leagues from La Ferté-Milon where Racine was born, and seven leagues from Château-Thierry, the birthplace of La Fontaine.

His earliest literary memories included tracing the epitaph of Demoustier in the local cemetery. The day before Demoustier's death, which took place on 2 March 1801, Dumas' mother sat beside the bedside of a man she dubbed one of the gentlest, most sympathetic that ever breathed. Her son remembered that 'though hopeless herself, she tried to instil hope into him'. Smiling sweetly, Demoustier had placed his hand on that of Mme Dumas with the words, 'We must not delude ourselves. I can take neither broth nor milk nor water any longer. So I must die.' And with a smile on his lips, the next day he breathed his last.

At Villers-Cotterêts Dumas met and rejoiced in the fragile beauty of Pauline Bonaparte, 'so slight, so graceful, so pure'. Here he twice saw the defeated emperor, passing through the town on his way to Paris. The first time Napoleon was returning from Elba, 'his face pale, sickly, impassive'. The second time was just before Napoleon's decisive defeat at Waterloo, which Dumas later came to see as a blessing for the French people.

'Everyone rushed forward to the emperor's carriage, myself naturally amongst the first,' he recalled. 'Napoleon was seated on the right at the back, clad in a green uniform with white facings, sporting the star of the Legion of Honour. His face, so pale and sickly, seemed to have been carved out of a block of ivory. It leaned slightly forward onto his chest.' Lifting his head Napoleon asked, 'Where are we?' Someone answered 'At Villers-Cotterêts, sir.' Napoleon responded with the question, 'Is that six leagues from Soissons?' and receiving the answer yes, sank back into a semi-stupor. The stable-lads cried '*Vive l'empereur*'; the whips cracked, the emperor acknowledged the greeting with a slight inclination of his head; and at full gallop the carriages disappeared around the corner of the Rue de Soissons. A few days later came the news that the French army had been annihilated at Waterloo and that the English, the Prussians and the Dutch were marching on Paris.

The route back to Soissons from Villers-Cotterêts is romantically named Route de Charlemagne and runs through the north-eastern section of the forest of Retz. While you are still in the forest, keep watch for the D2, which will take you off to the right for 4 km to see the abbey at Longpont. This ruined Cistercian abbey, founded in 1131, envelops a picturesque village which rejoices in a château which, one is told, is based on the monastic cellars. Not content with serving as the basis of such a magical building, part of the cellar also supports Longpont's parish church.

Now return back to the Route de Charlemagne (or the N2, to give it its more prosaic name), driving through Vertes-Feuilles and turning north-east to Soissons. Since we are making for Laon it is possible to take a minor ring-road around the city. The N2 continues north-east. Just beyond Urcel I suggest a charming drive through a series of villages boasting domestic Romanesque churches, before we reach the majesty of Laon. At Nouvion-le-Vineux the mid-nineteenth-century village water supply is a stream spouting through a wooden water-trough which is sheltered by an arcade dated 1841. The pointed and round arches of the twelfth- and thirteenth-century parish church shelter slender pillars and capitals, while the west portico has preserved its ancient colours and carvings. Fortified, walled, buttressed and dog-toothed, the splendid Romanesque tower still manages to smile down at us. Inside is a matching font. Presles, the next village, appears through the woods, its thirteenth-century château protecting an eleventh- (some say ninth) and thirteenth-century church, again three-aisled like that at Nouvion-le-Vineux, but much simpler in design. Instead of mini-apses, here we are offered one squat pepperpot tower and a stone roof. The carvings on the apse are stylized, delightfully so. Again the church boasts a porch with extremely fine carvings (including an angel bearing a scroll with the words '*Venite adoremus*' at the centre of an ogival arch). The apse is perfect, tiny, round-arched.

Drive on to Vorges, where a quite remarkable thirteenth-century church, fortified during the Hundred Years War, stands in the peaceful village square. Three-aisled, with two transepts and a great tower at its crossing, this church is opened up by early Gothic tracery. Over the west door is a mutilated statue of Jesus and what I take to be a nineteenth-century rose window. When you venture inside you are rewarded with a seventeenth-century wooden pulpit and sounding board, an ancient font and stone tombs, as well as an ogival crossing whose arched windows scarcely relinquish the Romanesque.

The Place de l'Église at Vorges is picturesque, with its plane trees, Hôtel de Ville, and a gabled house whose external steps are shaded by a vine. Scarcely a kilometre away is Bruyères-et-Montbérault with its twelfth- to fifteenth-century church, a massive, square thirteenth-century tower pressing down on the south transept. This church has been greatly altered over the centuries. You can make out where the south aisle abuts on to a blocked-up arch. The interior is complex and beautiful, its fifteenth-century transepts each held up by a single round central pillar from which spring graceful arches. The nave is still roofed by a flat wooden ceiling, and the organ gallery dates from the seventeenth century.

These humble yet remarkable treasures stretch along a distance of no more than 8 km. Then ahead along the D967 rises the outrageously arrogant cathedral of Laon, and you wind your way back up again to the Porte d'Ardon.

5

THE FRONTIER WITH BELGIUM

Beginning life as a small feudal town based on an island in the navigable River Deûle, Lille grew rich in the Middle Ages by reason both of its market place at a Flanders crossroads and its textiles. In the twentieth century Lille remains at the heart of the wealthiest economic region of France. Today the centre of the old city of Lille, once known as the Grand'Place (and still signposted as such), is named after Charles de Gaulle, who was born here in 1890. At the centre of the Place du Général-de-Gaulle rises a granite column which carries a bronze statue of a lady who represents the city. The citizens dub her 'la Déesse', the goddess. She was sculpted by Théophile Bra in the mid-nineteenth century and she and her column were raised here to commemorate an extraordinary feat of resistance in 1792, when the defenders of Lille withstood an Austrian siege lasting from 29 September to 8 October, and then forced the enemy to retire. The statue is a reminder that the prosperity of Lille has been achieved in spite of wars, sieges, occupations and countless vicissitudes. Yet such adventures have by no means destroyed the architectural, artistic and gastronomic heritage of Lille. Indeed to sample them in a couple or three days will tax anyone's stamina.

The southern corner of Place du Général-de-Gaulle is occupied by a chastely elegant building (chaste at any rate in terms of the exuberant architecture of this part of France), the former guard-house. Built in 1717 by Thomas-Joseph Gombert to house the royal guard, its façade is decorated with pediments and trophies and reached by a monumental open-air staircase, the whole complemented by a stepped gable. As if not to be outdone, the gabled newspaper offices next door (which belong to the *Voix du*

Nord) are much more extravagant, though they were built only in the mid-war years.

Surrounded by similar picturesque buildings, the finest of this square must undoubtedly be the former stock exchange, a building that exudes all the luxuriant excess of seventeenth-century Flemish baroque. Consisting altogether of twenty-four houses, its architect was Julien Destré, who began the building in 1652 when the Spaniards ruled Lille. When the time came to embellish the façade Julien Destré's inspiration caught fire. Medallions, swags, caryatids, varied pilasters, garlands of fruit and flowers, windows topped with triangles and windows topped with arches enliven the building, the whole ensemble rising to its belfry. Inside this former Bourse he designed a courtyard with an arcaded and decorated gallery. The inscriptions which adorn the gallery speak of the commercial achievements of Lille. The decorations are almost as lavish as those on the outside. As for the statue of Napoleon Bonaparte (by the sculptor Philippe-Honoré Lemaire), this was made in 1854 out of bronze melted from cannons captured by the French at the Battle of Austerlitz – Napoleon's greatest victory. Dressed in his Roman garb, the emperor looks slightly out of place.

Alongside the former Bourse runs Rue des Manneliers, taking you to the cobbled Place du Théâtre. Although the theatre was built only at the beginning of this century, the architect (the ubiquitous and all-purpose Louis-Marie Cordonnier) chose the late-eighteenth-century Louis XVI style. Then Hippolyte Lefebvre sculpted the triumph of Apollo for its pediment. The whole sensuous ensemble exudes theatrical excess. Cordonnier also designed the brick-and-stone Palais de la Bourse on the north side of the Place du Théâtre. This time he chose the Flemish seventeenth-century style, crowning his work with a splendidly offset belfry.

Looking from the theatre down Rue Faidherbe (named after the general and governor of Senegal who was born at Lille in 1818) you can see a decided curiosity: Lille's railway station was brought here in 1862, having already served as the Gare du Nord in Paris. You can discern the date of its transfer on the front of the building, which today is introduced by an inventive fountain. As you walk along Rue Faidherbe towards it, turn right into the short Rue du Priez. At the end of this street rises Lille's finest surviving

medieval church, Saint-Maurice. A flamboyant Gothic hall
church (or *Hallekerque*) whose five aisles are of equal height,
Saint-Maurice was built between the fourteenth and the fifteenth
centuries and widened in the 1870s, when it was decided to
rebuild the façade. In my judgement the restorers worked well,
the five gables indicating the five naves within, a spikily crocketed,
open-work spire rising from the centre. As you walk around the
church to reach the west end, you realize that the church is much
bigger than it looks from the end of Rue du Priez. Inside, the five
naves are of the same height and uniformly Gothic, their vaults
rising from slender columns with sculpted corbels.

The finest paintings in the church are by the Flemish artist
Jacques van Oost the younger, who lived from 1639 to 1713.
They include depictions of St Francis, St Charles Borromeo and
St Therese. Charles Borromeo, who died in 1584, is a particularly
fascinating choice as a subject, for he was an uncompromising
opponent of Protestantism as well as a determined reformer of the
laxities of the Catholic church of his own day. In his work for this
church Jacques van Oost the younger is deliberately mingling
subjects familiar to us from the Holy Scripture (the Adoration of the
Shepherds, and Jesus's Presentation in the Jerusalem Temple)
with images of the Counter-Reformation (not only Borromeo
but also Jesus appearing to St Rose of Lima and the glorification
of St John of the Cross). Less polemical but extremely moving
religious art from an earlier era includes a polychrome sixteenth-
century statue of the flagellation of Jesus, in the chapel of the
Dieu-de-la-Pitié in the north transept. The frescos just further on,
depicting St Joachim and St Anne, were painted in 1603.

Now explore the quarter to the north of the Place de la Gare.
Flemish houses of the sixteenth, seventeenth and eighteenth centuries enliven the cobbled streets. Due north of the railway station,
scarcely a hundred paces away along Rue Saint-Hubert, stands
the Porte de Roubaix, an orderly, battlemented, three-arched
gateway built in 1621 of white sandstone and brick and designed
by Michel Wattrelos. A little stone guard-house sits on top of the
gateway. The walls are surprisingly thick inside the arches, two
today reserved for motor traffic and one, mercifully, for terrified
pedestrians. The far side of the gateway is ornamented with coats
of arms and a fearsome statue of Victory, brandishing her sword.
A plaque tells you that the gateway of 1621 was restored in 1875.

A little further north is a touching monument to a heroine of the First World War, Louise de Bettignies, who died in enemy captivity in 1918. Maxime Réal de Satre sculpted her memorial. In times of conflict Lille has been blessed with other redoubtably brave women. In 1559 the city was under siege by a band of marauders. Its defenders would have given in save for the valour of a singer named Jeanne Maillotte, one of the many women in this part of France who, as we have seen, stood in the stern tradition of Joan of Arc. Jeanne Maillotte simply refused to let the menfolk surrender. The city has also honoured Louise de Bettignies by naming a square after her, and this is our next objective, reached alas from the Porte de Roubaix by the deeply unattractive Rue Cannoniers.

Turn speedily left at the Rue des Urbanistes into Place aux Bluets, where the environment instantly improves. Rue Saint-Jacques takes us past a smart courtyard which belongs to Lille's university and is flanked by the eighteenth-century residence of its principal. As it picturesquely twists along, Rue Saint-Jacques is enlivened by more and more noble, tall Flemish houses, reaching Place du Lion-d'Or whose houses are grand indeed. Place Louise-de-Bettignies lies immediately to the right and is again a square surrounded by patrician Flemish Renaissance houses. The finest is the Maison Gilles de la Boé, a ravishing blend of seventeenth-century Flemish and French architecture.

Two fascinating buildings rise nearby, namely the Hospice Comtesse and the cathedral. From Place Louise-de-Bettignies the way to the hospice is signposted down Rue de la Monnaie, which itself is filled with beautiful Renaissance houses complete with assertive gables. Before you reach this hospice, burrow to the left through the archway of the Hôtel de la Treille to find yourself confronted with yet another curiosity in a city of many: Lille cathedral.

I cannot quite make up my mind about this huge building, which is dedicated to Notre Dame de la Treille (Our Lady of the Vine). Begun in 1854 to replace a collegiate church destroyed at the Revolution, the basilica is another oddity in this city, first because its architects, Henry Clutton and William Burges, were British and secondly because the churlish French architectural establishment of the time deliberately frustrated their work. Notre-Dame-de-la-Treille was begun in 1854 during an era when

Victorian Gothic architects were sweeping their European contemporaries and rivals aside. In the 1840s Gilbert Scott, for
example, had won the competition to design the Nikolaikirche in
Hamburg. A few years later Burges and Clutton were collaborat-
ing on a work which was published under Clutton's name as *The
Domestic Architecture of France*. Then the city of Lille set up a
competition for the design of its new church of Notre-Dame (for it
was not deemed a cathedral till Lille became the seat of a bishopric
in 1913). Anyone, of whatever nationality, could enter. The
church was to be larger than the cathedral at Noyon, almost as
long as that of Reims and built in the style of the early thirteenth
century. The sum of £120,000 had been set aside to build it.
Burges and Clutton knew that only cunning could overwhelm the
amour propre of the French. They submitted their competition
design in French packing-cases in order to trick the judges. On 13
April 1856, the panel announced that the design of Clutton and
Burges had won.

Runner-up was another British architect, G. E. Street, and the
British took altogether eight of the nineteen prizes on offer. To
one's lasting regret, although Burges and Clutton took the prize
money the cathedral they designed was never properly built.
French Catholics were outraged at the victory of the Anglicans.
'We have met with a second Agincourt,' declared one of the
judges. As the British *Ecclesiologist* put it, 'the divided factions of
the judges and the executive committee', backstairs politics, 'political, national, and ecclesiastical influences', and French chauvin-
ism meant that in the end the cathedral was built to the composite
designs of several of the submitted schemes, co-ordinated by one
of the defeated candidates named Charles Leroy. 'Intrigue,' the
Ecclesiologist fulminated, 'has done its work.'

To give him his due, Charles Leroy painstakingly respected
many aspects of the submission of Burges and Clutton. But although I am a passionate devotee of Burges in particular, this
particular church in the end seems to me too much of a pastiche
of earlier Gothic to work as a building in its own right. One could
judge better if it had ever been finished, but the west end is
horribly bricked up. Yet a fair amount of Burges's vitality remains.
The apse is overwhelmingly grand, and the free-standing belfry
to the left as you walk to the façade is delicate (one might say tiny
by Flemish standards). The conical roofs of the chapel derive

from Burges's study of the cathedral of Noyon, as do the windows of the transept. Because of his assiduous love of the architecture of the gateway to France, Laon cathedral and that at Amiens are paid due homage here. If you go inside you will find that part of the cathedral is modelled on the Sainte-Chapelle in Paris and houses a miracle-working, Romanesque statue of the Virgin Mary.

On the north side of Notre-Dame-de-la-Treille rises the elegant classical home of the canons and cathedral authorities. The little Passage de Notre-Dame-de-la-Treille leads back east from here to Rue de la Monnaie. Turn right for a few paces and then walk through a ruined gateway to the green square which is surrounded by brick houses and the stone apse of the chapel of the Hospice Comtesse. Jeanne, Countess of Flanders, founded the hospice in 1236, but the present beautifully proportioned brick-and-stone buildings date from the fifteenth and seventeenth centuries. Today they serve Lille as the Musée d'Arts et Traditions Populaires, enabling all of us to visit above all the abbess's room and the delightful *salle des Malades*, with its fifteenth-century décor, the ceiling like the hull of an upturned ship. This hall, like the courtyard in which the sick would once have convalesced, exudes peace. The entrance is at no. 32 Rue de la Monnaie, and the museum is open every day save Tuesdays.

As you walk around the apse of the hospice chapel, Rue Comtesse takes you back to Rue de la Monnaie. The elegance of this street is matched at the end by the little conservatory, given over to dance and theatre and the park which constitutes the Place du Concert and houses a statue of André, who was mayor of Lille in 1792. Take Rue d'Angleterre (so named after Thomas à Becket had stayed here) in order to explore two aspects of Lille, that which once belonged to the bourgeoisie and that which belonged to the late-seventeenth- and eighteenth-century nobility. Rue d'Angleterre itself is stylish, some of its houses seventeenth century, some late eighteenth, some exuberantly nineteenth. At the end appears the square tower of the three-naved *Hallekerque* of Sainte-Catherine. It was added in 1793 to a church that was built in 1538 and houses a painting of the martyrdon of St Stephen by Rubens himself.

If you want to admire that sector once belonging to the bourgeoisie as opposed to upper-crust inhabitants of the old city, turn left at the end of Rue d'Angleterre. The superb bourgeois houses flank Rue Esquermoise, three of them decorated with garlands, cherubs and grotesque masks. Then turn into the Place Rihour for another delightful sight, the sumptuous Gothic remains of the Palais Rihour which Philippe the Good ordered to be built in the mid-fifteenth century. Completed in 1473, the Palais Rihour has now been commandeered by Lille tourist office. The war memorial slapped against the palace unfortunately hinders one's complete enjoyment of its chapel. Nor do I warm to the figures on this memorial: miserable captives in bowler hats; miserable soldiers; miserable angels.

No doubt by now one's calves are aching, but I have always found it worthwhile strolling back along Rue Esquermoise and then up the aristocratic Rue Royale as far as the church of Saint-André. Sumptuous palaces, created after Louis XIV annexed Lille in 1667, line the way to the equally sumptuous church, which was built for the Carmelites in 1702 by the Lille architect Thomas-Joseph Gombert. Nearby rises the *Grand Magasin* of 1730. Rue Magasin leads left here to Lille's lovely green esplanade, rendered even more pleasant by its welcome benches. A couple of bridges cross the Canal de la Moyenne-Deûle to reach a splendidly preserved masterpiece of military architecture, Vauban's citadel. Built within three years after Louis XIV became master of the city, this pentagonal defensive barracks houses its own chapel. The inscription over the entrance lauds Vauban's patron, Louis XIV. In 1669 Vauban himself wrote that he intended this to be 'the queen of citadels.' In fact all his skill failed to deter the duke of Marlborough and Prince Eugène, and in 1708 the citadel surrendered to their troops. Louis XIV received it back only when the Treaty of Utrecht, five years later, ceded Lille to the French crown.

This citadel is all that remains of Lille's once powerful fortifications, apart from the Porte de Roubaix which we have already seen and two other gates: the Porte de Gand further north which Pierre Raoul built in 1621; and the overwhelmingly monumental Porte de Paris which Simon Vollant constructed at the end of the seventeenth century to guard the southern entrance to the city. You reach the latter from the citadel by following long and wide Boulevard de la Liberté, which begins to fill itself with shops. On the way if you turn left at Rue Nationale (another useful shopping

street) and then right again into Rue de l'Hôpital-Militaire, you
will find the former Jesuit church of Saint-Étienne, its gracious
façade dating from 1692, its pulpit by the celebrated sculptor
François Rude who created the finest reliefs on the Arc de Triomphe in Paris. The military hospital referred to in the name of
this street occupies the former Jesuit college, another building by
Lille's eighteenth-century architect Gombert.

Continue down the Boulevard de la Liberté. Before reaching
the Porte de Paris the boulevard runs into massive Place de la
République, which houses both the Hôtel de la Préfecture and
the Musée des Beaux-Arts. Both buildings date from the second
half of the nineteenth century, the former from 1865 (though its
style is a fourteenth-century pastiche), the latter from 1885 to
1892. Its collection of paintings is outstanding. Scholars revel in
its remarkable accumulation of Italian drawings. For the rest of
us there are obviously some 'show' works that anyone with a
couple of hours to spare should certainly not miss. I find the
massive canvasses of Rubens persistently enthralling, and the
museum houses some of his marvellous altarpieces. Van Dyck is
well represented. The fifteenth-century Flemish master Dieric
Bouts is also represented here by his 'Heaven' and 'Hell', two
famous works of which the latter, as one finds almost invariably
with these subjects, is by far the more striking. The paintings of
another Flemish genius, Jacob Jordaens, hang close by, for
example his portrait of St Francis in ecstasy, a work venturing far
beyond the images of conventional seventeenth-century piety. A
bizarre treat (though it is said to be only a copy of the original) is
'The Concert in an Egg' by Hieronymus Bosch, where birds sit on
the heads of the musicians and generally misbehave, save for one
which lies dead in a basket.

Since the gallery hangs so many of them, French painters tend
to dominate the rest. The masters range from Poussin to Raoul
Dufy. Lesser paintings by Louis-Joseph and François Watteau
(respectively nephew and great-nephew of the great Antoine
Watteau) depict the daily life of Lille in their days and are rightly
on display here, since it was the former who in 1792 managed to
persuade the city fathers to promote a museum of fine arts. As for
the works of masters from further afield, Lille's Musée des Beaux-
Arts is renowned for a marble relief by Donatello depicting
Herod's Feast, as well as for two works by Goya, 'The Young Girl'

and 'The Ageing Woman'. The latter is a cruel painting. The former has a little dog vying for the attention of his mistress, who is preoccupied with what is apparently a love letter. It is fascinating to compare El Greco's tormented St Francis with Jordaens's ecstatic one. These undoubted treasures can easily obscure the quality of some of the other works hanging in this gallery: paintings by Jan Brueghel the Elder; the scenes of skating which the Dutch so relished; calculated calm interiors by Pieter de Hooch; Jakob van Ruysdael's endlessly mysterious landscapes.

Beyond this huge square, Boulevard de la Liberté continues as far as Boulevard Louis XIV. Turn immediately north here and walk towards Place Simon-Vollant and the Porte de Paris, beyond which you can see the massive belfry of Lille's new Town Hall. In the midst of the square stands the Arc de Triomphe, known as the Porte de Paris, and built to the designs of Simon Vollant between 1685 and 1692. Today the city has spread far beyond this monumental gateway, and it now rises in its little garden as a kind of traffic roundabout. It remains a noble affair. Like Vauban's citadel, this gateway glorifies Louis XIV. Its arcade is decorated with the arms of the sovereign alongside those of Lille. Above them Victory is crowning *le Roi-Soleil* (the Sun-King). To warn would-be intruders, statues of Mars and Hercules flank the portal.

Mention of the Porte de Paris is a reminder that one other legacy of the reign of Louis XIV is worth finding, not here but in the northern part of Lille. In 1675 the architect Simon Vollant laid the first stone of the domed church of Sainte-Marie-Madeleine, which stands in Rue du Pont-Neuf a few paces northwest of the Porte de Gand. When Lille was besieged in 1708, work stopped and the local architect Gombert took over the work in 1713. Yet this church remains an imposing example of the triumphalist architecture of the reign of Louis XIV. It is said also to house a silver tabernacle and paintings both by Van Dyck and by Rubens, but alas the building is no longer in use as a church and I have never managed to get inside.

I have wandered too far away from the Porte de Paris (at least on paper and in spirit) and should return. Immediately east of the gateway, in Place Roger-Salengro, rises the massive new Town Hall. I sometimes think it was designed with the same function in mind as the citadel and the gateway itself, namely to repel. But the thought is unworthy. For the administrative functions of the sixth largest city in France the architect Émile Dubuisson created an amazingly grandiose neo-Flemish building, adding a belfry – the tallest in Flanders – that pokes 104 m into the sky. The Flemish love their giants, and this civic architecture, completed in 1929, is certainly gigantic. The base of the colossal belfry is even decorated with sculptures of the two giants who traditionally founded the city, Phinaert and Lydéric. (For some reason their feet do not touch the ground.) In one form or another Lille has been celebrating its annual *Grande Kermesse* since 1270, and these giants have come to play a major role in the entertainment. Crowds still gather, enthusiastically applauding the statues of Phinaert and Lydéric as they are carried through the city. Then the citizens repair to their own quarters for legion of traditional forms of merriment and huge doses of traditional Flemish food (including liberal libations of beer and the juniper-berry liquor known as *genièvre*).

To return to the Grand'Place from Place Roger-Salengro, follow Rue de Paris. Its undistinguished motley buildings are suddenly graced on the left by the Hospice Gantois. Founded by Jean de la Cambe as a hospice in 1460, the building was enlarged in 1664, I think in order to shelter pilgrims as well. Its façade is ornamented by a statue of their patron St James of Compostela, accompanied by a dog who, I presume, accompanied him on his travels. On the right further on from the hospice is a classical house whose porchway bears the date 1626. Before walking back to the Grand'Place make a note that the main Sunday morning market at Lille takes place around Rue de Wazemmes to the south of the Porte de Paris.

Since 1976, when the protégé of Pierre Boulez, Jean-Claude Casadesus, founded the *Orchestre national de Lille*, a new artistic pleasure has been added to these traditional ones. An extremely generous public subsidy has allowed this orchestra not only to maintain a permanent company of 100 musicians but also to commission and promote works by modern French composers. This daring repertoire has brought international renown to the orchestra, to Casadesus and to Lille itself.

In a major cosmopolitan city such as this, one rightly expects to be able to dine in some quarters till the small hours – an expectation that would be disappointed in other parts of this region. One also eats well. In a recent *Guide du Boeuf* published under the aegis of the *président d'Interviandes Nord-Pas-de-Calais* and the *président d'Interbovi Picardie* I was not surprised to discover that of the thirteen recipes printed from celebrated chefs, three came from Lille. They were from M. Bernard Amedro (of the *Restaurant Amedro*), who offered the secret of his majestic *fillet de boeuf aux légumes et fruits de printemps, rognons et julienne de veau mignonette des trois viandes*, from M. Robert Bardot (of *Le Flambard*), who offered the secret of his *filet de boeuf sauce au persil et ses petits navets*, and M. Loïc Martin (of *Le Paris*), who offered the secret of his *pièce de filet de boeuf à la broche*.

At Lille one can also readily sample the cheeses of the *pays du Nord*, above all the chunky *mimolette*, the long *baquette de Thiérache*, the *vieux-Lille* which comes wrapped up like a loaf, the curiously tart *boulette d'Avesnes*, a slice of *maroilles*, or (my favourite) the fairly strong, slightly salty, satisfying *rollot*. As some of their names indicate, these cheeses are not of course unique to Lille. One of the oldest regulations regarding cheese in this region dates from 1245 and relates to four villages in Thiérache (namely Marbaix, Taisnières, Noyelles and Maroilles itself). In it the Bishop of Cambrai instructs the farmers to prepare their cheese on 24 June, the feast of St John, and deliver the mature product to the abbey of Maroilles on 1 October the feast of St Rémi.

Cheese is a product of the countryside, whereas Lille, with its population of 193,000 (not including the suburbs, where another 130,000 people live) is of course a huge and modern industrial city as well as an ancient one. In consequence the rustic paintings of Ruysdael in the city art gallery are a pleasing reminder that some words of Paul Verlaine written in the last century about this region of France, still remain true of the surrounding countryside. 'Manufacture,' he observed, 'is a tyrant in this *département*, but it has not yet driven out all poetry. Nearby are two forests, not extensive I admit but still lovely, their shaded tracks and clear open spaces, their hills and dales filled with the singing of blackbirds and doves.' It is time to explore that countryside.

Architecturally and industrially the two most important towns which attach themselves to Lille are Roubaix and Tourcoing. On the way to the former you should look out for the Renaissance Château de Fontaine. Roubaix is a town of ravishing parkland, and at its heart rises a huge Town Hall, built in 1911. The six bas-reliefs on its frieze depict the wool trade, the source of the

town's wealth. Its finest church, the Gothic Saint-Martin, stands
with the Hôtel de Ville in the Grand'Place. The tower hangs
thirty-eight massive bells, altogether comprising the heaviest carillon in France. Inside, its furnishings gleam with the artistic skills
of fifteenth-, sixteenth- and seventeenth-century Flanders.

Tourcoing lies close to the Belgian frontier, its Grand'Place the
home of the church of Saint-Christophe, built in the fifteenth
century but heavily restored in 1862. The carillon of Saint-
Christophe boasts ten more bells than that of Saint-Martin,
Roubaix, and its treasures include exquisite gold and silver work
of earlier dates as well as a relic of St Christopher himself. You
find the huge Town Hall by walking north from the church, and
the eighteenth-century hospital, with its lovely cloister and chapel,
by walking west. The latter is sweet, the former – built with a
ravishing belfry in 1860 – breathtakingly arrogant.

The richly cultivated landscapes around Lille offer scope for
entrancing excursions in the *département* of the Nord. To the
north-west lie Armentières and Bailleul. If you take the Avenue de
Dunkerque towards Arras you pass through the suburb of Can-
teleu, whose church is a copy of the Holy Sepulchre in Jerusalem,
and presently arrive at industrialized Lomme. This was the birthplace of Anne Delavaux, one of those remarkable eighteenth-
century women who, disguised as a male, followed a successful
career as a soldier. The fifteenth-century parish church of Lomme
shelters a sixteenth-century statue of the Virgin Mary. The commune also boasts the Château d'Isengheim, basically a reconstruction of an eighteenth-century pavilion. Armentières, 16 km from
Lille and celebrated in occasionally ribald song by the Tommies
in the First World War, was rebuilt after that conflict. The
Flemish gables of its houses are matched by the brick Town Hall
and is belfry (both the work of Louis-Marie Cordonnier), and
nearly so by the 81 m high tower of the restored church of Saint-
Vaast behind it – altogether a superb ensemble. At Armentières I
also confess to being impressed by the double towers of the
modern church of Notre-Dame, which you can discover by crossing the Town Hall square from the belfry and continuing up
Rue Sadi-Carnot.

Return from the church and turn left when you see the signs for
Nieppe and Bailleul. For a moment or two – as far as Nieppe –
our route is unpleasantly built-up, but then the countryside opens

up again. We are flanking the Belgian border, with Ypres sign-posted to our right. Bailleul is old enough to have been ravaged by the Normans in 882. Its belfry and yellow-brick Town Hall appear on the skyline as we approach. Brick-and-stone houses in the style of the Flemish Renaissance, the Town Hall with its arcaded balcony in the same style (save that the base of its belfry dates from the twelfth century), and the church of Saint-Amand contribute to the charm of this spot. Saint-Amand stands behind the Town Hall, proffering a Flemish stepped gable complement-ing those in the Grand'Place (even though all their designs vary enormously). On Wednesday mornings the market will elbow you out of your parking space in this Grand'Place.

As you leave Bailleul the elegant classical former Palais de Justice appears on the right, built in 1775 and one of the few buildings in Bailleul that needed no restoration after 1918. This is flattish country, save that to the north rise the Flanders hills, hence the strategic importance of such towns as Bailleul in past wars. You can see them better (and a vast panorama as well) from the top of the Town Hall belfry. Today the most exciting event in Bailleul is probably its Shrove Tuesday carnival, when the giant Gargantua is given his annual outing.

Drive due west for 11 km along the N42 from Bailleul to reach first Pradelles and then Hazebrouck. The churches are now the most impressive part of the villages through which you pass. At tiny Pradelles the fifteenth-century brick church boasts an earlier tower that hints at the Romanesque style, as well as a pulpit and choir stalls of the eighteenth century. Between Pradelles and Hazebrouck, the eighteenth-century church at Borre has another Romanesque tower which is half-brick and half-stone. The centre of Hazebrouck is delightful, watered by the little Borre. Its name means 'marsh of hares'. Its finest building is the former Augus-tinian convent, a *mélange* of styles, dating from 1518 to the seventeenth century. The façade of the Town Hall is also en-trancing – a long row of arched colonnades topped by a row of Doric pillars. If you walk through its colonnades you discover that they open out behind the building into an elegant semi-courtyard.

A Monday morning market fills the whole of the square in front of the Town Hall. To reach Saint-Éloi, the oldest church in the town, walk along the street at the far corner of this square. Its tower, built in 1532, rises at first extremely defensively, with only slits for light and with blocked-up arches, and then suddenly breaks out into playful tracery and little turrets. The rest of the church is fifteenth century, and its interior contains beautiful eighteenth-century furniture. Walk round it and you discover a handsome little *béguinage*, one of those public-spirited homes for widows and single pious women which have existed in these parts since the twelfth century. The well-laid-out public park opens at the angle of the *béguinage* and the church.

Shortly the landscape and the villages of this part of Flanders grow even lovelier, as we take a tour of some 30 km or so of fields devoted to flax, that pale blue and transient flower whose stalk can be transformed into the strongest of cloths. Make your way back from the church of Saint-Éloi to Hazebrouck's Town Hall square and follow the signs northwards for Steenvoorde. On the way to Steenvoorde a tiny detour east will take you to Eecke, whose seventeenth-century church is accompanied by a detached, decidedly quaint wooden belfry standing in the graveyard and known as the '*klockhuis*' (the house of bells). Just outside Steenvoorde we see our first windmill on this trip – one of the type in which only the top turns and not the whole mill. The church at Steenvoorde is seventeenth-century Gothic and is well complemented by the Flemish houses of the village, as well as two superb windmills. At Houtkerque the church was built two centuries earlier than that of Steenvoorde. You cross the River Yser and 11 km later reach Hondschoote on the Colne canal, with its Spanish Renaissance Town Hall, built in 1558, its painted houses and its fifteenth- and sixteenth-century brick church, whose superb tower has a stone *flèche* rising for 80 m. Inside are a mid-eighteenth-century pulpit and organ console. Market day here is Friday morning. On the penultimate Sunday in June is held an antiques and second-hand fair; and – most entrancing of all – on the first weekend of September the people of Hondschoote still bring in superb horses for their agricultural fair (or *Karyole Feest*, as their dialect has it). This is a fisherman's and rambler's paradise, and to the north of the town you can visit a twelfth-century windmill, one of the oldest in Europe.

To reach Bergues-Saint-Winoc drive north along the D947 until you arrive at the Canal de la Basse Colne. Here you turn left to wind alongside the canal whose picturesque drawbridges seem to come from a painting by Van Gogh. Bergues is a grander spot that Hondschoote, still partly surrounded by Vauban's fortifications and encircled by the canal. Its complex star-shape derives from these fortifications, and its complex name from its founder, a saint who set up a hermitage here at the turn of the eighth century. A few romantic vestiges of the abbey he inspired still remain, namely a monumental eighteenth-century gateway and two towers. Though both date from the twelfth century, these are oddly different, one squat and square, the other octagonal with an extremely steep slate roof that was added centuries later. Four gateways open into the town's ramparts: the stately remnants of the Porte de Hondschoote where we arrive; the Porte de Cassel to the south bearing the emblem of *le Roi-Soleil*; the Porte de Dunkerque flanked by a couple of towers; and the Porte de Bierne, again flanked by towers. Two more towers remain from the medieval château. Blessed by ancient gabled houses, the best in my view dating from the seventeenth and eighteenth centuries, Bergues-Saint-Winoc sleeps happily alongside its peaceful canal, save in summertime when campers swim in its heated swimming pool when they are not paddling canoes.

The town is best known for its yellow-brick belfry. Built in the fourteenth century and thus bearing Gothic embellishment, it is decorated with four polygonal towers and culminating in a wooden octagonal campanile (with a carillon of fifty bells) and an upside-down onion dome crowned by the lion of Flanders. Can one ask for more? You can climb the 191 steps to its top. The belfry rises from the gabled, arcaded tourist office and municipal museum. Across the square, on the Place de la République, stands the impressive classical Town Hall, built in 1665. Walk beside the museum along Rue de la Gare and you reach the church of Saint-Martin, which was rebuilt after a fire of 1558. Its belfry is free-standing. The ruins of the chapter house are eloquent of a monastic past. Here too is modern art and a twentieth-century organ. Inside the lovely church I was customarily preparing to dislike the stained glass, fired in 1959, when a lady rose from prayer and began to tell me how beautiful it was. Maybe it is not too bad. I suppose I could eventually grow to like the colours of the windows depicting St Martin and the Blessed Virgin Mary. Next to the church stands an almshouse built by Wenceslaus Coeburger in 1630, today the town's art gallery. As ever in these Flemish towns the gallery is rich in local artists. In-

side this elegant building, with its stepped dormer windows, its tall
chimneys, its elaborate gable-ends and its double-storeyed slender
windows, hang works by Pieter Brueghel, Cuyp and Jordaens.
The gallery also contains an unexpected masterpiece, one of the
two versions of Georges de La Tour's 'Hurdy-Gurdy Player'. The
city museum houses manuscripts of the poet Alphonse de Lam-
artine, who was elected deputy by Bergues from 1833 to 1839.

Bergues-Saint-Winoc is a few minutes' drive from Dunkerque.
Leave the town by the Porte de Dunkerque and take the D916 to
turn right at the hamlet of La Belle-Vue to find Esquelbecq, one
of the sweetest villages in the whole of the Pas-de-Calais. The brick
walls of its sixteenth-century hall church are delicately patterned.
This church is typical of many in the region, seemingly three
churches joined together in one and dominated by a squat square
tower. In the square, to the south side of the church, a plaque on
a house tells you that here St Foulquin, bishop of Thérouanne
and Charlemagne's German cousin, died in 855. Is that his statue
over the church doorway, beckoning us inside? All but the walls
of the church were burnt to cinders in a fire which raged all night
long on 11 April 1976. Everything has been perfectly restored,
save for some charred statues of Jesus and his saints (including
Foulquin). The interior is a delight, patterned brick and stone
rising to barrel-vaulted ceilings, with sixteenth-century statues
around the apse. Across the square (Place Alphonse Bergerot)
stands the moated feudal château of 1606, boasting no fewer than
nine pepperpot towers. Nearby is a children's park. Esquelbecq
also cares for an English war cemetery, which you can find by
crossing the River Yser on the way to Rubrouck, and nearby
along the same route is a sixteenth-century chapel.

A notice on the wall of the parish church at Esquelbecq points
you a couple of kilometres east to the village of Wormhout, which
is twinned with Llandudno. The citizens of Wormhout still use its
mid-eighteenth-century communal windmill, and the miller leads
guided tours at certain times of the year. Tiny enough, Wormhout
nonetheless possesses an enormous triangular square, Place du
Général-de-Gaulle, lined with shops and enlivened by a bandstand
and proudly guarding the town's war memorial. It is the venue of
the Wednesday morning market, the carnival on the Sunday
preceding Palm Sunday, a flea-market on the fourth Sunday in
September, and several annual fairs. The massive tower of its

church, which was built in 1613, is beautiful, even more so when its white stones gleam in the morning sunshine. Its eighteenth-century organ is elaborately carved with musical instruments. Curious Gothic capitals top its stone pillars, and the confessionals and panelling are exuberantly baroque. Three of the confessionals bear exquisitely carved roundels, one depicting St John the Baptist carrying the Lamb of God like a fur coat around his shoulders. The other two depict St Peter and the Virgin Mary at Golgotha.

This is where we turn south to reach Cassel, a spot remarkable as much for its site as its lovely buildings. On our way the trees lean left, blown that way by the prevailing winds. The very name of Cassel suggests fortifications. Known long ago as Castellum Menpiorum, the town stands on a hill which rises above the low Flanders plain. Wind up to it among trees to reach the cobbled Grand'Place by way of the Porte de Bergues, which dates from 1685. Once a Gaulish *oppidum*, then a well-defended Roman fort, Cassel's seventeenth- and eighteenth-century houses are built for the most part in brick. In the Grand'Place (home of the Thursday market) stands the former administrative headquarters of this region, the *lanshuys*, a noble Renaissance building with elegant windows and pretty dormers as well as marble columns flanking the entrance. Comical faces decorate its façade. It has been reduced to the status of a local history museum. Other houses of the same epoch, some of them with pretty wrought-iron balconies, line the sides of the square. From here Rue Notre-Dame leads to the massive, brick-built collegiate church of Notre-Dame, whose origins lie in the late thirteenth century. Eight bells hang in its square central tower. A portrait of St Francis inside is said to be by Rubens.

Behind this church is a second one, in the baroque style favoured by the Jesuits, its brick walls enlivened by stone embellishment. Climb up from here to the late-eighteenth-century château, a curious octagonal building. Rue du Château takes us through another gateway of the former fortress of Cassel, this one built in 1621. The shady, flowery Promenade du Château boasts a sixteenth-century wooden windmill, and an equestrian statue of Marshal Foch. Foch made Cassel his military HQ in 1914 and 1915, and the statue was sculpted by Georges Masseau in 1928. He and his alert steed peer over far-reaching views of the surrounding countryside and, on a clear day, the north sea. Today nobody uses the windmill, but its sails turn every Saturday afternoon and you can pay to visit its interior.

Cassel is enriched by a second château. Château Vandamme, named after General Dominique-Joseph-René Vandamme whose name became illustrious during the battles of the Revolution and the First Empire. He built the present château and laid out its park between 1805 and 1815. Although it remains in private hands, you can readily admire it from the roadside.

Equally rewarding is the journey south from Lille to Douai and Cambrai, provided that you occasionally leave the beaten track. Avoiding the motorway you reach Seclin after 12 km, where the hospital founded by Marguerite de Flandres in the thirteenth century now cares for its patients in a magnificent Flemish baroque building of the seventeenth century. You find this long, lavish, brick-and-stone building at the end of its ornamental garden by following the signs '*Vieil hôpital*'. Its gatehouses are as elaborate as the hospice. The collegiate church of Saint-Piat is even older, a thirteenth-century building rising from a Merovingian crypt where St Piat lies in his third-century tomb. Tall round pillars, a double row of ancient capitals, a classical east end and unobtrusive modern glass complete an extremely satisfying interior. Its belfry bears a modern carillon of forty-two bells.

From here the tree-shaded D549 runs south-east to Pont-à-Marcq. We are entering a region of little rivers, woods and farms in which are cultivated strawberries, pears, asparagus and endives. Bersée, the next village of substance, 5 km to the south, has two mini-châteaux and a fine sixteenth-century church with a brick-and-stone tower. Pierced with narrow defensive slits until it reaches the two lights at the top, this tower dominates the village. Beside the church a tree of liberty was planted on 21 March 1989, to celebrate the bicentenary of the Revolution. It was still flourishing a year later.

Raimbeaucourt arrives next (after Faumont), delighted to be called 'capital of the asparagus' and hosting an annual asparagus fair on the first Sunday in June. Here are campsites, riding schools and cool woodlands. The village stands just off the main road, its brick church blessed with a battered stone tower wearing a brick-and-tile hat. A number of new houses are springing up here, most of them with dormer windows and built out of the traditional brick. As you leave the village a row of trees leads off to the

eighteenth-century château which replaced a medieval one. The
treats of this tour succeed each other rapidly. Watch for the next
major crossroads to make a little excursion left along the D938 to
Flines-lez-Raches and find a thirteenth-century Gothic church
whose quaint, tiled belfry is at least a century older. Then drive
back to the main road and turn south to Raches.

Here take the D8 left and wind along it to cross the River
Scarpe at nearby Lallaing. Lallaing is a modern town, but its
complex, cobbled and irregular main square is pleasing, trees
sheltering the citizens, and a drawbridge leading over the moat to
the few remnants of its fifteenth-century château. Even the tele-
phone box is disguised as a little brick house. The furnishings of
the brick-and-stone seventeenth-century church are exceptional,
as are those in the sixteenth-century church at Pecquencourt,
4½ km further east. Watch out for the unexpected turning towards
the village, which boasts some excellent Renaissance houses. Once
this village was the home of the abbey of Anchin, of which a
couple of ruined wings remain. Unable to locate this abbey I
went into the bar opposite the church and asked an aged man for
directions. Said he, 'Ask the barman; he's older than I am and
probably remembers it better.' So pleased was he with this joke,
that he repeated it, twinkling merrily. The barman did know,
telling me that the abbey had been sold at the Revolution, that
nothing remains but a few stones and an eighteenth-century
gateway, that I could find these relics by driving east alongside
the church and that the site of the abbey now serves as an
agricultural institute.

He was right. Today the wrought-iron altar and some fine
tombs from the abbey church are housed in Pecquencourt's parish
church. And from here you can make your way west to Douai by
the D225 and the D13.

At Douai we have reached a city long renowned as the Athens
of the North on account of the fame of its university which is no
more (save in so far as its spirit transmitted itself to Lille in 1887
when the dons and students moved there). Although Douai is
nowadays a thriving industrial town, slowly replacing the coal
industry with others, it is enjoyable and easy enough to read in
her stones an illustrious history. Most of her historically redolent
buildings lie on the right bank of the River Scarpe, her modern
quarters stretching away on the other side of the water. As a

result of long-forgotten conflicts, the old city also preserves a remarkably homogeneous aspect, for most of it had to be rebuilt after two destructive sieges during the war of the Spanish Succession. The allies took fifty-two days of bombardment to take the town in 1710. Villars took it back on behalf of the French crown two years later in a less costly but still burdensome siege.

Philip of Spain founded its university in 1562 as a determined attempt to foster the Counter-Reformation. But the chief annual reminder of the eras before the eighteenth-century rebuilding of Douai is a three-day festival beginning on the first Sunday after 5 July. On that day in 1479 Louis IX decided to lift his siege of the town. The citizens of Douai recall the occasion by parading their giants. A family of huge mannequins made of wicker-work (father Pierre, mother Marie Cagenon and their three children, Jacquot, Fillion and Binbin) are paraded through the streets. Their costumes are those of the sixteenth century, for the citizens did not take up the idea of the festival till 1530.

By this time the Counter-Reformation at Douai was in full swing. Members of the English-speaking college, convinced that Protestants were mistranslating the Bible to subvert true Christianity, had already published their own version, a translation that came to be universally regarded as unreadable. Other devout Catholics of Douai had already been martyred for their beliefs. The first was a Devonshire priest, Cuthbert Mayne, who had returned to his own country to propagate his faith. Seized by the authorities, he refused to accept the supremacy of the British sovereign in religious matters. In 1577 he was sentenced to be hanged, drawn and quartered. Throttled on a gallows at Launceston, as he was being cut down for quartering the martyr fell and smashed his head on a beam. He was fortunately dead before his body could be sliced open.

Douai today is a complex little spot. Arriving from Lille by way of the Rue de Lille, veer right into Rue Morel (whose finest eighteenth-century house is no. 40), reach the Place Carnot and then follow Rue Saint-Jacques. The next main street to the left, Rue Victor-Hugo, is shaded by the eighteenth-century prefecture. As you continue along Rue Saint-Jacques the collegiate church of Saint-Pierre rises in its square to the right. A church has existed on this spot since the early eleventh century. Today's domed building dates from the early eighteenth century, the work of a Douai architect named Lefebvre. This was an age of luscious carvings, as the gilded high altar, the organ console of 1760, and the splendid woodwork of the sacristy testify. It was also an age when social status was prized, and for centuries only the canons and the members of the *parlement* of Flanders were allowed to worship God inside this church.

Walk west from the church along a picturesquely winding street, bordered on the left by the Palais de Justice. It faces on to the River Scarpe, its little Gothic doorway preserved from the sixteenth-century, the rest rebuilt in the 1780s. Until the Revolution this was the seat of the *parlement* of Flanders, and inside the Palais the former *salon de la Révision du Parlement* is worthy of the fact, decorated in sculpted oak, with allegorical panels by Benet and a portrait of Louis XIV by that arch-flatterer Hyacinthe Rigaud.

From here cross the river which is flanked by high brick warehouses and walk on, following the signs to the church of Saint-Jacques, which rises in its square (on the right, just before the police station). Begun in 1706 for the English order of the Recollects (who came to Douai in 1626), it took a century or so to complete. The baroque high altar is famous for its depiction of the miracle of the Holy Sacrament, an occasion in 1254 when a priest is said to have dropped a consecrated host on to the ground, at which the sacred morsel leapt back on to the altar of its own accord. Look out in here for the early-seventeenth-century painting of the Crucifixion of Jesus.

Three monuments of Douai which unusually pre-date the eighteenth-century stand in this quarter of the town. Its former charterhouse lies to the north of the church of Saint-Jacques and includes a brick-and-stone Renaissance building erected between 1552 and 1608. When the Carthusians bought it in 1662, they added first their lesser cloister, their chapter house and their refectory, which all date from the following years. In 1690 more monks' quarters were built. The church is a noble building of 1720. This former monastery now serves as the museum of Douai.

As with all these Flemish towns, the collection is rich. To single out the polyptych of the Trinity painted by the local artist Jean Bellegambe in 1510 is necessary. Consisting of nine panels of oak, the assiduous have counted that surrounding the panel depicting the Holy Trinity the artist has painted no fewer than 254 members

of the heavenly church. The panel of the Holy Trinity itself is
strangely moving. An almost naked Jesus sits on the lap of a
sumptuously robed and enthroned God the Father. The Christ
points with one hand to his wounded side and with the other to
the Gospels, characterized by Alpha and Omega, symbols of the
beginning and the end of all things. In the form of a dove the
Holy Spirit seems to have just landed on this book. Alongside the
most moving sections of his polyptych Bellegambe has brilliantly
set charmingly amusing details, such as cherubs playing with
sixteenth-century spinning tops or blowing bubbles. Yet this rarity
ought not to hide the fact that the museum of Douai also contains
a portrait by Veronese, some sculptures in bronze and terracotta
by Giambologna, works by Jordaens, David, Courbet and Renoir,
some smashing little paintings by Pissaro, Boudin, Jongkind and
our own impressionist Alfred Sisley, and a bronze of the
Prodigal Son by Rodin. Another unusually early feature of this
quarter of Douai is the Tour des Dames, a tower of 1425 which
remains from the former ramparts and today stands in a garden
north-east of the museum.

Make your way back from these treats to the heart of Douai,
the Grand'Place, or Place d'Armes, the wrought-iron balconies of
the Hôtel de Paris overlooking the jolly modern fountains which
burst up in the square. (These fountains are ornamented with
whole bronze lilies, the water glowing pearly white and green at
dusk.) Just to the west in Rue de la Mairie rises Douai's most
imposing building, the Hôtel de Ville. Two smaller doorways
flank its main one. Above them rise eight flamboyantly decorated
windows, with niches in between each and a balcony overlooking
the street. To the right of its belfry is a fifteenth-century wing
which was matched in the same style on the other side in 1860.
The five-storeyed belfry is superb, built in the fourteenth and
fifteenth centuries, its square tower reaching 61 m. Adorned with
corbels and little turrets, heightened by 14 m of woodwork, it was
topped by a massive gilded brass lion holding the banner of
Flanders in 1470. Its platform offers superb views, and the belfry
carries the greatest (or at least the biggest) carillon in Europe,
sixty-two bells which chime every quarter of an hour. The Master
bell-ringers of Douai, a continuous line of thirty-four cam-
panologists since 1390, give concerts on this carillon throughout
July and August, during the annual September fair, on Mondays

at 09.00 and on Saturdays at 12.45. The rooms of the Town Hall are as splendid as its carillon and are reached by a double-ramped Gothic staircase. They include the *salle de Fêtes* of 1860, the eighteenth-century *salon Blanc*, the *salle Gothique* and the double *halle aux Draps* which rises on fifteenth-century sandstone columns, and finest of all the former chapel or *salle de la Rotonde*, whose arches rise from one single central column.

You see the Hôtel de Ville in all its glamour if you take the trouble to walk through its great doorway to espy it from the other side as well. After this almost any other building might seem slightly drab, but no. 16 in the square, the Maison du Dauphin, built in 1754 with a sweet forged-iron balcony and armorial decorations, is worth more than a glance. So is the white sandstone church of Notre-Dame, which you find by taking Rue de Valenciennes from the east end of the Grand'Place. Though the façade dates from 1852, Notre-Dame has a thirteenth-century porch, and the transept and choir date from the next two centuries. The spire was restored in 1971. Covered with a fifteenth-century wooden vault, the church is illuminated with modern stained-glass windows by J. Schreiter and by the firm of Hermet and Gaudin.

Rue de Valenciennes has another claim to fame, for Douai's local poet, Marceline Desbordes-Valmore, was born at no. 36 in 1786. Although Marceline died in 1859, the civic authorities raised her statue outside the apse of Notre-Dame only in 1958. Yet contemporary testimonies to her were legion. M. Raspail, to whom she dedicated her last volume of verses, described Mme Desbordes-Valmore as 'a Flemish girl such as I see in the paintings of Van Eyck and Van Dyck long before she becomes one of the glories of our French Helicon.' According to Alfred de Vigny, 'Hers was the finest female mind of her time.' Sainte-Beuve was content to add that 'Hers was the most courageous, tender and passionate of female souls.'

An actress as well as a poet, Marceline Desbordes-Valmore derived her inspiration chiefly from an ardent, unhappy love-affair. Her poems about it do give the impression that she half revelled in her plight as she wandered in the autumnal Flemish countryside bemoaning her fate:

> *Seule, je m'éloignais d'une fête bruyante;*
> *Je fuyais tes regards, je cherchais ma raison.*

20. The rich entrance to the Town Hall of Hesdin.

21. A serene swan graces the lake that surrounds Château d'Olhain in the Pas-de-Calais.

22. The formidable fifteenth- and sixteenth-century defences of Château de Liettres, south-west of Aire-sur-la-Lys.

23. Magnificent Château de Rambures, built mostly out of brick in the fifteenth century.

24. Statues of the patient beasts who helped to build the cathedral at Laon peer down over the city from its towers.

25. Part of the medieval fortifications of the city, the thirteenth-century Porte d'Ardon at Laon still glares fiercely at intruders.

26. These thirteenth-century arches in the Hôtel-Dieu at Laon once sheltered the sick.

30. Rodin's celebrated Burghers of Calais bemoan their fate in front of the city's Flemish Renaissance Town Hall.

31. The belfry of Boulogne's eighteenth-century Town Hall was built in the twelfth and thirteenth centuries as the keep of the former palace of the counts.

32. The city belfry and the tower of the church of Saint-Vaast dominate the Flemish houses which surround the market square at Béthune.

33. Melancholy beauty: the ruined abbey of Ourscamp.

34. This thirteenth-century Madonna smiles a welcome to those who visit the massive Gothic church at Marle.

35. An inescapably
pompous statue of
Napoleon Bonaparte stands
in the lavishly decorated
former Bourse at Lille.

36. The Porte de Paris,
Lille, built in the late
seventeenth century to
glorify King Louis XIV.

Mais la langueur des champs, leur tristesse attrayante,
A ma langueur secrète ajoutaient leur poison.
Sans but et sans espoir suivant ma rêverie,
Je portais au hasard un pas timide et lent.
L'Amour m'enveloppa dans ton ombre chérie,
Et, malgré la saison, l'air me parut brûlant.
Je voulais, mais en vain, par un effort suprême,
En me sauvant de toi, me sauver de moi-même.
Mon oeil, voilé de pleurs, à la terre attaché.
Par un charme invincible en fut comme arraché.

[Alone I quitted a boisterous festival;
Fleeing your glances, I sought my reason.
But the languor of the fields, their enticing sadness,
Added their poison to my secret languor.
Following my reverie, without goal and without hope,
I let my timid and slow steps take me where chance beckoned.
Love enveloped me with your cherished shadow,
And in spite of the season, the air seemed to burn me.
Vainly I wished by a supreme effort
To save me from myself by saving me from you.
Clouded with tears and fixed on the ground, my eye
Was torn away as if by an invincible spell.]

As she warms to her theme, the gloom becomes unbearable:

A travers les brouillards, une image légère
Fit palpiter mon sein de tendresse et d'effroi;
Le soleil reparaît, l'environne, l'éclaire,
Il entrouvre les cieux . . . Tu parus devant moi.
Je n'osai te parler: interdite, rêveuse,
Enchaînée et soumise à ce trouble enchanteur,
Je n'osai te parler: pourtant j'étais heureuse;
Je devinais ton âme, et j'entendis mon coeur.

[Through the mist a gentle image
Made my breast palpitate with tenderness and fear;
The sun reappears, surrounds and illuminates it,
Half-opening the sky . . . You appeared before me.
I dared not speak to you: astonished, a dreamer,
Enchained and submissive to this enchanting agitation,
I dared not speak to you: yet I was happy;
Guessing your soul, I listened to my heart.]

The same street, Rue de Valenciennes, takes us to a roundabout

in the centre of which stands the second gateway to survive from
Douai's medieval ramparts, the Porte de Valenciennes, built in
1453, strengthened in 1562 and still boasting a couple of round
towers and guard-houses. The way to Cambrai takes us through
the Porte d'Arras, a fourteenth-century gateway to the south of
the church of Saint-Jacques and at the end of Rue d'Arras. Part
of the second line of Douai's medieval defences which were begun
in the thirteenth and finished in the fifteenth century, this gate
was built in 1312. Defended by two round towers, its drawbridge
still in place, the Porte d'Arras is nonetheless also defended by a
couple of pillars from the eighteenth-century fortifications of
Douai, pillars which also once bore a drawbridge. At the crossroads just beyond them you turn left for Cambrai.

The N43 runs directly south-east from Douai to Cambrai, a
route which passes by the lakes to Sensée, relished by fishermen
and canoeists. Look for the signs just beyond Lumbres pointing
south-west to Gœulzin, for here is a splendid, though ruined,
seventeenth-century château. This road, the D65, next crosses the
Canal de la Sensée and reaches Arleux, a town so celebrated for
its garlic that at the end of August and the beginning of September
it hosts a garlic festival when everyone downs gallons of garlic
soup. Standing out amid the brick houses are the stones of the
early Gothic church. Its big square tower is capped by a classical
brick belfry and a slate spire.

Paul Verlaine spent some time at Lécluse, 5 km west of here,
staying with his cousin Élisa Moucomble. He decided that Lécluse,
with its red-tiled roofs, in itself was not of an 'exclusively transcend-
ental picturesqueness'. He mocked its sole street as 'implacably
straight and as clean as a new pin, with two footpaths – the Rue
de Rivoli in miniature'. Still, a diversion towards Lécluse would
reveal half-way there at Hamel a prehistoric dolmen, which the
locals dub 'the witches' kitchen'.

What Verlaine did like was the surrounding countryside,
marshes shaded by many kinds of trees, poplars, elms, willows,
filled with reeds and white and yellow water-lilies, and bordered
with chickenweed, watercress and forget-me-nots. 'Sometimes,
book in hand, I go out and sit before the melancholy Flemish
landscape,' he wrote, 'staying there for hours, dreamily following
the blue kingfisher, the green dragon-fly and the pearl-coloured
wood-pigeon as they fly uncertainly around.'

Drive south amid the lakes and wooded walks around Palluel, whose classical church built out of bricks stands next to the Town Hall and rises from a powerful stone base. Here you take the D21 which crosses the Canal du Nord and passes through such pretty villages as Oisy-le-Verger and Épinoy. Near the former stands the 3 m high menhir of Oisy-le-Verger, said to have been dropped by the devil who was startled by a cock crowing. The church at Oisy-le-Verger is massive, resembling the fortified ones we saw in the Thiérache valley. There is a British war cemetery at Épinoy, where I tend to close my eyes to the parish church, a concrete-and-brick edifice with a statue of Bishop Nicolas over its porch. At Épinoy you reach the N43 again and turn right to drive on to Cambrai.

Although greater Lille boasts a population approaching a million and Cambrai not a quarter that number, ecclesiastically the bishopric of the prefecture of the Nord *département* remains subordinate to that of its smaller neighbour. Cambrai, however, dates back certainly to Gallo-Roman times, whereas Lille was founded only in the eleventh century. St Vaast, who lived roughly from 499 to 540, was its first bishop. For a time Cambrai was even a capital city of the small realm of the Franks, till in 509 Clovis reunited that realm with his own lands. The wealth once deployed by Cambrai can be gauged from the contrast between its brick suburbs and the expensive white stone of the inner ancient city. Its most picturesque survival is the 61 m high belfry which once belonged to a church now gone. Begun in the fifteenth century, the belfry assumed its present form only in 1746.

Cambrai lies on the right bank of the River Escaut, which, like many other rivers of the Nord, has been tamed as a canal and is the home of peaceful barges. Peace at Cambrai was savagely interrupted in 1917, when the British temporarily dislodged the Germans who had occupied the city since the beginning of the war. The Germans fought back with spirit and managed to retake the city. When they finally retreated in 1918, they took care to mine much of Cambrai, so as to make the allied occupation of the city as difficult as possible. The local tourist office has prepared a free memoir setting out the surrounding sites and describing in detail the deeds and sufferings of these battles. The home of the tourist office is the *Maison Espagnole* – so called because when its was built in 1595 Cambrai lay under Spanish rule – the oldest house in the city, an overhanging wood-and-brick building enhanced by pretty bronze animals and caryatids.

One casualty of the Great War was the Hôtel de Ville, which stands in the same Avenue de la Victoire as the *Maison Espagnole*. A neo-classical building of 1877, it was burnt down by the Germans in 1918. Cambrai hastened to make good its losses, rebuilding its destroyed Town Hall in a classical style, restoring too its belfry. A couple of *jacquemarts* created in 1512 and named Martin and Martine were brought out of hiding and once more stand beside the Town Hall belfry chiming the hours.

The partly damaged cathedral of Notre-Dame which rises in the same avenue was similarly restored. Built originally in the early eighteenth century, finished in 1783 and partly redone in the nineteenth century, its façade of broken pediments and Corinthian columns is decorated with classical motifs (the sun, the moon, coats of arms), the symbols of the Passion (a whip and crown of thorns) and initials of the Blessed Virgin Mary, for it is dedicated to Notre Dame de Grâce. The separate tower on the north side dates only from 1869. Perched incongruously on top of the tower are the symbols of the four evangelists, the bull of St Luke squatting on his haunches as no real bull ever did. The style of this tower seems to me scarcely to match the decorously ornate façade of the cathedral, but as Our Lady by tradition is crowned in heaven, the belfry makes up for this lack of decorum by carrying on its spire a suitably ornate crown.

Three early-nineteenth-century statues of ecclesiastics inside this cathedral are worth a moment's pause. That of Monsignor Louis Belmas to the left of the main entrance is notable for its sculptor, the celebrated David d'Angers. I warm to a second statue in the cathedral not so much as a work of art but because of the man it represents. This monument, to Cardinal Pierre Giraud, stands a little further along the north wall of the cathedral from the statue of Monsignor Belmas. Archbishop of Cambrai from 1842 to 1850, Giraud is depicted quill pen and paper at the ready to inscribe one of his celebrated denunciations of the terrible conditions of working men and women at that time. Walk on from his tomb to the next but one chapel for a stunning and unusual work of art, the eighteenth-century grisaille by Martin Geeraerts. Representing the agony of Jesus, his deposition and entombment, and an angel at the empty tomb, their *trompe-l'œil*

illusion is brilliantly executed. Jesus's legs seem surely to protrude
from the wall, but in fact they do not. At the opposite side of the
church Geeraerts has worked the same artistic miracle in scenes
from the life of Jesus's mother, painting for instance a quite
remarkable three-dimensional dog. This chapel also houses a
Byzantine icon of Notre Dame de Grâce. It arrived here circuit-
ously, sent as a gift to the Pope in 1419 by the Greek patriarch
after the Council of Constance. The Pope in turn gave it to his
secretary, who was a canon of Cambrai, and he handed it on to
his own cathedral.

The third unmissable statue in this cathedral is another masterpiece by David d'Angers and even more important because of its
subject, François de Salignac de La Mothe-Fénelon. A native of
Dordogne, in 1675 the extremely tolerant Fénelon had been
appointed head of a convent school in Paris whose function was
to educate converted Protestant girls in the Catholic faith. Louis
XIV next made him tutor to his grandson, the duke of Burgundy.
Preferment in the church for a man of his note was inevitable,
and in 1695 Fénelon was consecrated Archbishop of Cambrai.
But he was both courageous and indiscreet. He once accused the
king, in writing, of caring scrupulously about little matters and
scandalously neglecting important ones. He wrote a satirical
novel, *Télémaque*, which covertly attacked the political hypocrisy
of his day. He made an enemy of Bossuet, the bishop of Meaux,
who, mistrusting Fénelon's writings on mysticism, persuaded the
Holy See to declare them heretical. This combination of political
untrustworthiness and religious heterodoxy made Fénelon's downfall inevitable. Disgraced, he was banished to his diocese. He
comforted himself with the maxim that we are never better
disposed for the next life than when matters go badly for us in
this. Still a lover of all men and women, whatever their persua-
sions, when the military struggle for the Spanish Succession
reached Cambrai Fénelon was found comforting the wounded of
both sides. In 1715 he was dead, killed by a fever he contracted
while weakened by a carriage accident. In the same century his
celebrated *Télémaque* was to go through nearly 200 editions,
elevating the fame of the 'swan of Cambrai' far beyond that of
his detractors. In Cambrai cathedral he is sculpted behind the
high altar, half-rising from death, his refined face gazing up to
heaven.

Today the eighteenth-century palace in which his episcopal successors lived has become the head post office, gracing the same elegant avenue in Cambrai. At the opposite end of the Avenue de la Victoire from the Town Hall is the oldest gateway of Cambrai, the Porte de Paris, which was begun in 1390 and boasts two little turrets. The city is still protected by two other such gates. The fourteenth-century Tour des Arquets, almost perfectly preserved, spans the River Scheldt at the end of the Boulevard de la Liberté. The moated Porte Notre-Dame, fortified in 1554 by the Spaniards to protect the city from the direction of Valenciennes, was adorned with the symbols of *le Roi-Soleil* when Louis XIV besieged Cambrai in 1677. This gate is also elegantly decked with pointed stone whose purpose must have been to deflect cannonballs back at the enemy in unexpected directions. Cambrai has also preserved the Château de Selles, built on the site of a medieval one by Emperor Charles V and enlarged by the Spaniards in 1595. Today it houses senior citizens. From here you can wander in the fine garden of the esplanade, which stretches over 12 hectares and is flanked on two sides by the citadel. It contains a statue in honour of Louis Blériot, the pioneering aviator and designer of the monoplane, who was born here in 1872.

For another reminder of violent times passed, cross over the Avenue de la Victoire from the cathedral and find in the nearby Place du Saint-Sépulcre the swirls and torches of the baroque façade of the former Jesuit chapel, which was built in 1692. It is fronted by a truly inadequate modern statue of Fénelon. Ironically, in 1794 the former priest Joseph Lebon sat here when presiding over the revolutionary tribunal of the Nord. In a couple of short months he sentenced 169 citizens of Cambrai to the guillotine. Behind the chapel is the former Jesuit college, now the municipal museum, from whose courtyard you can see the elegant rear of the chapel. The museum houses a painting by Rubens of the Coronation of the Virgin, as well as several works by Henri Matisse, who was born at nearby Le Cateau-Cambrésis, and sculptures from the former twelfth-century cathedral.

To look out of an evening from the Hôtel de la Poste at the softly illuminated buildings of the Avenue de la Victoire is entrancing. Nearby the restaurant La Renaudière is a beautifully transformed old house, with ancient beams and brick walls reinforced by stone. The proprietor welcomes the British by translating his menus, speaking our language and hanging his walls with English sporting prints interspersed with hunting horns and a few reproductions of works by Matisse (whom we also love). Alas, though I have no objection to his rich soup and *brochette provençale*, I wish he also served regional dishes. That is my sole complaint. One day I saw a man's cigarette accidentally burn the proprietor's arm as he served, and remarked that his flesh had now been cooked medium-rare. He replied, 'These are the risks of my profession,' and as a reward for my feeble joke gave me a handkerchief stamped with the name of the restaurant and made out of cambric, that fine white linen first created in this city.

Cambrai describes itself as a city of three belfries, and you can see all three by strolling up Avenue de la Victoire towards the Town Hall, glancing left to spot the third one along Rue du 11-Novembre. If you turn left at the Town Hall you will also find the city's second lovely church, Saint-Géry, once the chapel of the monks of Saint-Aubert and built between 1723 and 1745. Standing beside three arches which survive from the former episcopal palace, its tower rises to 76 m. The interior is graced by a painting by Rubens of the entombment of Jesus, eighteenth-century furnishings and a beautiful screen of 1632, made by Gaspard Marsy out of black-and-red marble and ornate with reliefs and statues.

One treasure of this church, its altar, reminds us of a rare treat in this part of France, for it came from the Cistercian monastery of Vaucelles, which lies 12 km south of Cambrai. Open to the public in summer, this abbey is an exquisite survival of the twelfth century. St Bernard of Clairvaux himself was here in 1147, curing a soldier's crippled leg. The abbey church was demolished at the end of the eighteenth century, though its lovely tiled floor has been excavated; but the chapter house, completed in 1175, remains the largest of those belonging to the Cistercians in the whole of Europe. The auditorium dates from 1155; and the monks' scriptorium, 37 m long and 18 m wide, is an extremely graceful monument of the same era.

You reach Le Cateau-Cambrésis 22 km south-east of Cambrai by following a Roman road as straight as a ruler, save where it wobbles a little to greet the mighty tower of the mid-nineteenth-century church at Beauvois-en-Cambrésis and then swerves to thread its way through the twin villages of Beaumont-en-Cambrésis and Inchy. The church at Beaumont-en-Cambrésis is worth pausing at for its fifteenth-century retable and font. The late-fifteenth-century church at Inchy stands beside the River Erclin. The river winds north-west to water the park in which stand the keep and towers of the thirteenth-century Château de Clermont (which is close by the village of Béthencourt).

Situated amid lovely walking and camping country on the slopes of the green valley of the River Selle, Le Cateau-Cambrésis derives its name from a château fortified here by the bishop of Cambrai in 1001. The town witnessed the signing of a treaty between Henri II of France and Philip II of Spain in 1559, when France finally gave up her attempt to dominate Italy. Le Cateau-Cambrésis was also the birthplace of France's greatest twentieth-century painter, Henri Matisse, and has celebrated the fact by transforming the eighteenth-century Palais Fénelon into a Matisse museum, enriched by several works given by the artist himself. Fénelon's name adorns the Musée Matisse because this building was formerly the palace of the archbishops of Cambrai, built in the 1770s by Théodore Brongniart. I find it a dull-looking affair and the park behind it much livelier. Le Nôtre laid out the grounds, and Fénelon is here honoured by a bust.

Beyond the Musée Matisse stretches the Place du Général-de-Gaulle. The stone Town Hall which rises here is an elegant curiosity, built in 1553 in the style of the Italian and not the French Renaissance. Its belfry is slightly at odds with this elegance, for it was added by the architect Jacques-Nicolas de Valenciennes only in 1705. At the corner of the square alongside the Town Hall are inscribed words broadcast by de Gaulle from London in 1940, including the stirring sentence 'France has lost a battle, but France has not lost a war!' Oddly enough the bronze statue in the square is not that of the great general but of another noble warrior Napoleon Bonaparte's Marshal Édouard-Adolphe-Casimir-Joseph Mortier, Duke of Treviso, who was born here in 1768. On 28 July 1835, he was assassinated in Paris at the side of King Louis-Philippe. As the plinth of his statue records, the monument was erected by the king, by princes, by ministers, marshals and the duke's fellow-citizens. On Tuesday and Friday mornings a covered market bustles heedlessly around him.

Over the houses behind the doomed duke rises the belfry of one of the finest seventeenth-century churches in these parts. Saint-Martin belonged to the former Benedictine abbey of Saint-André, its bulbous tower and an elaborate baroque façade overlooking the Place Sadi-Carnot. Gaspard Marsy designed the broken pediments, medallions, coats of arms and enthrallingly offset features of this façade in 1634. One of the first churches built in this style in the Nord, even the mitres worn by cherubs are baroquely falling off their heads. The tower was built some fifty years later. I found the church a trifle gloomy inside until I discovered that you can light up its splendid roof by putting a coin into a device to the right of the door. Almost as splendid as this church are the honeyed sweetmeats known as the *'cagoulets'* of Le Cateau-Cambrésis.

From Le Cateau-Cambrésis an enchanting tour will take you as far as the Belgian border and back to Valenciennes. It passes through Landrecies, 12 km north-east of Le Cateau and is reached through leafy woodlands. Landrecies was the birthplace of Joseph-François Dupleix, who longed to establish a French empire in India but was frustrated by the British. He managed to hold on to Pondicherry for the French East India Council throughout a five-week siege by Admiral Boscawen. Though commemorated here by a bronze statue fronting the eighteenth-century Hôtel de Ville in the Place d'Armes, he died in poverty in 1763, chiefly because the Council he had served refused to make good the financial losses he claimed to have sustained in their service.

Twenty-four kilometres east of Landrecies is Avesnes-sur-Helpe, once a fortified town on its little hillock. The ancient heart of the town remains picturesque, with its eighteenth-century, blue-stoned Hôtel de Ville and the flamboyant Gothic church of Saint-Nicolas. The church houses paintings by Louis-Joseph Watteau and a mid-seventeenth-century funeral monument dedicated to two Spanish soldiers who died in each other's arms. Old slate-roofed houses contribute to the charm of this spot, a cheese-making town whose own speciality is the *boulette d'Avesnes*, supplemented by the *maroilles* made throughout the neighbourhood.

Drive from here due north to Maubeuge. Lying on the Belgian border, Maubeuge was so damaged in the Second World War that it has become virtually a mid-twentieth-century industrial town. The citizens have consoled themselves for their architectural losses by endowing a zoo. True, a baroque Jesuit chapel and the Porte de Mons, a fine edifice of 1685, were spared by the bombardments. Nonetheless my own instinct is to visit it only in mid-July during the annual beer festival.

Not so Bavay, which lies 14 km west of Maubeuge. This exquisite Flemish town dates back to Gallo-Roman times. Parts of
ancient Bagacum have been excavated and are open to view (the
entrance is in Rue des Gommeries), representing one of the most
important sites in the *département*. Altogether Bagacum's baths and
shops, its forum and pillared halls covered in the region of 9
hectares. The shape of its ramparts has been preserved, enclosing
a Town Hall of 1784 and a church of the same era, both in the
huge main square which is surrounded by lovely slate-roofed
houses. Although Bavay's gastronomic specialities include a
honeyed sweetmeat known as *chiques de Bavay* and the strong *bière
de Garde*, the Café de Paris in the Grand'Place claims to serve no
fewer than eighty different beers. In the porch of its eighteenth-
century church are a couple of fine late-seventeenth- and
eighteenth-century tomb-slabs.

No fewer than seven Roman roads meet here. They come from
Amiens, Soissons, Reims, Trier, Cologne, Utrecht and Tournai,
converging on a column erected at the centre of the Grand'Place
in 1872. It bears a statue of Queen Brunhilda, who for a time
ruled every Merovingian domain but was finally dethroned and
done to death in AD 613 by being dragged along by wild horses.
The inscription on the column informs us that Caesar Agrippa
constructed the seven Roman roads around 26 BC and that
Brunhilda mended them in the year of her death.

Our route now takes us south-west for 14 km to one of the most
impressive fortified cities in the region. Perhaps its position on a
slight rise in the ground made Le Quesnoy a prized military site.
Both the Emperor Charles V and King Louis XIII of France
fortified it. Vauban completed their work, his pink, moated walls
still intact, though today sections of the huge ditches and the
lakes which added a further deterrent to invaders serve as leisure
parks. The walls enclose a Town Hall built in 1585 with a belfry
whose carillon of 1700 plays sweet tunes before striking the hours.
The classical parish church, a gentle brick building with simple
stone features, dates from 1829 and looks out on to the cobbled,
irregular Place de l'Église. The interior of this church is extremely
fine: round granite pillars support the ceiling, topped by delicate
mouldings; the classical panelling of the apse rises to the clouds of
heaven which are filled with cherubs; the high altar has gone (a
result of the twentieth-century liturgical movement which insists

that Mass be celebrated facing the people), but a painting of the crucifix still survives in its original place on the east wall. Although the stained glass dates from the 1940s, it is light and airy, and laudably designed in the eighteenth-century fashion. Over the pulpit an angel trumpeter heralds the word of God; and as you emerge from the church you can walk east through its grounds to find the belfry.

Le Quesnoy is proud of its avenue of honour, leading to a memorial dedicated to New Zealand soldiers who fell defending the town in the First World War. A couple of kilometres south-east is Potelle, whose medieval château you can explore from the outside but not visit. Fourteen kilometres south-west is Solesmes, our route ambling through Beaudignies, with its imposing manor-houses. The farms dotted around this countryside are equally powerful, boasting impressive courtyards. At Solesmes a priory was founded in 705, and the ruins of its former buildings are still to be seen. Solesmes is also served by a huge church built in 1780, with a wooden spire some 65 m high.

The city of Valenciennes lies 21 km north of Solesmes. Quaintly enough Valenciennes, the fourth of the major cities of this *département* of France, used to describe herself like Douai as the Athens of the North. By reason of her artists alone I should uphold the title. Antoine Watteau was born here in 1684 (as were Louis-Joseph and François Watteau). So, in 1827, was the once notorious and to my taste still entrancingly sensuous sculptor Jean-Baptiste Carpeaux. This city too was the birthplace of the chronicler of the Hundred Years War, Jean Froissart. He thus gives Valenciennes a particular connection with Britain, for in 1361 Froissart became secretary to the English Queen Philippa of Hainaut. In researching his *Chronicles* Froissart visited the court of King David II of Scotland as well as journeying around England. He was a companion of the Black Prince and the Duke of Clarence on their travels. In 1369 he and Lionel, Duke of Clarence, were in Italy when Queen Philippa died. The chronicler hastened back to her court to mourn her. Around a year later her nephew, Robert of Namur, persuaded him to publish the first book of his four-volume history of the long struggle between England and France. He was living here in Flanders in 1390 when he wrote the third volume of his *Chronicles*. Ten years later he published the final book. By 1410 he was dead.

Froissart was even-handed in his treatment of the war (or, some historians have judged, he favoured the English when the English were providing his daily bread and switched to the French side when he entered the service of the lord of Beaumont, Guy of Blois). Inevitably, for the earlier years of the struggle he was obliged to rely on the testimony of others, particularly the writings of Jean le Bel of Liège, but after the struggle had reached the year 1377 his own researches played a much greater part in the story. Throughout his *Chronicles* this cleric relished acts of knightly valour, scenes of battle, and noble ladies. As Sir Walter Scott put it, 'In Froissart, we hear the gallant knights, of whom he wrote, arrange the terms of combat and the manner of the onset; we hear the soldiers cry their war-cries; we see them strike their horses with the spur; and the liveliness of the narration hurries us along with them into the whirlwind of battle.' Whether his account of the virtues of his favoured knights and ladies truly reflects their characters one can no longer very well judge; but most of us cannot help warming to his description (for example) of the 59-year-old Count Gascon Phoebus de Fois as 'so perfectly formed that no one could praise him too much'. Froissart, it must be added, had travelled throughout Flanders and much of France in the service of Gascon and even dedicated his poetic romance *Meliador* to this particular lord. Whether or not we can therefore trust the chronicler's statement that 'although I have seen very many knights, squires, kings, princes and others, I never saw anyone so handsome' may be open to doubt; but the life of a late-fourteenth-century nobleman comes alive when we learn first that every day Gascon distributed at his gate five florins in small coins as alms to all-comers, and that 'he loved dogs above all other animals, amusing himself with much hunting in summer and winter alike'.

In 1856 Valenciennes honoured the chronicler with a statue by Philippe-Honoré Lemaire which stands in the *Jardin Froissart* at the end of Rue Saint-Géry, surrounded by ten medallions of other Valenciennes notables. On its plinth the legend quotes Froissart's own *Chronicles*: 'Should anyone wish to know who I am, I am called Jean Froissart, a native of the beautiful and free city of Valenciennes.' For a contemporary portrait of the man, with his pursed lips and long nose, you must visit the municipal library at Arras. To enjoy Jean-Baptiste Carpeaux and Antoine Watteau

we can stay in Valenciennes. The Musée des Beaux Arts in Boulevard Watteau at Valenciennes rightly devotes a whole room to
the works of Carpeaux. Since they include the maquettes in
plaster of nearly every one of his works, you can see here for
example the erotic group 'The Dance' which was instantly mutilated by horrified spectators the moment it appeared on the
outside of the Paris Opéra in 1869.

Three thousand of Carpeaux's designs and paintings are also
housed in the same museum, for he was talented in these fields as
well as in sculpture. The gallery itself is not, I think one of the
most beautiful in Flanders, designed and built in the first decade
of this century and necessarily restored after the Second World
War. It derives nobility from its cratered, bullet-ridden walls, the
result of the battles of Second World War, as well as from its
undeniably rich collection. This includes a roomful of works by
Rubens, including a famous 'Deposition' as well as a powerful
painting of the stoning of St Peter. Alongside these hang masterpieces by Cuyp and Van Dyck.

In addition to being suitably honoured by the museum and by
having a boulevard named after him, Antoine Watteau also
merits a sumptuous bronze statue in Square (*sic*) Watteau, brush
and palette in hand – a tribute by none other than Jean-Baptiste
Carpeaux. The four figures around the statue represent the *com-
media dell'arte* which so much influenced Watteau's sensuous paintings. Geese and the heads of old men are used to add gaiety to the
luxurious monument by spouting water into the fountain below,
but they seem to have stopped spouting recently and the base of
the fountain is now filled with flowers. Shading this square are the
classically formal and simple brick-and-stone walls of the church
of Saint-Géry, founded on behalf of the Franciscans by Countess
Jeanne of Flanders, another native of Valenciennes. Built in 1225,
the church has retained from the thirteenth century only the
arcades of the nave and a couple more in the choir. The rest was
destroyed at the Revolution and had to be rebuilt. The tower is
modern. As if the depredations of the two world wars were not
enough, Saint-Géry suffered extensively in a fire of 1958. Splendidly the town seized the opportunity to make a beautiful restoration of the thirteenth-century interior.

Watteau's statue seems to be pointing not to this church but to
that of Saint-Nicolas in the Rue de Paris. Founded by the Jesuits

in 1602, Saint-Nicolas is for me quite as satisfying as Saint-Géry. A carving over its porch represents Bishop Nicolas (or Santa Claus) rescuing three children from a cooking pot. Its furnishings, mostly contemporary with the church, are splendid, especially the Renaissance screen in black and white marble and a late-seventeenth-century statue of Jesus by Antoine Pater. The former Jesuit college next door, like the façade of the church, dates not from the same century but from the next. Its brick-and-stone walls enclose the municipal library, and a plaque on its wall reminds us of another distinguished native of the second Athens of the North, Valentin Conrart, born here in 1603 and destined to found the Conrart circle, cradle of the Académie française. The library itself is a rich one, partly because the Jesuits who once lived here were fine scholars and partly because other manuscripts and *incunabula* were brought here from dissolved abbeys after the Revolution. One priceless treasure, the manuscript of the *Cantilène de Sainte Eulalie*, dates from 881 and is alleged (wrongly, I would argue) to be the earliest known work in the French language. The building still retains not only its eighteenth-century woodwork and furnishings but also numerous portraits of bygone Jesuit worthies.

The Revolution may have brought together much of this superb collection of ancient manuscripts, but as well as demolishing most of Saint-Géry those fanatical anti-Christians among its devotees also pulled down a thirteenth-century church which had arisen as the shrine of Notre-Dame-du-Saint-Cordon, a statue venerated since 1008 when it was reputed to have saved many citizens from a plague. You reach the present church of Notre-Dame-du-Saint-Cordon by walking along Rue de Paris from the Square Watteau as far as the Place d'Armes, where stands the mighty Flemish Renaissance Hôtel de Ville, built in 1868, its three storeys decorated with huge balustrades, gables and caryatids. For its main pediment Carpeaux contributed a sculpture of the town defending her ramparts during a terrible siege of 1793. The Town Hall overlooks a little fountain as well as shops and brasseries.

Behind the Hôtel de Ville is the Place du Marché, where the market of Valenciennes installs itself every Wednesday and Saturday. Follow Rue Delseaux on the south side of the square and turn left into Rue des Ursulines to find the crumbling stones and the graceful buttresses of the church of Notre-Dame-du-Saint-

Cordon, which was rebuilt in the mid-nineteenth century in the style of the one destroyed at the Revolution. Its elegant, slender spire reaches up for 78 m, and in it hangs a celebrated bell known as 'Jehanne de Flandres' (and also known as 'la Bancloque') which was founded in 1358. The Revolution ultimately failed to extirpate what it dubbed superstition, for on the second Sunday of each September the ancient, miracle-working statue is still paraded around the streets of Valenciennes.

Washed by the Escaut and the Rhonelle, Valenciennes lost her fortifications in the 1890s (though a morsel remains in the fifteenth-century sandstone-and-white-stone tower which rises in the Place de la Dodonne). Ravaged by wars, the town has nonetheless preserved, alongside the monuments we have been visiting, numerous Renaissance houses and some fine eighteenth-century buildings, including the prefecture. Valenciennes is an industrial town, though today the mining families (whose cause was notably championed by Émile Zola) are rarer and rarer here as the coal industry declines. It offers traffic-free oases, such as the Rue de Famars, with its cafés, boutiques, crêperies, restaurants and pubs serving draught cider, as well as the tree-shaded waters and walks of the Rhonelle park – another unexpectedly green oasis in what has become one of the major centres of France's iron and steel industry.

6

APPROACHING PARIS

As you drive through the forests and pastures of the gateway into France and begin to approach Paris, Noyon is the first city you reach in the *département* of the Oise. The Oise is a complex and richly varied part of Picardy. More than a fifth of its entire surface is covered with forest, today marked by the tourist authorities with over a thousand hiking and rambling routes. You can fish in more than a hundred lakes in these forests alone. Outside the woodlands the landscapes vary entrancingly. The contrast could scarcely be greater between the deep green of the forest and the lush agricultural area known as the French Vexin, where the local tourist boards direct you to picturesque villages along routes marked by the symbol of a wheatsheaf (whereas the symbol of the tourist routes through the Clermont forest is a doe). To the north and west of Beauvais the farmers cultivate apples and live in what they dub the *Oise normande* because of its proximity and resemblance to Normandy. South of the *Oise normande* lies the so-called *boutonnière*, or 'buttonhole', of Bray, a geological depression filled with a fine clay that has served potters since Gallo-Roman times. The *département* also includes the vast and rolling Picardy plateau. Every one of these regions is peaceful and ravishing; most of them contain ancient towns, cities and villages; and the forests, hamlets, cities and châteaux of the region named after the Valois are especially redolent of the glories of the vanished eras of the French nobility and monarchy.

Initially we find ourselves in the region known as the Noyonnais, whose landscape is more scenically turbulent and tortured than any other in the *département* and whose fields grow cherries and redcurrants. Noyon, its capital, began life as a Gaulish town, developing into an important Roman prefecture and, in 531, into the seat of a bishopric. This intimate little city surprisingly encapsulates not only much of the history of medieval France but also was the cradle of a later profound religious change in the western world.

Its first bishop was St Médard, a native of Picardy. Médard's father was an important royal servant and his mother traced her descent from the Romans. She converted her husband from paganism and so much instilled Christian charity in her son that when he saw an impoverished beggar, Médard outdid St Martin by giving the poor man not half his cloak but the whole. He would often go without dinner so as to offer his food to the needy. (As Alban Butler of St-Omer put it, 'Fasting was his delight in an age when children seldom knew what it was to curb their appetites.') His first see was based on present-day Vermand, which lies 10 km from Saint-Quentin, but his diocese was so ravaged by the Huns and the Vandals that Médard transferred it to the stronghold of Noyon.

Here he received as a nun Radegonde, the saintly wife of King Clotaire I. Clotaire himself, who was desperate to expiate his former cruelties, adored Médard, which is why the saint's bones reside not in his cathedral of Notre-Dame at Noyon but at Soissons, for after Médard's death the king transferred the saint's earthly remains to add lustre to the great church he was engaged in building there. Throughout the Middle Ages church and state were similarly bound together, and Noyon played its part in their interaction. In the centre of the Place de l'Hôtel-de-Ville rises an obelisk fountain, set up in 1493 and inscribed with the stirring information that King Chilperic was buried here in 721, that at Noyon Charlemagne was consecrated ruler of Neustria in 768, and that here in 987 Hugues Capet was crowned King of France. Meanwhile the life of a medieval farming community lingers on into the twentieth century around the obelisk in the form of the Saturday and Wednesday morning fruit and vegetable markets, while on the first Tuesday in every month a greater market, still selling cattle, stretches from here as far as the Place Saint-Jacques.

Three buildings are of especial note in Noyon, two – the cathedral and the Town Hall – because their magnificence symbolizes this ancient intertwining of spiritual and secular, the third because here was born one of the greatest of those Protestant Reformers who in the sixteenth century split the Catholic church. The Town Hall at Noyon, standing in what was once the Place du Marché-aux-Herbes and now is known more prosaically as the Place de l'Hôtel-de-Ville, was built between 1485 and 1523 and expanded in the seventeenth century. It begins below as a Gothic building with spiky niches and a decorated doorway, and ends with a classical upper storey. A monumental classical gateway leads into an exceedingly jolly Gothic courtyard. Here is a whiskery bust of Ernest Noel, a mayor of Noyon who died in 1925. Here too are beautifully decorated windows and a five-storeyed tower.

Over the houses to the north-west of the square rises Noyon cathedral. If you make your way towards it by Rue des Merciers and then left along Rue de l'Évêché you pass the former bishop's palace on the right. It abuts on to the Tour Roland, a tower remaining from the medieval fortifications of the city. The episcopal palace itself is a gabled stone-and-brick Renaissance building, with a round staircase tower and a fanciful dormer window. Today it serves as a museum of costume from the Revolution to the Empire. You reach the cathedral through the former episcopal garden, its seats under the trees sheltered by the south flank of the mighty church. From here you can see the massive simplicity of the cathedral. Its two massive towers, the nearer built first, are scarcely decorated, and only a couple of the aisle windows make any major attempt at tracery.

First World War memorials in France are usually inventive, and the one at the end of the episcopal garden here is no exception. A sculptor named E. Pinchon carved the moving reliefs depicting Noyon during the First World War: women and children weeping as their menfolk are taken hostage on 22 September 1914; the return of the 13th French corps on 18 March 1917; the city in ruins on 25 August 1918; and finally brave men receiving the Legion d'honneur and the Croix de Guerre in the presence of Marshal Joffre on 10 July 1920.

Two huge buttresses hold up the west end of the early Gothic cathedral, which also suffered in the war and was not finally restored until 1952. The robust towers reach a height of 66 m, the south one finished by the end of the twelfth century, the north one not until around 1320. The façade, dating from the end of the thirteenth century, once carried some 350 statues, every one of them destroyed in October 1793. Before going inside, walk around the north side and past the cloister to see the former canons' library. This long, delightful half-timbered building dates back to the sixteenth century and surmounts a beguiling arcade held up by wooden pillars. There seems to me too much dangerous dry kindling incorporated into a building which houses some 4,000 precious books.

Inside the cathedral are some utterly splendid chapels, the most magnificent that on the right dedicated to Notre Dame de Bon Secours. Bishop Charles I of Hangest founded it in 1528, and its pendentives bear the Hangest and Amboise coat of arms. The coat of arms of the order of the Holy Spirit (to which Charles belonged) decorates the centre one. Superbly carved niches today lack their statues. Enjoy the double frieze – a row of vines surmounted by one of the cockleshell symbols of St James the Great (or *coquilles de Saint-Jacques*). The next chapel, that of the Holy Sacrament, is enhanced by beautiful panelling, carved with musical instruments and brought here from the charterhouse of Mont-Renard. Its large classical retable, carved in 1735, also came from elsewhere, the monastery of Froment.

Although both transepts have early Gothic ceilings, the late Romanesque south transept is far less elaborate than that on the north side of the cathedral (a contrast mirrored in the decoration of the two towers of this cathedral). The high altar, whose bronze angels are defended by the eighteenth-century wrought-iron screen of the choir, dates from 1757. Both the chapter house and the cloister remain as they were in the thirteenth century.

Like the Town Hall square, Parvis Notre-Dame (the cathedral square), flanked by sixteenth-century canons' houses, once had a name more evocative of country life, namely the Place du Marché-aux-Volailles. Leave it by Rue Saint-Antoine and take the first street on the right to discover the former cloister of the Hôtel-Dieu, which was founded in 1178 and rebuilt in the eighteenth century. Then walk back down Rue Calvin to find the half-timbered brick house where on 10 July 1509, the Reformer John Calvin was born. The boy was brought up in the ambience of the Noyon cathedral, for his father, Géraud Cauvin (to revert to the French and not the Latinized form of the family name), was a diocesan solicitor and financial agent, procurator for the cathedral canons and the bishop's secretary. As his son later put it, 'From my youth upwards my father intended me for theology.' His mother must have brought a more down to earth element to the home, for Jeanne Le Franc was the daughter of an innkeeper from Cambrai.

As he grew up, the cathedral chapter financed John Calvin's studies by giving him first one and then two benefices (even though by this time he was scarcely eighteen years old). At the age of fourteen, along with three young relatives of the bishop of Noyon, he was sent to study in Paris. Just as young Calvin was about to matriculate as a Master of Arts, his father fell into dispute with the cathedral authorities over some property. The row flared, and he was excommunicated. This apparently prompted Géraud Cauvin to direct his son to exchange the study of theology for that of law, and so John transferred from Paris to the University of Orléans, moving on to the University of Bourges within a year. In May 1531 his father suddenly died, and the parental yoke was lifted. After hurrying back for the funeral John felt free once again to take up the study of theology.

Inevitably after his conversion to Protestantism Calvin's enemies would point to his father's dispute with the church as a reason for souring John's relationship with Catholicism. They also put out the calumny that he had for a time been imprisoned for sodomy. The truth is that both at Paris and at Orléans John had come into contact with Lutherans as well as humanists, some of whom were becoming increasingly critical of the laxities of the church. Among those he sought out were Lefèvre d'Étaples, whom we have already met as translator of the first French Bible. Lefèvre was now living with other religious reformers in comparative security, under the protection of Marguerite of Navarre, the sister of King François I. Moreover, Protestantism was by now attracting many whom no one could claim had a grudge against the Catholic church.

John Calvin's quite sudden conversion to fully fledged Protestantism occurred at the end of 1533 (or perhaps early in the next year). Returning to Noyon in May he surrendered his benefices. By the end of the year, in the light of increasingly hostile action against Reformers by the authorities, John Calvin was safe in Protestant Basel. Two years later he published his immensely influential *Institutes of the Christian Religion*. Among those influenced

by his teaching in his native land was no less a figure than the
bishop of Beauvais, Cardinal Odet de Châtillon, who, in 1562,
two years before John Calvin's death, declared himself a Calvinist.
He also took a wife and the title Count of Beauvais. The former
cardinal decided to remain as bishop, and the diocese of Beauvais
did not manage to oust him till 1569.

At Noyon John Calvin's birthplace is now a museum devoted to
his teaching and his memory; with audio-visual displays, a reconstruction of his study and copies of his books. It welcomes visitors
from 1 April to 1 November on every day save Tuesdays. And just
around the corner is the Town Hall where we started this little tour.

A leisurely, forested route from Noyon to Senlis by way of
Compiègne takes you first along the D145 south-east to Pont-
l'Évêque. As soon as you have crossed the canal and the River
Oise, turn right along the D164 following the sign for the abbey of
Ourscamp. From the roadside its exceedingly palatial eighteenth-
century quarters, along with the ruins of the twelfth- and
thirteenth-century abbey church, appear through the grille of a
gate wrought in iron in 1768. The great monastic reformer St
Bernard of Clairvaux refounded this abbey in 1129 on the site of
one established here in 649, and parts of its thirteenth-century
wall still survive. Behind the church to the right rises the long,
former infirmary of the abbey, which was built in 1269.

Through the oaks, hornbeams and beeches of the Ourscamp
forest you drive south-east along the D48 to Carlepont, where you
turn right for Tracy-le-Val. Site of a vicious battle in 1914, today
the peaceful village of Tracy-le-Val preserves its twelfth-century
church with a splendid set of carvings on the exterior and a dog-
toothed porch. Nearly everything has been excellently restored.
Do not miss the little carving of Adam and Eve with the serpent,
set in the two-storeyed belfry. Adam has his hand on his chest,
protesting his innocence and as ever blaming his wife for his Fall.
Opposite the little church square is an excellent though (I think)
slightly pricy restaurant for this little village. Drive on past the
chimneys, painted roofs and earlier outbuildings of an impressive
château built in the Empire style in 1882, to wind up to Tracy-le-
Mont. Be prepared here to discover suddenly on the left a church
replete with gargoyles, whose squat Renaissance tower sports a
double cupola. Its pulpit dates from 1662. The nearby towered
house was built a couple of centuries earlier.

Still running south-east towards Attichy, our route begins to flank the long white wall of someone's private domain. Be ready to leave the D16 and veer sharply right alongside this wall and along the D547 to drive to Saint-Crépin-aux-Bois. The road snakes down into the valley, across which towers the medieval and Renaissance Château d'Offemont, with its long and high balustraded parapet. Just before the village a notice directs lovers of evocative ecclesiastical architecture to the ruined eleventh- and sixteenth-century priory of Sainte-Croix-d'Offemont.

Saint-Crépin-aux-Bois, so named because it sits at the edge of the forest of Laigue, has a Gothic church with a Renaissance doorway. Exquisite villages succeed each other along this route. The D547 takes you south-west to one of them, Rethondes, whose white-walled houses with their stepped gables are washed by the River Aisne. To the south side of its Romanesque-Gothic church is a well, and on the church wall a plaque carries a relief of the head of Marshal Foch and the information that here on 10 November 1918 (the eve of the armistice), he and his faithful aide General Weygand came to pray.

Just beyond the west end of the church the road crosses the river and plunges into the Compiègne forest on its way to Vieux-Moulin. Nature lovers should look for the signposted tourist route which will take them by way of the little hills and lakes of the forest. This is a region nurturing beautiful wild flowers: the yellow wild tulips; the purple and brown bee orchids; buttercups; the hanging purple flowers of the fritillaries; the little white flowers of the sea-kale; the curious brown long-leaved sundews; the pink flowers of *Aster amellus*, with their yellow centres; white and pink orchids; the green, spiky fingers of buglosses; wild anemones with their white flowers turning yellow at the centre; and the deep purple pasque-flowers. Campsites and parking spots are clearly marked. Here are signposted rambles, hikes and tracks for horse-riding. With the little stream that once drove the old mill, its trees, gardens and exquisite houses, many decorated with dormer windows, Vieux-Moulin is an ideal centre for such pleasures. Here you can buy fishing licences and equipment. Its classical church, built in 1860 opposite an *auberge* (of which there are several in the village), boasts a pretty wooden porch and a greensward with concrete seats.

Drive on through the woods to the crossroads, crossing it and continuing past the lakes and campsites on the way to Pierrefonds. *En route* take care to pause at the fascinating little office of the national forest authority, with its display of the various trees which are shading us: cochineals, hornbeams, silver birches, chestnuts and oaks. At the D973 turn left to drive into Pierrefonds, which boasts another good campsite. Here I relish first of all simply parking by the lakeside to gaze up at the château, a riot of battlements, turrets and towers which Viollet-le-Duc matched only in his reconstruction of Carcassonne in the Languedoc.

This château, at once a military fortress and a domestic home, stands on a defensive site which has been occupied with some sort of fortification since at least the eleventh century. The present building was begun by Louis d'Orléans in 1392. One of the king's Master builders, Jean Le Noir of Senlis, devised the plans. Over the centuries it changed hands, occupied by Catholics and by Protestants and even once by the English. A royal army virtually dismantled the whole château in 1616, and we owe the reconstruction of this astonishing building to the two greatest Napoleons – Bonaparte, who bought it in 1810 because of its historical redolence, and Napoleon III, who charged Viollet-le-Duc with its restoration. If only to admire Viollet-le-Duc's scholarly, inventive (and often playful) genius, a visit is an enormous treat. (Between the beginning of October to the end of March it is closed on Tuesdays.) The architect's vision was breathtaking, but even more I adore his details, especially his comical corbels, gargoyles, and capitals.

Before leaving Pierrefonds, spare a glance at the much restored church of Saint-Sulpice, which has a choir in part dating back to the eleventh century and a mid-sixteenth-century Renaissance belfry. Exquisite Saint-Jean-aux-Bois lies through the forest 6 km west of Pierrefonds. Park in Rue des Meuniers opposite the entrance to its twelfth-century abbey church and chapter house. The abbey was founded for the Benedictines by Louis VI's widow Adelaide in 1152. Walk through a couple of medieval pepperpot towers with a porch in between to discover to the right a row of pretty cottages. Further to the right is a more substantial gateway with its own gatehouse. A row of trees leads you across the close to the tall slender windows of the abbey church, founded by the Benedictines in 1152. Once again the early-thirteenth-century church is embellished with grimacing faces, both human and bestial. You must walk round to the far side to get inside to enjoy the sight of the vaults which spring from leaf-decorated corbels. Two pillars support the crossing. Beauty here derives from simplicity. One ancient window, some of the glass thirteenth-century, still glows, especially its medallion of the Crucifixion. A polychrome statue of St John the Baptist depicts him with the Lamb of God around his neck. The eighteenth-century pulpit has a mischievous-looking cherub situated behind the preacher's head. The chapter house is even earlier, built in the late twelfth century, two central pillars supporting its roof. It opens every afternoon.

From here drive on to the D322 and turn right to reach Compiègne after 9 km. The armistice which ended the First World War was signed in a railway carriage just outside Compiègne. The Clairière de l'Armistice is a memorial and museum of this long-awaited moment, beautifully laid out in the Compiègne forest, and the event is annually commemorated here on 11 November.

Just under a couple of decades ago, when my elder daughter was seven and my younger daughter only one year old, my family and I wondered whether to stay overnight in Compiègne. Said my elder daughter, 'It's not our kind of town.' Recently I asked my younger daughter whether she agreed. She replied, 'Compiègne is an untidy sort of place.' So (apart from its château) it remains, though there are some treats that no one should miss here. At the heart of the Place de l'Hôtel-de-Ville is a statue of Joan of Arc, defender of the town. Placed here in 1895, the plinth proclaims her words, '*Je yray voir mes bons amis de Compiengne* [sic]' (I shall come to visit my friends of Compiègne). The impressive, late-Gothic and early-Renaissance Town Hall was built in the first half of the sixteenth century and extended in 1870. Two turrets flank its mansard roof, and either side of the main building has a classical extension. In niches on its façade stand a bishop, a queen, a knight, a cardinal and a king. In the centre, where traditionally would have been placed a relief of the Assumption, is an equestrian statue of King Louis XII, placed here in 1869. Medieval knights with plumed hats and swords guard its powerful belfry. They turn out to be the three *jacquemarts* who strike the hours on an ancient bell known as 'la Bancloque'. The Town Hall houses a museum with a staggeringly immense display of model soldiers in military uniforms from all over the world, some of the figurines still fighting battles won and lost long ago.

The Town Hall square was once the garden of an abbey founded by Charles the Bald in 877. The ruins of the fourteenth-century cloister of Saint-Corneille today usually form a deserted haven in the busy shopping street, Rue Saint-Corneille, that runs from the Place de l'Hôtel-de-Ville. Walking around this cloister you come upon a couple of tombstones set in the wall, one depicting a knight in armour, the other a priest in his vestments. A few plants grow from its Gothic walls, as they do from the huge twelfth-century keep known as the Tour Beauregard a little further on. Beside it, in a sweet garden decorated with more vestiges of the ruined cloister, is the Musée Vivinel, housed in a nineteenth-century mansion and displaying Greek antiquities. Opposite the Tour Beauregard rises the Gothic front of the Hôtel-Dieu, which was founded by St Louis himself. For the most part it is locked, unless open for a concert. Walk along Rue du Grand-Ferré and the side of the building to admire the Renaissance portal at the other end.

Rue du Général-Leclerc takes us further into the busy shopping thoroughfare of Rue Solférino, where we complete the tour of the centre of Compiègne by walking back to the Town Hall square. Beyond it rises the curious stone tower of the church of Saint-Jacques, Gothic with a classical cupola. Buttresses shore up the aisles of the church. Behind the east end stands the Palais de Justice, in the former Hôtel de la Chancellerie, and if you look north you see a shop known as the Cave Saint-Vincent – one of the few half-timbered houses to have survived in this city.

From here you can follow either Rue des Cordeliers to see the early-fourteenth-century church of Saint-Antoine, or else Rue du Château to visit Compiègne's magnificent château. Built for the most part in the mid-eighteenth century, it became a fashionable residence for the courts of Napoleon Bonaparte and Napoleon III, the latter's Empress Eugénie making their autumn season at Compiègne a social paradise for about seventy guests, each of whom was invited for a week. Dressed in the green uniforms of the court of Louis XIV her guests would hunt stags or indulge in lavish though amateur plays. Their glamour is recalled today in the Musée de l'Impératrice of the palace, as well as in the wing sheltering the Musée du Second Empire. Less exotic but equally interesting is the Musée du Véhicule housed here, whose contents begin with a reconstituted Roman chariot and continue through coaches and bicycles to motor cars.

Just as in a hurry one might ignore the circuitous forest route I
have described from Noyon to Compiègne and simply drive the
fast 25 km route directly from one town to the other, so the
straight route from Compiègne south-west to Senlis is not to be
despised if you want to reach the latter quickly. Our route runs
through the enormous Compiègne forest (which in all covers
some 15,000 hectares) and emerging remains tree-lined as far as
the bustling town of Lacroix-Saint-Ouen. Verberie, the next
town, is situated on the banks of the Oise and is pleasingly
decrepit, save for the splendid Château d'Aramont whose Renaissance façade flanked by simpler classical outhouses can be seen
from the road to the west of the town. Today, like many a French
château, it takes in guests. Verberie's Town Hall occupies a
sixteenth-century royal guard-house. The Carolingian nobility
relished this little town and the countryside surrounding it, building here a palace that has long disappeared, to be survived by the
numerous medieval houses of the old streets. As for the parish
church of Verberie, it dates from the thirteenth and fifteenth
centuries, with a lovely porch from the latter era. The Virgin
Mary stands meekly at the doorway, the sole remaining Gothic
statue of six. Inside at the crossing are polychrome capitals.

Two interesting churches flank this town. Three kilometres
west at Rhuis is one of the oldest Romanesque churches in this
part of France. Built in the eleventh century, it boasts a three-
storeyed belfry and stone tower rising from the north aisle. Inside
is one of the earliest ogival apses in the country, though alas the
church is usually locked. At the other side of Verberie, 1 km
south-east, is Saint-Vaast-de-Longpont, whose very-early-twelfth-
century church has a square belfry topped with a stone *flèche*.
Then from Verberie wind south up into open country to reach
Villeneuve-sur-Verberie. The name of this spot ('new town above
Verberie') was accurate in the late eleventh century. Villeneuve-
sur-Verberie was created as a result of forest clearances, at a time
when the population was increasing and fresh agricultural tech-
niques were being developed to feed many newly born mouths.
Today even its church is ancient, dating from the eleventh and
twelfth centuries, its nave rebuilt in 1510, its two sweet porches
dating one from the twelfth and the other from the fifteenth century.

Far more entrancing than driving straight on to Senlis is to take the signs from Villeneuve-sur-Verberie to Château de Raray. Built at the beginning of the seventeenth century in basically the same style as that at Verberie, this château is far more elaborate, its long central quarter flanked with two segments bearing tall pointed roofs. Again you can see it from the road and on Sundays are welcome to visit the exterior to explore its decorative motifs, which include Diana the huntress and her various victims. Golf too is promoted here. And Château de Raray has become famous because it entranced the poet and film maker Jean Cocteau, inspiring his legendary film *La Belle et la Bête*. Today the village of Raray sports not only a sixteenth-century manor-house, its walls strengthened with a medieval pepperpot tower, but also a Rue Jean-Cocteau. Here are more lovely cottages and walled farms, and the Gothic church at Raray has a little Romanesque tower.

Just as at Noyon church and state were intertwined from the Middle Ages, the same blend can be seen in the architecture of the villages we shall shortly meet, most of them protected both by a fine church and an equally dominating château. These churches include some of the finest rural Gothic buildings in France. To explore them and the châteaux return to the fork outside the village of Raray and veer right, to turn right again at the next crossroads and drive to Néry, where you turn left to see the eighteenth-century château at Béthisy-Saint-Martin. Béthisy-Saint-Martin also boasts a twelfth- and fifteenth-century church, standing like the château in the upper part of the village. The church tower bears a sixteenth-century magnificent spire, and in an inscription over its doorway the dead speak to the living, praying to be forgiven their sins and warning that 'we were like you and you will be like us'.

The Gothic church at Orrouy, 6 km east, is blessed with a Romanesque belfry and houses sixteenth-century Renaissance stained glass. If you are not careful you will miss this church, for the road bypasses the village, which rises to the left. As you are driving up to the church you pass on the right the eighteenth-century Château de la Douye. Now belonging to the commune, its park is open all the time, and parts of the château have been usefully given over to reading rooms, a billiard club, a public library and such like. In some of the village shops you can buy a guide to the marked ramblers' paths that thread through the surrounding countryside. We are also close to some impressive

Gallo-Roman remains, at Champlieu 4 km north of Orrouy. Its baths, a temple and a theatre are open to view in the mornings and afternoons in the summer season (though only from 14.00 to 16.00 for the rest of the year). The handwriting of Viollet-le-Duc characterizes some of the restorations here.

From Orrouy drive on eastwards, crossing the D332 and following the D32. At Fresnoy-la-Rivière a sign points left to Morienval, whose stupendous Benedictine abbey church with its three towers suddenly appears before you. To the left of the main door are deteriorated but still lovely Renaissance panels, with statues of Jesus and the Madonna. The main door is decorated with Renaissance linenfold panels. The interior is a religious box of treat after treat. You descend steps to the original level of the floor. This church, part of a monastery founded by Charles the Bald, has a late-eleventh-century nave, though this was given an ogival vaulting in 1662. The vaulting of the choir, by contrast, dates from 1130. The apse contains a remarkable deambulatory, around which pilgrims would circulate to venerate the bones of St Annobert. Above it five squinting little windows let in more light.

The roof boss above the crossing is sculpted with a seventeenth-century coat of arms, while other, simpler bosses include one bearing the three nails with which Jesus was crucified. As for the furnishings they include choir stalls with misericords, one of which depicts what I take to be a bat. The most extraordinary tomb is that of a recumbant crusader. Florent de Viri de Hangest was killed in 1191, aged only thirty-eight, while fighting on the third crusade at the siege of St John of Ancre. His body, save for his heart, was mummified and brought back here in a lead coffin. Exhumed earlier in our present century, in spite of mummification the corpse had dissolved into a skeleton.

Close by, behind a grille in the north crossing, are a goodly set of works of religious art from many periods. I much like the statue of St James the Great, booted and accompanied by his dog, though his hat is decorated not with the customary cockleshell but with crossed keys and the face of Jesus. There are also a couple of statues of St Sebastian, though the arrows which killed him have dropped out of both of these. Against the north wall are ranged the tombs of abbesses of Morienval.

Return to Fresnoy-la-Rivière, whose Gothic church, though fine, can only be a disappointment after Morienval, and continue

south-east along the D32 to the hamlet of Pondron, with its Romanesque church and its château, a merry affair with turrets, a
stepped gable, brick chimneys, and an ornamental flight of steps
up to its main doorway over which rises a stone balcony. I judge
that this château must be a nineteenth-century pastiche. We are
driving through the valley of the Automne and fine walking
country. High across the valley rises the Gothic belfry of the
church at Bémont. Then appear two unexpected delights. First
you come upon a stupendous church in a garden. The royal
abbey of Notre-Dame-du-Lieu-Restauré is so called because its
twelfth-century church had to be restored after the Wars of Religion. Its church boasts a stunning flamboyant rose window.
Part a ruin, part an archaeological museum, its owners tell you to
wander here at will provided you avoid the dangerous ruined sections.

As you round the next bend the second treat appears. The
château of Vez perches on a cliff, its great keep to the left, its
seigneurial building to the right. Turn right along a narrow road
to look up at its curtain wall and turrets. Unlikely as it may seem,
this road winds up to the village of Vez itself, where a number of
new modest houses have recently sprung up west of the twelfth-
and thirteenth-century church without properly imitating the old
stones of the village. Drive through Vez and wind down back to
the D32 past the château walls. Fortified in the fourteenth century,
built mostly two centuries earlier, Château de Vez owes its present
sparkling look chiefly to a restoration by a pupil of Viollet-le-
Duc.

It is time to cross the valley, for we are on the edge of the
département of the Aisne. A country road (the D2) which we come
upon at the bottom of the hill out of Vez will take us the $3\frac{1}{2}$ km to
Vauciennes, winding up past the hamlet of Saint-Mord with its
gabled houses, farms and fourteenth-century turreted manor-
house. The woods give way to a fertile plateau, and then we reach
the N2 and the malodorous manufactory of Vauciennes (which
nonetheless boasts a thirteenth-century church a little further
east). Turn right (in the direction of Paris) and then fork right
along the N324 for Crépy-en-Valois.

Here is another British connection, for the first church you see
as you enter the town is the ruined Saint-Thomas-de-Canterbury,
dedicated to Archbishop Thomas à Becket after his murder in the

Canterbury cathedral. It stands outside the town walls and ceased to be a church in 1793. Thirteen years later the beautiful church was mostly demolished. Over the door you can still see inscribed the creed of the Revolution: '*Le Peuple Français Reconnoie l'Être Suprême et l'Immortalité de l'Âme.*' (The French people believe in the Supreme Being and the Immortality of the Soul.) Now the church is fronted by a pretty little park.

Bear right to reach the ramparts and the remains of the old château, whose great hall now houses a curious combination: the Musée Valois de l'Art Religieux and a museum of archery. Crépy-en-Valois is a complex town, but close together near the château you can see three buildings which all reveal the extreme peril brought by the Revolution to religious architecture. The church of Saint-Thomas, like that of Saint-Thomas-de-Canterbury, was sold at the Revolution but was fortunately brought back into use in 1802 and thus escaped demolition. It had already lost its spire, so a new one was built in 1850. At its west end, to the left of the square, rise the former abbey buildings and excavations of Saint-Arnoul, founded in the eleventh century and left to rot after 1793. Much has been restored, and today you can visit its early-twelfth-century crypt, part of the thirteenth-century cloister and what remains of the fourteenth-century church. Then pass through the city walls to find a sixteenth-century towered house followed by the thirteenth-century door-way of the former Ursuline convent. Sold at the Revolution it became for a time a calico factory.

Wind on into Place Gambetta with its lime trees and stately houses. Should you wish to spend more time at Crépy-en-Valois, the tourist office (in Rue de Soissons) offers lists of local *gîtes*, as well as details of campsites and hotels. The same tourist office organizes walks and cycle tours of the whole region. Crépy-en-Valois has an exquisite park, with a couple of lakes on which swim swans and wild ducks. When these have sufficiently en-tranced you, at the far corner of Place Gambetta a sign points the way to Senlis. As you leave Crépy-en-Valois you pass between two tall pillars, all that remains from the Porte de Paris of 1758. Senlis is a mere 20 km away.

Senlis is an intimate city, softly lit in the evening. I looked out of my window at the Hostellerie de la Porte Bellon across to another ancient house illuminated by the yellow glass of a lantern.

Then I went down to the bar to sip a Colvert, one of Picardy's tangiest beers, stronger than most Strasbourg beers and brewed at Péronne by Declerck and Co. Food in Picardy is entirely satisfying, though I do not pretend that it embodies the subtleties of those dishes of Périgord, the part of France where I have chosen to live. Picardy meals are sturdy, and Colvert beer is sturdy enough to match them. Refreshed after my *rognons de veau* described as *normande* (which means cooked in cream), I strolled up Rue Bellon to find at no. 15 the imposing gateway of the eighteenth-century Hôtel Dufresnoy, where Marshal Foch and his aide General Weygand chose to stay in November 1918, in preparation for the armistice which ended the First World War.

Rue Bellon meets Rue du Chancelier, where you climb up past half-timbered houses to reach the cathedral square of Senlis, the Place Notre-Dame. We owe its lovely building to Bishop Thibaut, who in the mid-twelfth century began rebuilding a church on the site of many earlier ones. The new cathedral was solemnly consecrated on 16 June 1191. Although many devout men and women enriched the cathedral over the following centuries (sometimes out of necessity, as after a dreadful fire of 1504, and after the mutilation of the west end during the Revolution), the south side which we first see represents French Gothic architecture at its earliest and, as one might put it, purest – save for the swirls of the crossing, built by Jean Dizieult and Pierre Chambiges in the late flamboyant style after the 1504 fire.

The statues of two persons who generously helped to pay for the rebuilding, King Louis XII and Queen Anne of Brittany, were unceremoniously thrown from their niches on either side of the doorway at the Revolution. God the Father still stands atop the gable. You enter a complex spot, enriched with hanging pendentives and sixteenth-century glass. In a south chapel of the transept a fourteenth-century Madonna carries an infant who has lost his head. Walk on to the crossing to admire round pillars which alternate with more elaborate ones, the latter rising to the ceiling and dividing the cathedral into three elegant aisles. Wait long enough to accustom your eyes to the darkness created by the modern blue glass of Senlis cathedral in order to admire the delicate capitals and roof bosses. As these bosses near the west end they grow more complex, for the cathedral was built westwards and the masons flexed their artistic muscles as the years passed.

Much of the lower nave dates from the twelfth century, the upper from the sixteenth. The eighteenth-century organ came from the former abbey of Saint-Vincent in Picardy. As for the choir, it soars in thirteenth-century splendour.

Then walk around the deambulatory, beginning in the south aisle. A Romanesque font and a fifteenth-century statue of the Virgin Mary weeping over the corpse of her Son are but two of the treasures on display here. On the right steps rise to one of the oldest parts of the cathedral, a chapel whose thirteenth-century arches are as simple and excellent as one could ask for. The chapel was frescoed with paintings of St Stephen and St Denis a hundred years later and now houses medieval statues, including St Roch (who is for ever scratching his bad leg) and my own patron the pilgrim St James the Great. The saint with a spade is the Irishman Fiacre, who died around the year 670 and has been adopted as patron of gardeners and Parisian cab drivers.

Flamboyant Gothic chapels now radiate around the apse. The easternmost chapel is bizarre. In 1847, quite voluntarily, the canons decided to demolish their ancient twelfth-century chapel and rebuild it in the nineteenth-century Gothic style. I have to confess that I like the little dragons which climb its pillars, as well as the fourteenth-century statue of the Virgin Mary which once adorned the nearby abbey of Sainte-Victoire. Our amble continues around the deambulatory to relish especially the ogival chapel of St Rieul, whose shrine encloses the relics of the first bishop of Senlis. Soon a plaque appears reminding us that on 15 August 1429, Joan of Arc led an army which defeated the troops of the duke of Bedford on Senlis plain and also stayed in the city from 23 April to 25 April the following year. As you reach the steps leading into the sixteenth-century chapter house you notice the rich hanging bosses of the vaults above, as well as a late-sixteenth-century statue of St Barbara. This fourth-century virgin and martyr holds the tower in which she lived while her savage father was away from home.

Then leave the cathedral to enjoy the superb west façade. Once Senlis cathedral boasted two virtually identical spires. The north one rises simply from its square base. From a similarly square base the south spire grows more and more elaborate as its architects drew their inspiration from that at Chartres. It hangs four early-nineteenth-century bells, which ring out in tonic sol fa the notes 're', 'mi', 'fa sharp' and 'so'. Traditional elements appear too: a tree of Jesse carries Old Testament sages, John the Baptist, Moses, Samuel, Abraham, Jeremiah, Simeon carrying baby Jesus, and David all make their appearance. The seasons of the year are depicted: sowing, harvest, killing a pig and the rest. All this pales beside a revolutionary concept which inspired the carving above the doorway, for what makes the west end of Senlis cathedral remarkable is its depiction of the triumph of the Blessed Virgin Mary. When these twelfth-century statues were being carved, the impassioned preaching of St Bernard of Clairvaux had raised the Adoration of the mother of Jesus to an extraordinary peak. As our faithful authority, Alban Butler of Saint-Omer, put it:

St Bernard was particularly devoted to the Blessed Virgin, as his works sufficiently declare. In one of his missions into Germany, being in the great church at Spire [Speyer], he repeated thrice in a rapture, 'O merciful! O pious! O gracious Virgin Mary!' which words the church added to the anthem Salve Regina.

For the first time in Christian iconography the power of St Bernard's word was translated at Senlis into a carved image that would be repeated again and again in Christendom. In depicting the mother of Jesus the west portal shows first her falling asleep. Then she is assumed into heaven (the first such depiction on a central tympanum), where as never before she is shown enthroned on the same level as her divine Son, albeit receiving his blessing. The triumph of the Virgin at Senlis is revolutionary both theologically and iconographically.

Before enjoying more of the cathedral, we surely must pause to relish the ensemble of buildings amid which we are standing. The west end looks over the brick-and-stone staircase tower of the twelfth- and sixteenth-century Hôtel du Vermandois and the gates of the splendid park of the Château Royal. To the right across Place Notre-Dame you can see the window, arcades and a blocked-up arch of the former episcopal chapel, which dates from 1221. The charming building adjoining it no longer houses the bishop of Senlis but instead the city's museum of art and archaeology. If you walk along Rue du Châtel to the south-west of the cathedral square you discover that the Château Royal abuts on to the sixteenth-century Hôtel des Trois Pots, the emblem of three jars set into its wall. Today this *hôtel* and part of the Château Royal have been transformed into a museum of hunting.

Walking the other way, around the north side of the cathedral of Notre-Dame, you find the north doorway carved with the salamander of King François I (who greatly enriched this cathedral) above a statue of his confessor Bishop Guillaume Parvi, who also taught the royal children. Here a little garden fronts the north façade of a former bishop's palace. It rises from a twelfth-century base, includes a Gallo-Roman tower and rises to Renaissance pilasters. The view from here of the gargoyles of the cathedral and especially of the forest of buttresses is thrilling. The Gothic church of Saint-Pierre appears on the right as you walk on, the gable of its west end rising far higher than the roof behind it. Its doorway is flanked by a couple of flamboyant porches, each with its own gable. As you continue around the church, enjoying the tracery of the windows, the north tower and spire come into view, the sole remaining twelfth-century elements of this building. The austere classical building on its right is the façade of the city library, built in the eighteenth century as a seminary.

Walk on down Rue Saint-Hilaire. The Romanesque apse of the church of Saint-Frambourg appears on the right. Saint-Frambourg was once a royal chapel, built in the last decade of the tenth century for Queen Adelaide in thanksgiving for the accession to the Frankish throne of her husband Hugues Capet in 987. Louis VII rebuilt the church in 1177. When T. F. Bumpus visited Senlis at the beginning of the twentieth century, Saint-Frambourg had been deconsecrated and adapted as a carriage repository, having previously served as a barracks for cuirassiers. (As he gazed one morning on the apse from where we are standing, its semicircular sweep seemed to him 'to compose a picture truly enchanting, standing out as it did against a sky of purest blue'.) Then, exactly 800 years after Louis VII rebuilt it, the church was given back its dignity and transformed into a concert hall, the Auditorium Franz Liszt. Its west façade preserves an intact and beautiful Romanesque porch.

Beyond the apse of Saint-Frambourg you reach what I regard as one of the most rapturous (though unpretentious) squares in Picardy. The cobbled Place de la Halle at Senlis is a long triangle ending in a stepped gable. It includes no major buildings, but every one plays its part in infiltrating one's heart with pleasure.

They enclose little shops and bars: a *charcuterie*, a pharmacist, newsagents, a bookshop, a restaurant and a brasserie, an optician, a fruit and vegetable shop, the ancient stones of the restaurant La Licorne. Their upper storeys are of all shapes and sizes. You can make out from their ends that once many were half-timbered and others held together in the past with wattle and daub. On either side the walls undulate slightly. The traiteur has crammed his window with white puddings, *foie gras de canard*, quails, *bouchées à la reine* and lashings of *ficelle picarde*. The fish shop opens out on to the street. A beautician, a florist, a perfume emporium, a Normandy butcher next to a purveyor of horse meat, a wine merchant, a cake, chocolate and coffee shop fail to exhaust the bustling establishments of this little corner of Senlis. If you look around the corner of the café-bar along Rue Saint-Jean you see in a niche a statue of the Madonna and her Child. In the evening the square is bathed in a gentle yellow light, and the shops stay open till late.

Rue de la Porte-au-Pain leads from here into another delicious square, the Place Henri IV. A bust of this king peers quizzically down from the façade of the Hôtel de Ville (which was built in 1498), with the legend (taken from his charter of 1590):

MON HEUR A PRINS SON COMMENCEMENT
EN LA VILLE DE SENLIS
DONT IL S'EST DEPUIS SEMÉ
ET AUGMENTÉ PAR TOUT NOTRE ROYAUME.

[My happiness was born
in the town of Senlis
and from there has disseminated
and increased throughout our kingdom.]

From the far corner of this triangular square take Rue de Beauvais, which starts off on the left with a couple of eleventh-century houses. One of them bizarrely retains its letter-box, while being otherwise completely blocked up. Soon you reach the church of Saint-Aignan which boasts a Romanesque tower, the rest fifteenth century save for a monumental seventeenth-century porch and doorway stuck on to the north side. For the most part we are enjoying a walk along a Renaissance and classical street, and the little tower we come across next once belonged to a sixteenth-century *hôtel*. The houses are ennobled by fine gateways. Place

Gérard-de-Nerval opens out on the left, plane trees shading its
parked cars. Across the road a bronze, declining head of Gérard
de Nerval himself adorns a garden. The face of this dissipated and
inconsolable poet exactly matches the inscription underneath,
which is taken from his '*El Desdichado*':

> *Je suis le ténébreux*
> *Le veuf*
> *L'inconsolé.*

> [I am the gloomy one
> The widower
> The inconsolable.]

This is the celebrated poem in which de Nerval goes on to
describe himself as the imprisoned prince of Aquitaine whose
guiding star is extinguished and whose lute is burdened with
melancholy. Yet the suicidal Nerval perfectly evoked the magic of
the old streets of Senlis in his '*Sylvie*'.

The square in which his bust has been set up is far from
melancholy; its classical houses are superbly balanced. Throughout our tour glimpses of the remarkably well-preserved Gallo-
Roman walls of Senlis have served as a reminder that the city is
ancient. Rue de Beauvais continues from Place Gérard-de-Nerval
to end at the Place des Arènes where, across a grassy square, you
find yourself in the city's arena. Opened up in 1863, these first-
century AD Roman remains were excavated in 1863 and can
be visited almost every day in the year. Ten thousand spectators
once crammed into this elliptical arena. The temple of Hercules
has been excavated, niches still visible in which statues of pagan
gods and goddesses once stood.

The former ramparts of Senlis are now marked by the boulevards which surround the city and stretch away south-east from
the arena towards the well-restored twelfth-century collegiate
church of Saint-Vincent, with its late-seventeenth-century cloister. To regain the centre of Senlis more easily (and more picturesquely), walk back to Place Gérard-de-Nerval and turn left
past his bust, noting the magnificent classical gateway and house
ahead. Half-way up this street a road runs off to the right, taking
you to the Rue des Vétérans. Follow the curve of the ancient
houses of Rue des Vétérans left as far as a T-junction, where you

turn left once more. Ahead rises the clinic of Saint-Joseph, and as you approach it, the Gallo-Roman fortifications appear again, along with another gateway of the Château Royal. Rue du Chat-Harêt, which runs on past the clinic, offers a yet more entrancing view, across the Jardin du Roy to the Château Royal, to the cathedral and to a tower of the crumbling fortifications, decorated by the Gallo-Romans with brick bands and arches. The lovely sixteenth-century house at no. 4 in this street once housed a privileged cathedral canon. If you turn right at the end of Rue Chat-Harêt you pass another church and another section of the Gallo-Roman wall to find yourself back in the cobbled cathedral square.

Arriving at Senlis one autumn, Gérard de Nerval wrote, 'I passed through the most beautiful and sombre land that one could ever see at that time of the year. The ruddy tint of the oak trees and the trembling of the dark green of the grass, the white trunks of the silver birches, all this rose amidst the heath and the brushwood.' He added that at Senlis he had yet to meet an ugly woman. As for the environs of the city, he adored the forests of Chantilly, Compiègne and Ermenonville, and the woods of Châalis, especially when the sun was setting, a time when far-away châteaux, their towers usually reduced to pigeon houses, peered through the dusk. As he walked through the red leaves and brown pine trees on the way towards the château of Mont-l'Évêque his Sylvain sang him a rhyme learnt from the local peasants:

> *Courage! mon ami, courage!*
> *Nous voici près du village!*
> *A la première maison,*
> *Nous nous rafraîchirons!*

> [Keep your spirits up, my friend!
> We're close to the village!
> There at the first house
> We'll sup!]

So they did, Nerval recorded, on a humble wine that was not disagreeable for someone on a journey. Their hostess, noticing that they were unshaven, concluded that they were artists and therefore bound for the abbey of Châalis.

So are we, but not till the end of this tour of the Oise. To make one of the most delightful round trips of all those described in this book, drive north from Senlis through the Halatte forest to Fleurines. Here in the central square opposite the Town Hall a tiny fruit and flower market sets itself up every Sunday morning, the fruit merchants lining up their stalls in one continuous stretch along the south side of the church. Rising from the same side of this church is a powerful tower, with but one opening save for the doorway. The church interior is as spruce as anyone could wish. Its single aisle exactly matches the dimensions of the nave. The stained glass, created by the Parisian firm of Avenat in 1891, depicts St Hubert in the forest through which we have been driving. Though he is the patron saint of hunters, Hubert is depicted preventing a dog from savaging a stag which bears a crucifix between its horns. In the next window (glazed by the same firm) St Gilles is sheltering a hunted deer from its persecutors. Heaven knows, such poor beasts need some protection from the avid huntsmen of the Oise. Speaking of game reminds me that at Fleurines Mme Yan Nivet of *Le Vieux Logis* is rightly proud of her traditionally cooked veal kidneys (or *rognons de veau gael*).

A little further on, before you have left the village, you come upon a sign pointing right to the hilltop village of Saint-Christophe. Unless you wish to become depressed I urge you not to follow it, for the village houses a vast thirteenth-century priory church no doubt haunted by the shades of the Cluniac monks who once worshipped here and now ruined and open to the elements. As compensation I should add that this is superb walking and riding country.

Drive on north-east as far as Pont-Sainte-Maxence, with its 1920s Town Hall and a flamboyant Gothic church whose unfinished Renaissance tower is so huge that it seems to be planning to take over the whole building. The lady after whom Pont-Sainte-Maxence is named was an Irish saint martyred on this spot in the fifth century. The bridge across the river brought the town prosperity, for this became one of the main crossings on the route from Flanders to Paris. Pont-Sainte-Maxence boasts not only some fine sixteenth-century houses but also subterranean caves inhabited till the recent past, some of them with fourteenth-century vaulting.

Our aim is to reach Creil, and we should therefore turn left at

the river (the Oise), but first I recommend a diversion to the
right, following the sign which directs us just outside Pont-Sainte-
Maxence to the royal abbey of Moncel at nearby Pontpoint.
Philip the Fair founded the abbey in 1309. Its church and most of
the cloister were pulled down in 1795, but much remains, evoking
the long-gone life of the followers of St Francis known as the Poor
Clares: the vaulted cellars; the chapter house whose vaults rise
from a central octagonal pillar; the refectory, with fourteenth-
century frescos and the pulpit from which one of the sisters would
read improving works or passages of holy Scripture while the rest
ate; the kitchen, whose massive seventeenth-century chimney is
decorated with a plaque depicting St Clare's patron, St Francis,
receiving the stigmata. You can visit the abbey daily from 09.00
to noon and from 14.00 to 19.00, save in August.

Pontpoint church is Romanesque, its simple ogival apse slightly
out of true, with a stone belfry topped by a stone pyramid. The
arches in the north chapel are even simpler. Those in the south
crossing rise from a lovely central pillar whose capital is decorated
with oak leaves. From the village return now to Pont-Sainte-
Maxence and continue along the D120 to Beaurepaire, with its
moated château, built here in the thirteenth century and continually extended until the eighteenth. Skirting the Halatte forest our
route now follows the valley of the Oise by way of Verneuil-en-
Halatte, whose church was begun in the twelfth century, though
it was partly rebuilt in the fifteenth and sixteenth centuries. Its
tower is as pretty as its fifteenth-century porch. Nearby are
the remains of a Renaissance château. Then, still flanking the
river, we reach the busy and sizeable town of Creil (the second
urban centre in Picardy). Here you can watch the long barges
plying the wide Oise. The unexpected treats of this industrial town
include the museum in its late-eighteenth-century Hôtel de Ville
(itself built on the Gothic cellars of the former château) and the
thirteenth-century church of Saint-Médard whose tower, added
in the sixteenth century and embellished by squatting lions, has a
spire rising to a height of 31 m. Creil boasted a celebrated ceramic
factory from 1797 until it closed down in 1895. Many of its
ceramics today enhance the collections of the discerning and rich.
You can admire some of them here in the Musée Gallé-Juillet.

Drive north-west from Creil through Nogent-sur-Oise to
Clermont-en-Beauvaisis. Although the château at Nogent was

almost completely rebuilt in the nineteenth century, it retains the charming Renaissance medallions of its predecessor. The thirteenth-century cemetery church well merits a visit, its treasures including the shrines of St Brigid and St Maure, two Irish virgins martyred in the fifth century, and a statue of Jean Bardeau, who kneels on his tomb, sculpted in 1632 by Michel Bourdin.

Tumbling down its hill which was once a Gaulish *oppidum*, Clermont-en-Beauvaisis (which entered written history in 1023) has seen a long and often vicious history. It received its civic charter from Count Louis of Blois in 1197, but charters never stopped the covetous and strong forcing their authority on humbler citizens. The medieval château of the counts was as much a symbol of their domination as of their desire to protect their subjects. In consequence in 1358 the revolt of the poor against their oppressors which is known as the *jacquerie* proved particularly violent here. The following year King Charles the Bad of Navarre took on and defeated the army of the *jacquerie*. The king invited the leader of the insurgents to parley with him in the town, and then arrested him and put him to death. His followers were massacred.

A year later Captal de Buch took control of Clermont and set about encircling it with walls. Three parts of his fortifications survive to this day: the Porte de Nointel, the Tour des Gloriettes, and the west façade of the Town Hall. These fortifications proved strong enough to deter the English in their attempt to take Clermont in 1420. Clermont was less fortunate during the Wars of Religion. Declaring for the Catholics the town was taken by the troops of Henri IV and pillaged for seventeen days. And if in more modern times the Franco-Prussian war and the First World War proved disastrous for Clermont, her sufferings in the Second World War were more murderous than ever, as witness the sad list of names on her war memorial.

Today on Saturdays a peaceful market straggles down the hillside into the triangular town square. It is best, I think, to drive up to the top of the hill and park in front of the thirteenth-century church of Saint-Samson, most of which was rebuilt in the mid-fifteenth century after a fire in 1436. Another fire at the end of the eighteenth century burnt down the tower, which had to be rebuilt a second time. I very much like the sixteenth-century stained glass in the choir. The east window depicts Jacob's dream, angels sliding up a ladder into heaven, the patriarch wrapped in a blushing red cloak. Drive around the north side of the church and through the narrow, fourteenth-century Porte de Nointel. Rue du Donjon runs off left into the park, which embraces the tree-shaded Promenade du Châtelier with its magnificent views, as well as the eleventh-century keep and some of the ancient walls of the former château of Clermont.

Clermont-en-Beauvaisis is twinned with Sudbury in Suffolk which, I think, gets the best of the bargain. Its Rue de la République houses the Town Hall, built in 1359 after the first fire and ornamented with statues of St Louis, his son Robert de Clermont, and Charles IV the Fair who was born in this town in 1294. Drive back to the main road (the N31) and travel west to reach Agnetz (which lies just off the main road), where the twelfth-century church, extended over the next 200 years, is full of minor masterpieces of religious art. The N31 emerges from the forest of Hez at La Neuville-en-Hez, where you can indulge in horse-riding and rambling. La Neuville-en-Hez is one long street, save for its church, whose belfry dates from the twelfth century and whose choir dates from the fifteenth.

Five kilometres further the twelfth-century apse of the parish church of La Rue-Saint-Pierre appears in a field on the left, its Romanesque porch lovely, its simple Romanesque tower no more than a wall with a couple of holes to carry bells. Bresles, 3½ km further west, boasts a church with a Carolingian nave and an eighteenth-century Hôtel de Ville which once was a retreat of the bishops of Beauvais. In spite of such delights and the fact that we are almost at enchanting Beauvais, please turn off the main road to call at Therdonne. Among the brick houses of the village are a couple of half-timbered ones. Ahead, just outside Therdonne, rises the elaborate apse of its cemetery church. Once surrounded by a village (named Saint-Ouen), the church alone survived a fire in the eighteenth century. It was begun in the twelfth century, but much modified subsequently. Its nave, simpler than the apse, is flanked on one side by a Romanesque tower which was actually built in 1674. Inside, I know, is a fourteenth-century statue of the Madonna and Child and a sixteenth-century statue of St Ouen, but I have never seen them. After all, one cannot hang around waiting for a funeral to get inside a normally locked church; and even if one does, it is impolite to wander around during the obsequies.

From this remarkable spot you can drive straight on into
Beauvais, provided that you take care to make a sharp turn right
outside Therdonne just beyond the church.

In spite of such massive destruction during the last war that
almost the entire ancient quarter disappeared, Beauvais displays
in its two mighty churches the spiritual effect of medieval wealth.
Flanking the River Thérain on which the city rises, woollen mills
multiplied in the Middle Ages. From as early as the eleventh
century this ancient stronghold, the former capital of the Bellovaci
tribe whom Caesar successfully put down, began to grow rich on
the cloth trade. Its first bishop was installed in 1015, and his
successors became great temporal as well as ecclesiastical lords.

In 1664, two years after Colbert had founded the state tapestry
factory at Gobelins, the citizens of Beauvais had begun making
tapestry too. They used a different technique from the Gobelins
workshops, weaving on looms with horizontal as opposed to
vertical warp. Alas, this seventeenth-century factory was bombed
out of existence by the Germans in June 1940, along with more
than 2,000 old houses, many of them half-timbered and dating
from the same era as the tapestry works. To see the ones that
survived, in Rue Racine, Rue du Tournebroche, Rue de l'École,
Rue du Chant and Rue de la Banque is a poignant reminder of
what has been lost.

Events were often turbulent here long before 1940. Philippe-
Auguste had fortified Beauvais in 1190, which enabled the city to
repulse Edward III fifty-six years later. By contrast the bishops of
Beauvais usually allied with the dukes of Burgundy and the
English, a policy which rarely had the support of the citizens. The
most notorious of these bishops, Pierre Cauchon, who was responsible for the execution of Joan of Arc, put the city in the
hands of the English around 1420. Poor Cauchon has always had
a bad press. Would he ever have exclaimed, as George Bernard
Shaw had him do in his play *Saint Joan*, that 'The heretic is
always better dead,' and that 'mortal eyes cannot distinguish the
saint from the heretic'? To quote Shaw again, did Joan, like
Socrates, really combine 'terrifying ability with a frankness, personal modesty, and benevolence which made the furious dislike to
which they fell victim absolutely unreasonable'? Whatever our
answer, her contemporaries at Beauvais had little time for her
persecutor. Nine years after Joan's death his supposed subjects

forced the bishop into exile at Rouen. The same century was made glorious at Beauvais by the ferocious patriotism of other women. When Charles the Bold and 80,000 men besieged Beauvais in 1472, the wives and daughters of the city, led by Jeanne Laîne whose nickname was Hachette (which means hatchet), seized the enemy's standard and rallied the city's defenders.

As you arrive at Beauvais the unmistakable contours of the cathedral of Saint-Pierre rise ahead. Saint-Pierre remains one of the most daring buildings in northern France. The architects who in 1227 began building the present cathedral under the rule of Bishop Milan de Nanteuil intended to create the largest Gothic church ever built. Their aim over-reached their skill. The choir was vaulted in 1272. Twelve years later it fell down. Patiently the builders began again, reinforcing the bulwarks of the choir with immense buttresses, adding more pillars, until by the outbreak of the Hundred Years War in 1337 the new structure was virtually complete. Already it was the tallest church in France.

No one attempted to finish the rest till the beginning of the sixteenth century. Beauvais was served by this gigantic choir and by the little Carolingian church which its nave was intended to replace. In 1500 the architect Martin Chambiques began building the transepts, and his work was continued in 1532 by Michel de Laliet. Daring again bred architectural arrogance when in 1550 Jean Vast decided to build over the new crossing the highest church belfry imaginable. Its *flèche* rose over the tower to a height of 158 m. On the feast of the Ascension in 1573 both *flèche* and tower crumbled. Instead of turning to the nave, the architects of Beauvais were obliged to rebuild the transepts. Finally the grandiose plans for the nave were abandoned, and the west end was closed up. It remains a concrete blank, the daring buttresses and tiles around it unable to conceal a fantastic failure.

Beauvais cathedral remains remarkable, by no means simply for its height. The façades of the crossings must instantly impress any visitor. Dating as we have seen only from the first half of the sixteenth century, they are masterpieces of French flamboyant Gothic architecture. Their statues disappeared at the Revolution, but their sinuous tracery, especially that of the rose window in the south façade, and the fantastic clusters of embellishment, growing all the more elaborate as your eye reaches the gable and the crocketed pinnacles, is so outrageously daring that I find myself

increasingly impatient with the remarkable number of com-
mentators who seem obsessed with the notion that the failure to
complete this cathedral was a punishment for some sort of hubris
on the part of its builders.

The exquisite early Renaissance sculptures on the doors are
by Jean Le Pot, those on the south door (alas partly damaged by
bombs) depicting episodes in the lives of St Peter and St Paul, the
four doctors of the church and the four evangelists. That of St
Paul's conversion is my favourite here, the saint tumbling helpless
from his horse, a symbol of his helpless resistance to the Christian
gospel. The sculptures on the north door are in much better
condition, less animated but still entrancing, every figure on the
door wearing subtly curving robes, and a tree of Jesse culminating
in the salamander symbol of the French royal family – a testimony
to the generosity of François I to this cathedral.

The cathedral statues were not the sole sufferers at Beauvais
at the time of the Revolution. When that devout Britisher T. F.
Bumpus revisited the city at the beginning of this century, he
recorded how, among the curios brought together in the museum
hard by the cathedral, he

regarded with melancholy interest a fair embroidered mitre. It belonged
to F. de La Rochefoucauld, Bishop of Beauvais at the time of the
Revolution, who with his brother, the Bishop of Saintes, the venerable
Dulau, Archbishop of Arles, and nearly two hundred non-juring
ecclesiastics of every grade, so bravely met death at the hands of a horde
of hired ruffians in the convent of the Carmelites at Paris on the night of
2 September 1792.

Their crime was to refuse in 1790 to accept the Civil Constitution
of the Clergy, reluctantly signed by Louis XVI, which would
have deprived the Pope of his temporal power in France and
subjected the church to the state. For this La Rochefoucauld and
eighty or so other bishops, along with countless parish priests,
were forced out of their sees and livings. In spite of their bishop's
example and the fact that Pope Pius VI had condemned the
demand that all French clergy swear an oath to the new Civil
Constitution, most of the clergy in La Rochefoucauld's diocese
did take it. In spite of their capitulation, their diocese was suppressed in 1801 and not restored till 1817.

Albeit of several different styles, the interior lives up to one's

first taste of the glamour of Beauvais cathedral. In spite of lacking
a nave, it stretches a breathtaking 72½ m from the west end to the
apse. As you enter, the birds in the glass of the rose window of the
north transept display their plumage, a stunning introduction to
the rest. Yet this is not the finest stained glass in Beauvais cathedral. In 1582 Engrand Le Prince designed the glass in the chapel
of the Sacré-Coeur to illustrate stories from the life of Jesus as well
as St Hubert and St Christopher. Glowing red at its heart, this
glass explodes in bursts of yellows and blues.

Whereas the choir itself, with its exquisite windows and extremely slender tracery, dates from the thirteenth century and the
transepts from the early sixteenth, the south aisle, swept away by
the collapse of 1573, had to be rebuilt in the next quarter of a
century. Most of the glorious sixteenth-century stained glass was
put away for safe-keeping in 1939, to be brought back after the
war. In the rose window of the south crossing the artist has shown
God creating the world, as well as stories from the Old Testament.
We know the names of some of the artists. The glass in the
galleries of the south crossing (depicting the prophets, St Peter
and St Paul, the four evangelists and four doctors of the church)
was made by Nicolas Le Prince in 1551.

Before enjoying the windows and splendid lines of the choir,
most of us are drawn to the extraordinary astronomical clock of
Beauvais. Built in the 1860s by a brilliant engineer from Beauvais
named A.-L. Vérité, this entertaining device which tells the time
of several world cities (including Beauvais), gives information
about the movements of the planets and the seas and tells out
both the secular and the ecclesiastical calendars, is built up of
more than 90,000 parts. Christ sits in judgement at the top of the
clock, and the scene of the Last Judgement is played out five
times in the afternoon. Such is its intrinsic merriment that one
forgets the sombre message of this clock. Its complexities ought
not to blind one to the cunning of another clock nearby, made in
the sixteenth century and topped with a little bell, nor to the
beauties of the sixteenth-century *pietà*.

Although John Ruskin probably went too far in judging that,
'There are few rocks, even among the Alps, that have a clear
vertical fall as high as the choir of Beauvais', his enthusiasm was
certainly pardonable. It rises for 48 m and extends east for
nearly 37 m. Glass dating from the fourteenth to the sixteenth

centuries fills its windows. That in the easternmost window depicts Christ crucified, while his twelve Apostles flank him in the six windows on either side. Look too for two lovely thirteenth-century stained-glass windows in the chapel of Notre-Dame, the gift of two of the medieval guilds of the city.

The cathedral still boasts its cloister, filled with medieval and Renaissance fragments of sculpture, with a chapter house sheltering a Renaissance *pietà* painted on wood. But the most remarkable and ultimately pleasing result of the continual crumbling of this great building is that where the projected Gothic nave should be lie the remains of the earlier cathedral, a rare Romanesque building of the very late tenth century (save for its thirteenth-century south porch). By contrast with the choir of this cathedral, this '*basse-oeuvre*' as it is called measures no more than 28 m in length, and is but 22 m wide and 27 m high. The pattern of its window is at once simple and delicate.

Beside the cathedral sits the powerfully fortified gateway of the former Palais de Justice. This palace has a long history. A Romanesque tower remains from the former fortress which the counts of Beauvais built on the old Gallo-Roman wall. By the early eleventh century the bishops of Beauvais had already claimed it for themselves, and one of them, Simon de Clermont, built the gateway and its couple of pepperpot towers in 1306. Walk across the garden to a complete contrast, the exquisite Renaissance building that Louis de Villiers de L'Isle-Adam constructed as his episcopal palace after the previous one had been sacked by the Burgundians in 1572. A polygonal staircase tower, gaily decorated dormer windows, part of the chapel and a round tower which becomes a belfry help to make up this façade. Arcades rise to the left and a Gothic fountain spouts in the middle of the garden. Since 1972 the palace has housed the Musée du Département de l'Oise. If you go inside you find that the Renaissance architecture is a skin stretched around the Gothic. The treasures of the museum include a statue of St Barbara by Jean Le Pot and a splendid sixteenth-century tapestry depicting a mythical history of the Gauls. Another room is devoted to the rare and brilliant mannerist works of Antoine Caron. Court painter to Catherine de Medici (Henry II's queen), he had learnt his skills from the Italian master Francesco Primaticcio. The gallery is also proud of the art nouveau and art deco collections which it houses, all created by comparatively unknown artists of the Oise such as Max Blondat, Maurice Denis and August Delaherche.

To the south of the cathedral, in Rue Saint-Pierre, stands France's Galerie Nationale de la Tapisserie, housed in an ugly little building. To mention but one group of superb pieces of work inside, the weavers produced a charming series of illustrations to the fables of La Fontaine, designed in the first half of the eighteenth century by the local artist Jean-Baptiste Oudry. Behind this museum you can see the remains of the Gallo-Roman wall which once guarded the city. This corner of the wall is today guarded by a statue of one of France's three greatest dramatists, Jean Racine, who in the 1620s was a pupil at the college of Beauvais for no more than three years. Rue Racine, which stretches from his statue along the north side of the cathedral, is precious for being lined with some of the few half-timbered medieval houses of Beauvais. I should very much like to have seen the half-timbered one which Victor Hugo described in a letter to his wife, its walls decorated with what he described as the most curious painted ceramics and pottery in the world.

Across the street from the museum of tapestry, the ruins of the sixteenth-century church of Saint-Barthélémy have been intelligently adapted as a branch of the city tourist office (dispensing its information from April to September). Beyond it Rue Saint-Pierre becomes an inexpensive but attractive shopping street, with graceful lamps and a bronze fountain. As you walk along it, if you glance left along Rue de la Taillerie you glimpse the tower of the church of Saint-Étienne. Turn right at the fountain to reach the huge Place Jeanne-Hachette, now the centre of the city. Only those who visit this spot in January enjoy the carrousel whose prancing horses arrive promptly half-way through the month and as promptly disappear. Jeanne Hachette's statue, sculpted by Vital Dubray, was set up at the heart of this square in 1851 and today stands over a modern fountain. I have met women like her and decidedly fear them. Hachette wields a battle axe in one hand and clutches a standard in the other. On the last Sunday of June this square and the streets surrounding it are the scene of the annual festival of Jeanne Hachette, with colourful processions, the participants wearing medieval costumes. At the far end of the square stands the Hôtel de Ville, the classical pilasters and balustrades of

its mid-eighteenth-century façade having survived the Second
World War.

Take Rue Desgroux to the right of the Town Hall and walk
further south to find the partly Romanesque, partly flamboyant
Gothic church of Saint-Étienne. From the outside the nave and
transept of the church remain as they were built in the twelfth
century. Inside they house early-Gothic vaulting. As for the
choir, built between 1506 and 1522 it exudes all the magic of
French flamboyant Gothic. Before going inside walk round the
building to admire the gabled north crossing with its wheel of
fortune (with carved human beings rising and falling around it)
and the greatly decayed but still fragrant thirteenth-century west
façade and portal.

A notice on the north wall tells you that from a pulpit here the
mayors of Beauvais between 1629 and 1789 would swear to
wound no one through enmity nor advance another through
friendship, comporting themselves as a good mayor and a decent
man ought to do. A plaque on the other side declares that
beneath and around the church tower was once a Gallo-Roman
bath. I think that the tower, topped by incongruous classical
towers, is decidedly leaning to the west.

Saint-Étienne contains masterpieces by the same men who
worked in the cathedral: iridescent stained glass by the family Le
Prince; statues of St Sebastian, St Roch, an Ecce Homo, St Martha
and St Margaret by Jean Le Pot; a sixteenth-century Deposition.
Of these gems the window depicting the tree of Jesse by Engrand Le
Prince is indisputably the finest. How I wish some British airline
would once again run flights to Beauvais so that one could
regularly enjoy such treats! When I lived in Lancashire my family
and I used to take a flight from Ringway over a long weekend,
stay for a couple of days at the Hôtel de la Poste, wander around
the Saturday market in the Place des Halles (which also sets itself
up there on Wednesdays), eat a *salade de haddock et saumon fumés* for
lunch and whisk ourselves from the railway station to Paris-Nord
within an hour for a day and a half in the capital of France.

From Beauvais take a trip north-west along the D901 and D133
to Gerberoy, an exquisite village founded at the end of the tenth
century whose houses are half-timbered, whose Town Hall is an
eighteenth-century gem and whose collegiate church was rebuilt
in the fifteenth century, having been sacked during the Hundred

Years War. Gerberoy had been powerfully fortified in the eleventh century, but the fortifications were dismantled in 1592 under an agreement made between Henri IV and the duke of Mayenne. In 1078 and 1079 these fortifications had enabled Robert Courtheuse to repulse the attacks of his brother, William the Conqueror. Emboldened by this success, Robert pursued William's troops into the Bray valley and routed them. At the beginning of the twentieth century an enlightened philanthropist and painter named Henri Le Sidaner conceived the notion of transforming what remained of the fortifications into a delightful terraced garden.

From Gerberoy take the D930 south-west to the splendid Normandy town of Gournay-en-Bray, where you turn south-east to reach Saint-Germer-de-Fly. St-Germer founded an abbey here in the mid-seventh century, and the superb Romanesque church which once served that foundation was built between 1150 and 1159 just as architecture in this part of France was about to transform itself into early Gothic. Though the building is large, it encapsulates a moment in architectural history when a monumental style seemed suddenly fragile and all the more precious. The architect of the eighteenth-century tower on top of the church must have felt something of this, for he has done all in his power to restrain any attempt to draw attention away from the clear lines of the original building. The Sainte-Chapelle, built beside it to link the Romanesque abbey church with the abbey buildings, demonstrates the next supreme achievement of religious architecture in northern France. Finished around 1260, its great rose window represents the triumph of Gothic over the architecture of an earlier age. Two thirteenth-century stained-glass windows gleam succulently in the choir. Today the ensemble is a perfect setting for *son et lumière* performances in summer.

This part of *Oise normande* utilizes the apples grown in the region to enhance its cuisine. In the restaurants the locals display the quick wit and courtesy that I have found in restaurants throughout Picardy. Eating in Saint-Germer-de-Fly I once regretted to the waiter that there was no soup on the menu. '*Si*,' he said, contradicting himself (in a measure), and speedily brought me a bubbling green potion made out of endives. As well as possessing one of the most modern ceramic factories in France, Saint-Germer-de-Fly assiduously courts its tourists, rallying them out of season with its flea-market on the first Sunday in October, hosting special weeks of music and running an annual antiques fair on the last weekend of the same month.

Instead of taking the main road back to Beauvais, follow the more picturesque D129 south-west through Le Coudray-Saint-Germer, with its sixteenth-century church, turning north at La-landelle (whose church dates from 1863) to join the N31 at La-chapelle-aux-Pots. The name of this quiet spot rightly indicates this is a centre of fine ceramics (for we are still in the clay country of the 'buttonhole' of Bray). The Hôtel de Ville houses a little ceramic museum. Numerous other potters' villages dot the region: Savignies, Saint-Germain-la-Poterie, Saint-Paul, Auneil and Ponchon.

To return from Beauvais to Senlis by way of the left bank of the Thérain, drive along the N31 for 4 km to Therdonne, turning right here along the D12 towards Bailleul-sur-Thérain, with its broken-down château. Nearby rises a Gaulish *oppidum* dubbed *Mont César*. If you have time, make a short and rewarding excursion from here to Villers-Saint-Sépulcre, where you will find a twelfth-century church housing a nondescript tile which happens (so it is claimed) to be a fragment of the Holy Sepulchre of Jerusalem as well as a magniloquent entombment of Jesus which I guess dates from the seventeenth century. Then continue south-east along the D12 to Bury. The entry to the centre of Bury is well signposted. At the T-junction you turn right to discover a superb church, partly Romanesque but becoming flamboyant Gothic as you reach the east end. Its buttresses must have been inspired by those at Beauvais, and its retable was created in the sixteenth century. At the west end rises a turret topped by a tall stone spire.

If you take the right fork at the end of the village you can drive on to reach Mello, whose thirteenth-century church was in part rebuilt at the Renaissance, followed by Saint-Vaast-lès-Mello, which is dominated by an eighteenth- and nineteenth-century château which rises on the left. The church here and its furnishings have scarcely changed since the twelfth century. At the bustling town of Montataire, 6 km south-east, you come across not only a medieval château and a Romanesque church but also another quaint modern church built out of aluminium. I prefer to ignore the last by driving up Rue de l'Église to the top of the town to admire the older church of Notre-Dame, winding round to view the château and then driving down again to the centre of the town to look up at the whole ensemble.

To find the splendid village of Saint-Leu-d'Esserent take the D12 south. The landscape is speckled with lakes, crumbling farm-houses, manors and ancient churches, finally succumbing to indus-trial nastiness, a squalor entirely made up for by the sight of the apse and the twin towers of the church of Saint-Nicolas which rise high on your right. Park and walk up the narrow ginnel which is called the Sente de la Jacquerie (for poverty and despair caused repeated and desperately vicious uprisings here in the fourteenth century). A green park on your right leads up to the brick-and-stone façade and elegant external staircase of the Hôtel de Ville. At the top of the Sente de la Jacquerie appears the stone wall of the château. Turning right here you walk alongside the ancient buttressed walls, emerging beside the formal garden of the Hôtel de Ville and climbing the steep steps to the front of the church. Apart from its weedy modern stained glass, this is one of the finest early Gothic churches in the whole region. Inside is a model of its complex and beautiful roof-beams. Next to the church stand the cloisters, sweetened by the priory garden, entered by a majestic battlemented double gateway.

After relishing the rest of this picturesque village, walk back past the church down Rue de l'Église, passing next a twelfth-century Benedictine wine cellar (which is now a local tourist office). You can slide your hand against the rough-chiselled stones of the houses, noting the narrow Ruelle de Mouton and the incredibly slim Ruelle François-Villon. Turn left at the Bar de la Mairie into Place de la Mairie and make your way back down Sente de la Jacquerie to rejoin your car. Better, first try to find time to eat one of the traditional Picardy dishes here (spotting perhaps a hint of nearby Normandy in the cream sauces or the Calvados that enlivens your *tarte aux pommes flambée*) and to make your way to the delightful quarter on the south side of the town where houses line a loop in the River Oise. Those who can stay longer in summer will find pleasure in fishing or sailing here, while during the tourist season the craftsmen and women of Saint-Leu ply their wares with gusto. The town boasts fine campsites, and in the summer evenings as dusk falls Saint-Leu illuminates its great church.

Through gentle countryside again the D44 leads you 6 km south-east to Chantilly, passing a caravan site that has cunningly dubbed itself the '*pré des Moines*' (or 'monks' meadow') and

crossing the River Oise by a suspension bridge. Whereas the
name of Saint-Leu derives from the Picardy dialect for St Loup,
who was bishop of Senlis in 609, Chantilly stems from Cantilius,
the name of a Gallo-Roman who built a villa here. Over the
centuries strongholds and châteaux were built, partly destroyed
and then rebuilt, until in the mid-sixteenth century the celebrated
Constable Anne de Montmorency returned from the Italian wars
fired with a vision of transplanting Italian architecture into his
own lands. Within ten years Jean Bullant had built for him what
we now call the Petit-Château of Chantilly. Bullant also designed
here seven little chapels, more or less hidden in the forest.

Once renowned for its lace, Chantilly derived yet greater
renown from its new château. The Petit-Château was once much
bigger, but after the duke of Enghien, later to be known as the
great Condé, won the Battle of Rocroi in 1643, Anne of Austria in
gratitude gave Chantilly to his widowed mother. So the great
Condé set Mansart to work rebuilding much of the château,
while he employed Le Nôtre and La Quintinie to create a superb
garden with statuary and waterfalls, and to tame the royal forest
with long avenues. Le Nôtre diverted streams and had canals dug
to surround choice buildings with water. The new home of
Condé's mother, an exquisite house in the woods, was called the
Maison Sylvie after the nickname which the flirtatious poet Théophile de Viau gave her. Building did not end there, nor the
vicissitudes of the châteaux at Chantilly. Between 1719 and 1735
Condé's successor, Louis-Henri de Bourbon, Prince of Condé,
employed Jean Aubert to create exquisite stables, the *Grandes
Écuries*. A *Jeu de Paume* was added in 1756.

The Revolution nearly destroyed everything when the prince
of Condé went into exile in order to attempt to organize an army
of opposition. At the restoration Mansart's work was in ruins.
When the Condé line died out in 1830, rescue was at hand, for
Prince Louis-Henri-Joseph left his inheritance to King Louis-
Philippe's son, the duke of Aumale. A passionate acquirer of
superb art, the duke took the opportunity to have the Grand-
Château completely restored in order to house his quite remarkable and vast international collection. The building work was
finished in 1883, and this is the château and art gallery we can
visit every day save Tuesdays, to see his legacy (or at least the
part of it that can be shown at any one time).

As for the *Grandes Écuries*, they have been transformed into a museum of living horses, whose dressage is on display again daily except Tuesdays. The *Jeu de Paume* and the Maison Sylvie are usually open at weekends. Le Nôtre's park has been augmented by a nineteenth-century garden laid out in the English style. The whole ensemble is entrancing, though of course no one can remotely take it all in at once. Inevitably the presence of the great stables has encouraged others in the area to train and breed horses, and the environs of Chantilly are peopled with ninety professional trainers, looking after some 3,000 horses for 800 owners. Racing takes place at Chantilly in June.

If you are staying for any length of time at Chantilly, be sure to make an excursion to one of the musical events at the thirteenth- and fourteenth-century abbey of Royaumont, which lies 6 km south-west beyond the sports centre. Though the church of 1235 is today only a ruin, much of the abbey is beautifully preserved. Its former abbot's palace, built just before the Revolution, remains in private hands, today calling itself the Château de Royaumont.

Chantilly is 24 km north-west of Ermenonville. The forest route is magical. Leave Chantilly by the Rue du Connétable, which runs east from the Hôpital Condé and Place Omer-Vallon. You pass by the church of Notre-Dame, designed by Mansart at the end of the seventeenth century and to me a cold, unwelcoming building. It stands by a gate of the *Grandes Écuries*, against which a plaque records that the Abbé Charpentier, a member of the French Resistance, was executed at Mathausen by the Gestapo on 23 January 1944. From here you continue into the park through great broken arches. Usually someone will be riding into the *Grandes Écuries* behind you. Pause by the lakeside to admire once again the Petit-Château with its chapel and Mansart's long building over to the right, its four porticos and two storeys of windows as elegant as ever.

Our route now becomes breathless and beautiful. Follow the D924A, crossing the River Thève at Montgrésin, to reach La Chapelle-en-Serval with its sixteenth-century church. Continuing south to Survilliers, where you must be prepared to discover the sixteenth-century priory church on the right just as you are leaving the town, turn left along the D922 to find Plailly (where there is a thirteenth-century church) and Mortefontaine (whose Renaissance château, a fine building with a central lodging and

two smaller wings, was built only in 1897). Here Gérard de Nerval
spent most of his youth. Seven-and-a-half kilometres futher east
we plunge into the Ermenonville forest. At Ermenonville itself the
eighteenth-century château, with its long, decorated façade and a
couple of wings, has been transformed into a hotel. The waters of
its moat, fed by the River Launette, ripple over dams. South-west,
in the direction of Meaux, you reach the Town Hall. The Town
Hall square sports a curious crucifix with a snake coiling itself
around the stem. Beyond it is a fortified farm. The priory church
of Ermenonville is accompanied by the Hôtel du Prieuré, defended
by a massive belfry. Jean-Jacques Rousseau himself sits meditating
in the centre of the town, sitting in a grove, an angel hovering over
his shoulder, sculpted by Henry Bazaud. In the cool, rustic park his
first tomb (for his remains are now in the Panthéon in Paris) bears
the inscription, 'Here lies the man of Nature and Truth.'

The route from Ermenonville back to Senlis (a mere 13 km
away) is filled with wonders. A zoo is signposted to the east. Very
shortly a sign directs you to the abbey of Châalis, which is
reached down a 50 m alleyway of plane trees. Founded by King
Louis VI in 1136, Châalis abbey grew rich by exploiting the
forest of Ermenonville, so that at the beginning of the thirteenth
century the monks could undertake the building of a church some
80 m long. Ambition occasionally over-reached the finances even
of this rich foundation, but in the eighteenth century, fired by the
work of Jean Aubert at Chantilly, the monks called upon him to
transform their living quarters. Shortly afterwards, like many an
other in France, the abbey was suppressed and sold.

Today Jean Aubert's sumptuous building houses an art exhibition ranging from antiquity through the Italian Renaissance to
souvenirs of Jean-Jacques Rousseau. Its prize possessions are two
paintings by Giotto, one of St John the Evangelist, the other of St
Lawrence, both of them panels from an altarpiece that once
graced the church of Santa Croce in Florence. As for the rest of
the monastery, two eighteenth-century pavilions guard the
wrought-iron gate where you enter; an exquisite north transept
survives from the thirteenth-century abbey church; and the chapel
of the abbot's lodging has also survived, though only as
a nineteenth-century restoration. In the nineteenth century too
were designed the flower beds and pools and cunningly contrived
vistas of the superb park which surrounds this abbey.

Directly opposite the abbey of Châalis is a pleasure park, with its own Ferris wheel, and the unequalled sea of sand (the *Mer de Sable*) of the Ermenonville forest. Our way back to Senlis from here runs through Mont-l'Évêque, where the bishops built a château and where we find yet another of those churches with a simple nave and a prolix chancel, against which rises a mighty offset tower. The château still stands, half-hidden behind the walls of a massive farm.

Scarcely have you left this village to return to Senlis when you notice a mighty double row of chestnut trees on the left. They lead to the ruined abbey of Victoire. Philippe-Auguste founded it to celebrate a victorious battle in 1224. Louis XI loved staying here. Today the late-fifteenth-century church is in ruins, but the eighteenth-century abbey remains intact. As you drive back to the main road you spot other monastic buildings dotting the park. Then, within a couple of minutes, you are back in Senlis.

Though Senlis is close to being my favourite city in the whole of Flanders, Artois and Picardy, I do not wish to finish my book here, but with a more recent phenomenon of this part of Picardy, the Asterix Park, at the very southern corner of the *département* of the Oise. Asterix the Gaul was but thirty years old when the fun park was created at the end of the 1980s. In consequence his inventors, Goscinny and Uderzo, were still on hand to supervise the work. Asterix, some 3 m high, sits on a polystyrene rock at the entrance of the park to welcome visitors. Roman soldiers lie defeated, while Asterix's companion Obelix chomps away at the remains of a wild boar. As I strolled down the Via Antiqua, whose shops are replicas of buildings visited by Asterix and his companions in their cartoon voyages throughout the world, I could not help thinking of the model ancient houses at Samara near Amiens. The northern French have a gentle way of laughing at themselves. If I had to choose between the Asterix Park and the remarkable exhibitions at Samara, of course I should choose the latter – but only just.

FURTHER READING

'L'Aisne', *Richesses de France*, 68, Bordeaux, 1986.

Ardagh, John, *Writer's France, a Regional Panorama*, Hamish Hamilton, London, 1989.

Bentley, James, Introduction to *Lives of the Saints*, Alban Butler, Bestsellers Publications Ltd, 1990.

Bernanos, Georges, *Journal d'un curé de campagne*, 1936 (tr. by Pamela Morris as *Diary of a Country Priest*, London, 1937).

Boussel, Patrick, *Guides des champs de bataille en France*, Pierre Horay, Paris, 1981.

Brandicourt, Jacques, Destombe, Michel and Duclercq, Philippe, *Voyage à travers la Somme*, Éditions S.A.E.P., Colmar-Ingersheim, 1975.

Bumpus, T. F., *The Cathedrals of Northern France*, London, 1910.

Carlyle, Thomas, *The French Revolution*, London, 1837.

Crook, Joseph Mordaunt, *William Burges and the High Victorian Dream*, John Murray, London, 1981.

'Le Département de la Somme', *La revue géographique et industrielle de France*, 46, S.I.R.C., Paris, 1972.

Dumas, Alexandre, père, *My Memories*, tr. by E. M. Waller, London, 1907–9.

Dumas, Alexandre, père, *Twenty Years After*, tr. by W. Barron, London, 1846.

Ferniot, Jean, 'Les fromages des frontières du Nord', *Cuisine et Vins de France*, 369, Paris, October 1981.

Flandre-Picardie: La France et ses Trésors, Librairie Larousse, Paris, 1988.

Gamblin, André, *Le Nord – Pas de Calais: 20 circuits touristiques*, Éditions S.A.E.P., Colmar-Ingersheim, 1984.

Hilaire, Yves-Marie, ed., *Histoire du Nord Pas-de-Calais*, Privat, Paris, 1982.

Hugo, Victor-Marie, 'En voyage', *Oeuvres complètes*, vol. 2, Paris, 1910.

Lambert, Élie, *Le Style gothique*, Librairie Larousse, Paris, 1943.

Meuret, Jean-Paul, *Guide des églises fortifiées de la Thiérache*, Société archéologique et historique de Vervins et de la Thiérache, Vervins, 1988.

Le Nord Touristique, Librairie Larousse, Paris, n.d.

'L'Oise', *Richesses de France*, 54, Bordeaux, 1963.

Parker, Geoffrey, 'Why the Armada Failed', *History Today*, 38, London, May 1988.

'Le Pas-de-Calais', *Richesses de France*, 22, Bordeaux, 1955.

Pays du Nord, Christine Bonneton, Paris, 1989.

La Picardie, Librairie Larousse, Paris, 1978.

Picardie, Christine Bonneton, Paris, 1989.

Pierrard, Pierre, *Flandre, Artois, Picardie*, Arthaud, Paris, 1970.

Ruskin, John, *The Bible of Amiens*, London, 1884.

Seydoux, Philippe, *Abbayes de la Somme*, Nouvelles Éditions Latines, Paris n.d.

    Églises de la Somme, Nouvelles Éditions Latines, Paris, n.d.

'La Somme', *Richesses de France*, 51, Bordeaux, 1962.

Le Touquet et la Côte d'Opale, Librairie Larousse, Paris, 1981.

Thiébaut, Jacques (introduction), '59 Nord', *Le Guide des Châteaux de France*, Hermé, Paris, 1986.

    '62 Pas-de-Calais', *Le Guide des Châteaux de France*, Hermé, Paris, 1986.

Vergnet-Ruiz, J., and de Kersant, A., *Châteaux de l'Oise*, Nouvelles Éditions Latines, Paris, n.d.

Verlaine, Paul, *Confessions*, 1899 (tr. by Joanna Richardson as *Confessions of a Poet*, London, 1950).

Vermand, Dominique, *Églises de l'Oise*, Nouvelles Éditions Latines, Paris, n.d.

Waddy, Etheldred, *Stacy Waddy*, London, 1938.

INDEX